Being White, Being Good

Being White, Being Good

White Complicity, White Moral Responsibility, and Social Justice Pedagogy

BARBARA APPLEBAUM

LEXINGTON BOOKS

A Division of

ROWMAN & LITTLEFIELD PUBLISHERS, INC.

Lanham • Boulder • New York • Toronto • Plymouth, UK

Published by Lexington Books
A division of Rowman & Littlefield Publishers, Inc.
A wholly owned subsidary of The Rowman & Littlefield Publishing Group, Inc.
4501 Forbes Boulevard, Suite 200, Lanham, Maryland 20706
http://www.lexingtonbooks.com

Estover Road, Plymouth PL6 7PY, United Kingdom

Applebaum, Barbara. "White Privilege/White Complicity: Connecting 'Benefiting From' to 'Contributing To'" in *Philosophy of Education*, ed. Ronald David Glass, 292–300. Urbana, Illinois: Philosophy of Education Society, 2008.

Applebaum, Barbara. "White Ignorance and Denials of Complicity: On the Possibility of Doing Philosophy in Good Faith" in *The Center Must Not Hold: White Women and the Whiteness of Philosophy*, ed. George Yancey. Lanham, MD: Lexington Books, forthcoming.

Applebaum, Barbara. "Engaging Student Disengagement: Resistance or Disagreement?" in *Philosophy of Education Society*, ed. Barbara Stengel, 335–345. Urbana, IL: Philosophy of Education Society, 2007.

British Library Cataloguing in Publication Information Available

Library of Congress Cataloging-in-Publication Data

The hardback edition of this book was previously cataloged by the Library of Congress as follows:

Applebaum, Barbara, 1953–
   Being white, being good : white complicity, white moral responsibility, and social justice pedagogy / Barbara Applebaum.
      p. cm.
   Includes bibliographical references and index.
   1. Racism. 2. Whites. 3. Responsibility. I. Title.

HT1521.A67 2010
305.8—dc22
                                                                                2009054094

ISBN: 978-0-7391-4491-6 (cloth : alk. paper)
ISBN: 978-0-7391-4492-3 (pbk. : alk. paper)
ISBN: 978-0-7391-4493-0 (electronic)

Contents

Acknowledgments

THE HEBREW WORD FOR GRATITUDE IS "HAKARAT HATOV" WHOSE LITERAL MEANING
is "recognizing the good." Although used in many ways, it can refer to the
acknowledgment of the good another has done for you. Hakarat hatov is not
merely an expression of thanks but also a demonstration of respect and value
of the person from whom one has received something important. It is to show
appreciation for being inspired, for being supported, for being helped.

If I were able to show my appreciation for all those colleagues and friends
who have directly and indirectly inspired me, the acknowledgments would
span and take the place of the entire book. Instead I will limit myself to just
thanking a few who have been especially supportive and central to helping me
complete this project.

A number of outstanding scholars have been especially influential in
shaping my thoughts on white complicity. If you see echoes of their insights
throughout the book, it is because they have been, as people and as scholars,
such an inspiration. Linda Martin Alcoff, Cris Mayo, Audrey Thompson and
George Yancy—my project stands on your profound shoulders. I would be
remiss if I did not acknowledge Dwight Boyd whose mentorship when I was
a graduate student many years ago opened doors for me both with his own
scholarship and with the scholarship he introduced me to. Dwight helped me
to understand that philosophy can be extremely personal.

Kenneth Strike—thank you for being my publishing mentor. Without your
sage advice, this book might never have gone to press. I am grateful to Sari
Knopp Biklen, my mentor and friend, who is not only a source of encourage-
ment and intellectual stimulation but is a model of leadership for me. I also
am so fortunate to have a colleague like Emily Robertson. Emily, thank you
for being such an amazing listener, for your friendship and for our ongoing
conversations. Your critical, but always respectful, comments challenge me to
formulate my ideas more clearly. The Dean of the School of Education, Doug
Biklen, has been especially helpful in providing me with the sabbatical time to

think through this project. But more than that, his confidence in and support of his faculty makes working at Syracuse University such a special experience. I am grateful to Sally Sayles-Hannon, my research assistant, for her help in proofreading and compiling the index for the book. I also want to thank the Wege Foundation in Michigan for providing financial support for the typesetting of the manuscript.

Some sections of this book have been previously published. I am grateful for permission to reprint them.

Most of all, I want to thank my family and my spouse for the faithful support they have given me in writing this book. Penina, Sara, Mordechai, Shani, Jason and Liraz, you give me pride and much joy. Thank you for being the people you are and for your patience during all the dinners to which I brought the progress and frustrations of writing a book. Adiv, Amir, Natai and Thalia, my grandchildren, thank you for making being a grandmother so much fun. Nissan, my amazing and loving spouse, has tirelessly walked me through the difficult work of writing. Thank you for always being there even when we are hundreds of miles apart.

CHAPTER 1

Introduction

"You are guilty!!" Andrew Schaap[1] opens his erudite essay on collective responsibility with the words that were pasted on signs across Germany after World War II by the Allies in their efforts to denazify the German population. Accompanying these words was a picture of one of the concentration camps and an accusatory finger pointed at the viewer. As Schaap notes, this charge was met with denials and moral resentment. Common responses to the charge were: "We didn't know" or (even if they did know) "We could not have done anything anyway." How can ordinary people be responsible for evil they did not directly perpetrate, might not have known about or might not have been able to affect even if they did know? Intention and causality, the hallmarks of responsibility, were often conspicuously absent in the case of the ordinary German people.

Why should the ordinary German, those who did not intend nor cause harm, be responsible for the evils perpetrated by the Nazi regime? After observing the trial of Adolph Eichmann, a high-ranking Nazi administrator, in Jerusalem, Hannah Arendt[2] coined the piercing concept "the banality of evil" to suggest that evil is perpetrated not only by depraved and malevolent monsters but also by regular people who uncritically follow orders and go about their daily lives. According to Arendt, Eichmann, who helped the Nazis carry out unthinkable crimes, did not seem to be a crazy fanatic but rather an ordinary person who claims to have been simply doing his duty. In her writings subsequent to *Eichmann in Jerusalem*, Arendt distinguishes between guilt and responsibility when she argues that in their support of the Nazi regime, the German people were responsible although not all guilty.[3] Arendt refuses to equate being guilty with being responsible because she insists that the German people could not all be guilty for the evils of the Nazi regime. This would stretch the meaning of responsibility to meaninglessness. Guilt, she intimates, implies a direct causal connection to the harm. Moreover, as she puts it,

"Where all are guilty, nobody is."[4] While all Germans may not be guilty, however, they were responsible. The ordinary German was responsible by virtue of the fact that s/he was a member of a political community that committed atrocities even when s/he did not directly cause harm.

In *The Question of German Guilt*, Karl Jaspers[5] upholds the guilt of the ordinary German for the atrocities of the Holocaust by distinguishing between moral guilt and metaphysical guilt. The former, Jaspers argues, is exclusively contingent on *what one does or does not do*, while the latter is based on *who one is*. Guilt, we are told, does not have to be exclusively focused on what one does or does not do in terms of directly causing the harm. Jaspers grounds metaphysical guilt in the "solidarity among men as human beings that makes each as responsible for every wrong and every injustice in the world, especially for crimes committed in his presence or with his knowledge."[6]

By introducing the notion of metaphysical guilt, Jaspers emphasizes a connection to evil that is centered not specifically on *the actions one chooses to do or not to do* (and that directly bring about such evil) but rather emphasizes the question, *who does one choose to be?* Jaspers attributes metaphysical guilt to German "survivors"—those who *chose* to live rather than contest the Nazi regime.

> We survivors did not seek it. We did not go into the streets when our Jewish friends were led away; we did not scream until we too were destroyed. We preferred to stay alive, on the feeble, if logical, ground that our death could not have helped anyone. We are guilty of being alive.[7]

Despite their differences, both Arendt and Jaspers allude to the question of complicity, the focal point of this book. Both assume that complicity involves a choice of some sort that connects one to evil and, most significantly, that one can choose not to be complicit. One's moral standing depends on that choice.

In the last several years, the notion of complicity has also been a recurrent theme in critical theories of race and racism, as well as in feminist theory. Questions about complicity have arisen in discussions around "internalized racism" and, especially, in debates about whether victims of racism can be implicated in their own oppression.[8] Feminist theorists who have tried to understand how women can perpetuate their own oppression have also turned their attention to questions of complicity.[9]

Recently, however, another type of complicity has appeared in the scholarship that focuses on the ways that the systemically *privileged*, rather than the marginalized, are complicit in the perpetuation of systemic injustice. In the field of critical whiteness studies, for instance, questions of complicity are especially notable in the academic discourse around social justice education.

Here we find a claim about complicity that is addressed to all white people regardless of and despite of their good intentions. What I refer to as "the white complicity claim" maintains that white people, through the practices of whiteness and by benefiting from white privilege, contribute to the maintenance of systemic racial injustice. However, the claim also implies responsibility in its assumption that the failure to acknowledge such complicity will thwart whites in their efforts to dismantle unjust racial systems and, more specifically, will contribute to the perpetuation of racial injustice.[10] Recognizing that one is complicit, according to the claim, is a necessary (albeit not sufficient) condition of challenging systemic racial oppression. Most significantly, since the white complicity claim presumes that racism is often perpetuated through *well-intended* white people, being morally good may not facilitate and may even frustrate the recognition of such responsibility.

What does it mean to claim that white people are complicit in the reproduction of racist systems despite their good intentions and even when they might want to renounce the privileges they accrue because of their whiteness? How can white people be responsible for their complicity if they cannot choose to be not white? Even if white people are well intended, even if they consider themselves to be paragons of anti-racism, how might they still be unwittingly complicit in sustaining an unjust system they claim to want to dismantle?

What is of specific interest about white complicity is the claim that white people can reproduce and maintain racist practices even when, and *especially when*, they believe themselves to be morally good. Some feminist philosophers have been acutely aware of this problem. Marilyn Frye queries, "Does being white make it impossible for me to be a good person?"[11] Similarly Linda Martin Alcoff asks

> What is it to acknowledge one's whiteness? . . . (is) it to acknowledge that one is inherently tied to structures of domination and oppression, that one is irrevocably on the wrong side?[12]

I take an important cue from Fiona Probyn's provocative assertion that "Complicity . . . is the starting point and the condition of ethics itself."[13] Thus, this project not only explores the meaning of complicity presumed by the white complicity claim, it also considers the notion of moral responsibility that is attributable to white people in the context of such complicity.

This book will be of particular interest to those who practice and research social justice pedagogy. White denials of complicity are particularly widespread in courses that teach about social justice. Not unlike the ordinary German who denied being guilty of complicity with Nazi crimes, white students often conflate complicity with guilt, the guilt that arises from direct causality to harm. Such notions of responsibility support and encourage denials of complicity. White students believe that they are justified in denying their complicity because they claim that they do not have any "bad intentions" or any "causal connection" to the harms of systemic racism. Often white students *refuse to even engage* with the possibility that they are complicit. Most white students see themselves as good people and take the charge of complicity as a serious affront to their moral being. They perceive their moral being as transcending their whiteness. Denials of complicity go deep and are maintained, as will be demonstrated, by certain conceptions of responsibility.

Moreover, currently "white privilege pedagogy" is the prevailing approach in social justice education, especially in schools of education across North America. Yet the notion of privilege that is the focal point of such pedagogy, as will be explained in Chapter 2, is extremely problematic.[14] Instead, this book advocates "white complicity pedagogy" that highlights and compensates for some of the more problematic aspects of white privilege pedagogy. White complicity pedagogy is premised on the belief that to teach systemically privileged students about systemic injustice, and especially in teaching them about their privilege, one must first encourage them to be willing to contemplate how they are complicit in sustaining the system even when they do not intend to or are unaware that they do so. This means helping white students to understand that *white moral standing* is one of the ways that whites *benefit* from the system. It also means linking such benefits to their complicity even when such links might not be specifically causal ones.

Acknowledging that one is complicit, however, does not relieve one of responsibility but rather, as Probyn insists, complicity is where responsibility begins. If privileged social groups are to take responsibility for their role in the perpetuation of systemic injustice and be able to form effective political coalitions with the marginalized, both understanding white complicity and the type of white moral responsibility it entails require elucidation.

This book examines and elucidates the particular meaning of complicity assumed by those who maintain the white complicity claim. My project, however, is not to "prove" that white people are complicit in systemic racial injustice. Instead I endeavor to elucidate what white complicity means when critical scholars of race and racism refer to it. A key task of this book is to demarcate some of the required moves that must be made in our conceptual landscape to make white complicity visible—in particular, shifts in our conceptualization of the subject, of language, and of moral responsibility.

More specifically, the main objectives of this book are to explain what scholars mean by white complicity, to explore the ethical and epistemological assumptions that white complicity entails, and to offer recommendations for how white complicity can be taught. The primary question the book attempts to take up is: What can it mean for white people "to be good" when they can reproduce and maintain a racist system even when, and especially when, they believe themselves to be good? In my attempt to answer this question I argue that social justice pedagogy must shift its understanding of the subject, of language and of responsibility in ways that incorporate deconstructive and post-structural insights.

Traditional conceptions of moral responsibility, it will be shown, not only fail to expose white complicity but also contribute to the normalization of denials of complicity that protect systemic racism from being challenged. One of the problems with traditional conceptions of moral responsibility is the presumption that moral innocence is attainable. Because such notions of responsibility center the question "what can I do?" rather than the question "what needs to be done?" they can encourage moral solipsism, heroism and white narcissism. I call for a rearticulated notion of moral responsibility that is based on the works of Iris Marion Young and Judith Butler. This rearticulated notion of moral responsibility does not focus on guilt but instead emphasizes uncertainty, vulnerability and vigilance. Significantly, the rearticulated notion of moral responsibility this book calls for does not function to make white people feel better because it is grounded in the understanding that preserving white moral innocence is impossible. Yet the arguments in this book also support the possibility for white people in the context of white complicity to act in ethically responsible ways.

A superb illustration of the complexity of white moral agency and its dangers is evident in Sara Ahmed's discussion of her white students who so consistently ask her, "but what can white people do?" Although such questions on face value reflect white moral agency, Ahmed argues that such speech acts reinscribe privilege rather than challenge injustice. Ahmed explains the solipsism implied in this question when she writes that

> (t)o respond to accounts of institutional whiteness with the question "what can white people do?" is not only to return to the place of the white subject, but it is also to locate agency in this place. It is also to re-position the white subject somewhere other than implicated in the critique.[15]

Such moral agency recenters the white subject as the authority who brings about change and also assumes that the white subject can transcend the critique of whiteness that provokes the question being asked. Yet Ahmed also insists that this question is not totally misguided,

> . . . although it does re-center on white agency, as a hope premised on lack rather than presence. . . . The impulse towards action is understandable and complicated: it can be both a defense against the "shock" of hearing about racism (and the shock of the complicity revealed by the very "shock"); it can be an impulse

to reconciliation as a "re-covering" of the past (the desire to feel better); it can be about making public one's judgment ("what happened was wrong"); or it can be an expression of solidarity ("I am with you"). But the question, in all of these modes of utterance, can work to *block* hearing; in moving on from the present towards the future, it can also move away from the object of critique, or place the white subject "outside" that critique in the present of the hearing. In other words, the desire to act, to move, or even to move on, can stop the message getting through.[16]

I read Ahmed as acknowledging that for white people to join in alliances with the victims of racism to challenge systemic racial oppression white people have to acknowledge their complicity. This means being vigilant about white moral agency because such moral agency can ironically obstruct a genuine engagement with those who experience racial oppression.

Ahmed, for instance, cautions white people to examine their desire "to do something" because it can also function to protect one's moral innocence and the social system on which such innocence is based. "If we want to know how things can be different *too quickly*," Ahmed cautions, "then we might not hear anything at all."[17] This book is about the type of white moral responsibility that is possible given the depths of white complicity.

Finally, I introduce "white complicity pedagogy" that is grounded in this rearticulated notion of responsibility. I contend that white complicity pedagogy can potentially increase the development of alliance identities by facilitating the type of listening on the part of white students that can foster a willingness on the part of the systemically marginalized to engage in dialogue with white students.

In the remainder of this chapter, the white complicity claim will be examined in further detail. The white complicity claim has been articulated in at least two ways in the scholarship. The first focuses exclusively on *unconscious* attitudes and beliefs. While this approach has been enormously helpful in understanding white complicity, a second approach that forefronts white "ways of being" or the phenomenology of whiteness[18] has drawn attention to two practices that keep complicity hidden: systemic white ignorance and the discourse of denials of complicity. Such white "ways of being" do not entail whiteness as essence but instead point to habits of whiteness and whiteness as performativity. Chapter 2 focuses on white ways of being by examining how white ignorance and white denials of complicity that are socially sanctioned conceal white complicity. Systematic white ignorance will be shown to be a form of white knowledge that is upheld by denials of complicity.

One way that I have found to explain to white students how they are complicit is to link systemic white ignorance and denials of complicity to the type of benefits that protect their moral innocence. Students often want to understand how they are implicated and ask especially about the link between "benefiting from the system" and "contributing to the system." Systemic white ignorance makes denials of complicity seem justified and this, in turn, protects white moral innocence, on the one hand, and shields unjust systems from being interrogated, on the other. As long as white complicity is not acknowledged, I explain, the status quo remains beyond challenge. Yet my students still struggle with their responsibility since the notion of responsibility they work with forefronts causality, control, knowledge and/or intentions. Moreover, they insist that in order to be responsible they must be able to transcend the system that constitutes them as white.

To understand what notion of moral responsibility under complicity is possible, first the notion of person that grounds the white complicity claim is examined and then, second, how discourse works is addressed. Chapter 3 takes up the conception of subjectivity that the white complicity claim presumes by turning to the work of Judith Butler. The limitations of Butler's conception of the subject are also addressed. When, however, Butler's ethical and critical concerns are brought to the forefront, I argue, the critiques of her conception of the subject can be negotiated. Chapter 4 focuses on the conception of discourse that helps to explain how seemingly moral utterances can function as denials of complicity. To understand how denials of complicity work, one must shift one's epistemological framework from language as representation to language as discourse.

Chapter 5 examines traditional conceptions of moral responsibility asking whether they are able to expose rather than hide white complicity. Many accounts of complicity in the philosophical scholarship rely on a notion of responsibility that emphasizes causality, knowledge, control, choice and/or intention. Such notions of responsibility, however, when applied to white ways of being whose ethical relationship to systemic racism can be disputed not only cannot capture how such ways of being are connected to the perpetuation of structural injustice but also focus too much on whether guilt or blame is attributable to particular individuals. The consequence is that well-intentioned white people are able to effortlessly let themselves off the hook since they can honestly claim they did not intend to perform anything wrong, and they were ignorant of or had no control over the wrongful outcome.

Chapter 6 begins with Iris Marion Young's critique of liability models of moral responsibility and considers her social connection model of responsibility. Some limitations of Young's model are noted but I argue that Butler's recent work on responsibility can expand Young's work and can help to flesh out a notion of vigilance as a key feature of white moral agency that is always on guard for white denials of complicity. Such a notion of responsibility also underscores the importance of and possibility of collective action.

Finally, Chapter 7 describes how encouraging such vigilance can be a crucial element in white complicity pedagogy by contributing to the development of alliance identities that collectively play a part in challenging the systems that create and maintain social injustice.

THE WHITE COMPLICITY CLAIM

While many scholars of color have eloquently written about white complicity,[19] it is only recently that white academics within the area of critical whiteness studies have given this concept attention. The growth of critical whiteness studies as an academic field provides a background for understanding the place of white complicity in this scholarship. Critical whiteness studies has developed as a result of a shift in understanding racism as exclusively a matter of overt practices involving prejudice or antipathy to an understanding of racism as a system in which covert and subtle forms of institutional, cultural and individual practices produce and reproduce racial injustice. Along with this shift in the conceptualization of racism as a system rather than only an attribute of individual people, there has been a general consensus about the social construction of race as a category. As scientific evidence for race as a biological concept has been shown to be lacking[20] and that the meaning of race not only varies geographically but also changes over time within particular societies, research became focused on the ways in which the meaning of race is constructed and reproduced via social institutions such as law, media and education.[21]

To acknowledge that race is socially reproduced through social institutions is to underscore how such construction is hidden via the processes of normalization. As a discursive construction that marks social differences, race is a concept that involves the mutually constituted locations of groups within a system of social relations in which one group is considered the norm and other groups are evaluated as "different" or "deviant" on the basis of that norm. As Martha Minow[22] emphasizes, the norm from which "difference" is demarcated is taken for granted and is invisible to those who benefit from it. Given the invisibility of whiteness to white people, many critical theorists of race and racism recognize that studies must be turned "from the racial object to the racial subject; from the described and imagined to the describers and imaginers; from the serving to the served."[23]

An incident that took place during a panel discussion on a predominantly white university campus, and of which I was a participant, illustrates how whiteness is normalized and tends to be invisible to white people. Participants on this panel were asked to address how they taught about race and racism in their courses. Many white professors reported how their courses included sections on U.S. Antebellum slavery, Martin Luther King Jr. and the Brown vs.

Board of Education decision. For them, teaching about race and racism meant teaching about the racialized "Other." The invisibility of whiteness was conspicuous as white faculty equated race with the *victims of racism* and implicitly assumed that *whiteness is race-less*. As one of the panelists of color explained, this invisibility of whiteness to these white professors is implicated in the persistence of systemic racial injustice. Moreover, she continued, as long as racism can be attributed to "bad white people" and the violence and discrimination that victims of racism endure, then ordinary, often well-intentioned, white people do not have to consider their complicity in the perpetuation of systemic racism.

Critical whiteness studies begins with the acknowledgement that whiteness and its concomitant privileges tend to remain invisible to most white people. In order to dislodge whiteness from its position of dominance, whiteness must be studied in order to "make visible what is rendered invisible when viewed as the normative state of existence."[24] From this perspective, racism is essentially a white problem. Whiteness is mainly invisible to those who benefit from it. For those who don't, whiteness is often blatantly and painfully ubiquitous. For white people then, it is impossible to gain an understanding of systemic racism without naming whiteness and understanding how whiteness works.

While the definition of whiteness is difficult to pin down, there is widespread agreement that whiteness is a socially constructed category that is normalized within a system of privilege so that it is taken for granted by those who benefit from it.[25] Ruth Frankenberg defines whiteness as

> . . . a location of structural advantage, of race privilege. Second it is a "standpoint," a place from which White people look at ourselves, at others, and at society. Third, "Whiteness" refers to a set of cultural practices that are usually unmarked and unnamed.[26]

Cheryl Harris[27] suggests that whiteness is best understood as a form of property rights that is systemically protected by social institutions such as law. Thus whiteness is not merely about skin color alone but involves a culturally, socially, politically and institutionally produced and reproduced system of institutional processes and individual practices.

A major area of study in critical whiteness studies involves white privilege. Whiteness, as Barbara Flagg explains, is a "location of power, privilege, and prestige."[28] Peggy McIntosh's influential essay lists the social, political and cultural advantages of being white in the United States. Her metaphor of white privilege as an "invisible knapsack of unearned assets which I can count on cashing in each day, but about which I was 'meant' to remain oblivious"[29] is often cited in courses that teach about systemic injustice. McIntosh maintains that without acknowledging the "colossal unseen dimensions"[30] and the "silences and denials"[31] surrounding white privilege, white people cannot contribute to the eradication of racism and, in fact, contribute to its maintenance. Whiteness benefits all those ascribed whiteness and it is white people's investment in whiteness that can obscure how white people *even with the best of intentions* are implicated in sustaining a racially unjust system. It is the complicity of *well-intentioned* white people that is the central focus of this book.

The concept of white complicity turns up in various manifestations in the critical whiteness scholarship. There are at least two types of the white complicity claim that should be discerned. First, white complicity is often addressed as the product of unconscious negative attitudes and beliefs about non-white people that infect all white people and has an effect on their practices. This is one way to explicate how well-meaning white people play a role in the perpetuation of systemic racism. Barbara Trepagnier's recent work is a good example of this first approach to white complicity. Trepagnier refers to "silent racism" and argues

No one is immune to the ideas that permeate the culture in which he or she is raised. Silent racism . . . refers to the unspoken negative thoughts, emotions, and assumptions about black Americans that dwell in the minds of white Americans, including well-meaning whites that care about racial equality.[32]

Silent racism, according to Trepagnier, is not about some discrete individual's psychology but rather is a "cultural phenomenon."[33] It is silent in that these beliefs and emotions are unspoken yet they fuel everyday racism and other racist actions. Trepagnier underscores that all white people are not affected in the same way, yet all white people are "infected." White supremacy, according to Trepagnier, "inhabits the minds of all white people."[34]

Trepagnier studies the paradox in which racism in the United States remains an enduring social problem yet few white people perceive themselves as "racist." Her research is focused on well-intentioned white people who claim to be "not racist" yet who are involved in acts of "everyday racism." As an illustration of such silent racism, Trepagnier draws attention to an observation commonly reported by Black women in academia that many white people subtly express surprise when they encounter a Black person in a position of authority. This, Trepagnier explains, is an excellent demonstration of the "silent, insidious racism" on the part of people who are not hateful and do not intentionally want to marginalize. Such white people may even insist that they are "not racist."

Scholar and teacher educator Joyce E. King[35] similarly refers to a type of unconscious white racism that differs from outright racial bigotry. King refers to such unconscious racism as "dysconscious racism" which she defines as

> . . . a form of racism that tacitly accepts dominant White norms and privileges. It is not the absence of consciousness but an impaired consciousness. Uncritical ways of thinking about racial inequity accept certain culturally sanctioned assumptions, myths, and beliefs that justify the social and economic advantages White people have as a result of subordinating others.[36]

Because of their miseducation, King argues that whites have a distorted view of the reasons for racial inequality. Moreover, they unconsciously protect these beliefs because they support their self-image from the pain of being challenged. King emphasizes that dysconscious racism is not about hate or animosity towards people of color. She demonstrates how such unintentional and often unconscious racial beliefs are the predominant type of racism in contemporary society in the United States.

Some Critical Race Theorists also highlight the role of unconscious negative racial attitudes in perpetuating systemic racial injustice. Charles Lawrence III,[37] for instance, argues against the presumption of purposeful intent that is a condition of much anti-discrimination law. In order to seek redress for discrimination, the litigant must show the perpetrator's intent was to discriminate on the basis of race. This is counterproductive, Lawrence contends, when the source of racism is more often not attributable to overt, blatant acts of hate but instead attributable to unconscious negative attitudes and beliefs. Individuals raised in a racist society absorb attitudes and stereotypes often without even knowing. Such racism is deeply embedded in white people's psyches and influences behavior in subtle yet pernicious ways.

As an illustration of such unconscious racism, Lawrence recounts how as a student in a predominantly white college, his white companion once remarked, "I don't think of you as a Negro." As he contemplates the racist overtones hidden by this seemingly benign compliment, Lawrence realizes that its underlying presumption involves the belief that being considered a Negro is to be considered less than human. Such "well-intentioned" racism is deeply entrenched in the white unconscious. Unless the law is willing to expand its notion of discrimination to encompass these subtle ways that racism functions, Lawrence contends, racism will not only continue to endure but the legal system will also be complicit in its maintenance.

The work of psychologists Samuel Gaertner and Jack Dovidio[38] is also based on the acknowledgement of unconscious and unintentional racism that they refer to as "aversive racism." The characteristic feature of aversive racism is the denial of personal prejudice and unconscious negative feelings and beliefs. White people who perceive themselves and want to continue to perceive themselves as good liberal people possessing strong egalitarian values can still be perpetuating racist systems. According to Gaertner and Dovidio, aversive racists possess deep and unconscious negative feelings and beliefs about African-Americans although such attitudes and beliefs are not accompanied by hatred or animosity. Instead of hatred, there is often a fear or uneasiness that white people feel in the company of African-Americans which they attempt to hide because to acknowledge such emotions would conflict with their egalitarian self-image.

In the field of philosophy, the best illustration of scholarship that equates white complicity with unconscious negative racial attitudes and beliefs is to be found in Larry May's *Sharing Responsibility*.[39] Building on the same discussions of German guilt that opened this chapter, May attempts to explain how one can be linked to racially motivated harms that *other* people in one's group perpetrate. May wants to understand how can one be responsible for racially motivated crimes if one did not do anything to directly cause the harm. May argues that one is complicit if one contributes to the climate of racist attitudes that supports the harmful act. Although only certain members of a group might have directly perpetrated racial violence, May insists that "seemingly innocent" group members are also partially responsible if they share racist attitudes or if they fail to challenge these attitudes when exposed to them because in some deep sense they harbor such attitudes too.

While understanding white complicity through unconscious beliefs and attitudes has helped to expose the depth of white normativity in white psyches, such an approach remains limited because it is wedded to an individualist perspective that does not sufficiently appreciate how individuals are connected to larger social structures. Dwight Boyd[40] critiques the conception of persons, which he refers to as "the liberal individual," that haunts May's work. Although May refers to individuals as members of groups, Boyd argues that May still adheres to a notion of the subject that is presumed to be "ontologically unique" and "symmetrically positioned." In other words, May presumes that the subject is the center of consciousness and experience and distinct from others.

In addition, Boyd argues that May presupposes that, in terms of agency, all subjects are positioned equally and that the potential of agency is to be located in rational capacity. As Boyd explains,

> From this kind of perspective, socially recognizable action can be predicated only of individual subjective locations and only in so far as they engage in intentional behaviour to effect some desired state in the world.[41]

The danger is that such a focus on rational choice and intentions makes it seem as if social location is a function of individual choices over time. Such a notion of the subject obscures the ways in which whiteness gets constituted by being performed.

Boyd unequivocally rejects the presumption underlying the conception of the liberal individual that one's agentic potential for rational choice and intentionality involve a "capacity for transcendence." Such transcendence assumes a sense of autonomy understood as the possibility to overcome external constraints and "entails the possibility of standing outside of *any* existing social contingencies."[42] This understanding of the liberal individual is intricately connected to the assumption of the human as the pinnacle of reason. Social change, according to this notion of agency, is only possible to the extent that one can stand outside of social systems to enable one to critique them. Given Boyd's argument, two questions arise. First, what does it mean that one cannot stand outside of social systems? And, second, even if one does not need to completely stand outside of social systems to evaluate them, even if critique is possible from within a system, what does May's account with its emphasis on individual choice and the role of attitudes ignore? We will take the latter question first and address the former question only briefly here but will go in more detail in subsequent chapters.

The problem with May's account, according to Peg O'Connor,[43] is that it remains committed to the view "that people should only be judged morally responsible for those things that are under our control."[44] This emphasis on individual control overlooks and cannot account for the ways in which white people perpetuate racism through unintentional habits of their everyday practices and that are more accurately intertwined with white ways of being. In addition, May assumes that it is possible for a person not to have racist attitudes and become a good non-racist person. In doing so, he ignores that one can perpetuate systemic racial injustice even through one's seemingly moral acts.

Three features of May's account underestimate the larger social structures that connect individuals to systemic injustice. First, May reduces responsibility to having *negative* attitudes. It is often difficult to discern negative attitudes when practices that the white complicity claim points to are ones that are done with well-intentioned, not negative, attitudes or beliefs and are sanctioned by society's norms as "good." Second, May's approach explains how white people are *indirectly* responsible for overt harm that *other* white people directly perpetrate. This ignores the type of white complicity that involves practices that white people *themselves* live out and that are connected to the systemic privileges they experience. Finally, May presumes that white people can rid themselves of such negative attitudes if only they want to and try hard enough. In other words, May's approach neglects the ways in which power circulates through all white bodies in ways that make them *directly* complicit for contributing to the perpetuation of a system that they did not, as individuals, create.

Boyd and O'Connor allude to a second way that the white complicity claim gets fleshed out in the scholarship that is *not exclusively* focused on unconscious negative attitudes and beliefs towards people who are not white. This approach may or may not connect complicity with unconscious beliefs but is specifically focused on *practices and habits* of whiteness and *the consequences* of those practices and habits. Most significantly, this notion of white complicity is grounded in the belief that one cannot transcend the social system that frames how one makes meaning of oneself and the social world within which one is embedded.

Boyd offers perhaps one of the most useful metaphors to illustrate this relationship between individual qua social groups and a system of racial oppression and privilege. Boyd argues that racism is sustained by "mob-like" activity in which individuals are conceived qua members of a group similar to mob membership in which the "will of the mob does not seem reducible to the aggregate of the intentions of discrete mob members."[45] Boyd underscores the relational dimension involved in the constitution of social groups.

> One "finds oneself" in some particular social group *as and insofar* as one "finds" the other in a particular contrasting social group. For example, I am "white" insofar as others are deemed to be "black" (and other "colours"). (Further, I am "masculine" insofar as others are deemed to be "feminine"; I am "heterosexual" insofar as others are deemed to be "gay/lesbian," etc.) In every case, the "others'" social group identification depends on the reciprocal relationship.[46]

And this is not a reciprocity of equality as one group is always established as the norm from which other groups become "deviant."

Such a conception of complicity implies that the white subject has no identity as white except in contrast to that which has been contingently constructed as outside of its boundaries. Ruth Frankenberg succinctly articulates this although in terms of the "western self." She contends

> . . . the western self is itself produced as an *effect* of the western discursive production of its Others. This means that the western self and the non-western Other are co-constructed as discursive products, both of whose "realness" stand in extremely complex relationships to the production of knowledge, and to the material violence to which "epistemic violence" is intimately linked.[47]

Boyd further explicates that there is a sense of "proxy agency" in which, "'I' am unavoidably part of something that is doing something in me, for me, through me, as me."[48]

This second approach to white complicity can be found also in some of the scholarship that addresses white privilege. Wildman and Davis, for instance, contend that white supremacy is a system of oppression and privilege that all white people benefit from. Therefore, all white people

> . . . are racist in this use of the term, because we benefit from systemic white privilege. Generally whites think of racism as voluntary, intentional conduct done by horrible others. Whites spend a lot of time trying to convince ourselves and each other that we are not racist. A big step would be for whites to admit that we are racist and then to consider what to do about it.[49]

If racism involves a system of group privilege that white people benefit from and that simultaneously marginalizes people of color, such systemic privilege is not something that white people can renounce at will. Even when white people become aware of white privilege and want to disown it, the world continues to reinscribe privilege. White privilege, thus, cannot be renounced through individual volition.

In her discussion of white guilt by reason of privilege, Sandra Bartky similarly describes white complicity as culpability that does not stem from any particular individual act but is rather a product of something "far more global, namely, the very structure of the social totality itself that positions some as privileged, others as underprivileged."[50] White people perform and sustain whiteness continuously, often without conscious intent, often by doing nothing out of the ordinary. Bartky explains that

> . . . most white people in this country are complicit in an unjust system of race relations that bestows unearned advantages on them while denying these advantages to racial Others. Complicity in this system is neither chosen nor, typically, is it acknowledged, because there are both powerful ideological systems in place that serve to reassure whites that the suffering of darker-skinned Others is not of their doing and because the capacity of whites to live in denial of responsibility is very highly developed.[51]

I emphasize that for those in systemically privileged locations white complicity is not easily recognized because there are "powerful ideological systems in place that serve to reassure whites that the suffering of darker-skinned Others is not of their doing."[52] Moreover, the invisibility of white complicity is invoked when it is acknowledged that it is a privilege of being white that white people do not have to acknowledge their privilege because such privilege often consists in "what does *not typically happen to them*."[53]

Echoes of Boyd's mob metaphor can be discerned when Bartky argues that white complicity is not exclusively a matter of "doing" or "not doing" but often a matter of just "being." As she emphasizes, "On my view, I am guilty by virtue of simply being who and what I am: a white woman, born into an aspiring middle-class family in a racist and class-ridden society."[54] As I have previously underscored, this is not to imply that such being relates to an essentialist core but rather as will be discussed in Chapter 3 to contend that being and doing are inseparable and that doing constitutes being. The relevant point for now is that all white people are racist or complicit by virtue of benefiting from privileges that are not something they can voluntarily renounce.[55]

Such benefits are related to what Marilyn Frye refers to as whiteliness. Frye emphasizes the practices of whiteness in her discussion of "whiteliness" as a form of white being in the world. Frye equates "whiteliness" to "being masculine" as both masculinity and whiteliness are orientations towards the world or as Frye puts it "a deeply ingrained way of being in the world."[56] Shannon Sullivan likewise focuses on white ways of being by linking white privilege to unconscious habits that function invisibly in the way that whites do things and what they say "without thinking."[57] As an illustration of such habits of white privilege, Sullivan points to what she refers to as "white ontological expansiveness" or the tendency for white people "to act and think as if all spaces—whether geographical, psychical, linguistic, economic, spiritual, bodily or otherwise—are or should be available for them to move in and out of as they wish."[58]

One of the ways in which Sullivan's approach differs from those that equate white complicity merely with unconscious beliefs and attitudes is that Sullivan acknowledges that white people can be complicit *even when* they attempt to disrupt white privilege. For example, when a well-intentioned white person makes a conscious effort to disrupt her habit of living in an all-white neighborhood, "the sheer fact that she is able to make a choice about which neighborhood in which she lives, is . . . an effect of the privilege she has because of her race and economic class."[59] White ontological expansiveness involves, among other things, an unconscious arrogance in which white people presume they would be welcomed in all spaces. Moreover, privileged choice is that privilege to choose which spaces one can inhabit. Anti-racist white action, Sullivan insists, does not necessarily mean one has given up one's privilege and, in fact, can reinforce the very white privilege that the white anti-racist is trying to disrupt.

Such arrogance is emphasized in Frye's notion of whiteliness. Whiteliness, like being masculine, involves a belief in one's authority and in one's own experience as truth. In addition, whiteliness entails an unwillingness to be challenged that is protected by perceived white moral goodness. White people generally perceive themselves to be "morally good."

Whitely people generally consider themselves to be benevolent and good-willed, fair, honest and ethical. The judge, preacher, peacemaker, martyr, socialist, professional, moral majority, liberal, radical, conservative, working men and women—nobody admits to being prejudiced, everybody has earned every cent they ever had, doesn't take sides, doesn't hate anybody, and always votes for the person they think best qualified for the job, regardless of the candidate's race, sex, religion or national origin, maybe even regardless of their sexual preferences.[60]

Whiteliness involves the ways in which whiteness is performatively enacted. A conviction in regard to one's moral innocence or goodness is a characteristic of being whitely.

When the moral agency that one would call upon to raise awareness of such complicity conspires to camouflage the very complicity that needs to be exposed, white complicity becomes extremely problematic. In effect, whiteness becomes reinscribed and recentered in the very practices that attempt to work against social injustice. In his analysis of Lou Ann Johnson, the main character in the popular movie *Dangerous Minds* (played by Michelle Pfeiffer), Henry Giroux[61] provides a provocative example of this type of complicity. Johnson is depicted as an idealistic white teacher who is grappling with the challenge of academically motivating her "delinquent" students. Amidst a backdrop of the urban realities that construct these students as objects to be feared and as "rejects from hell," Johnson enters the story as "a good-hearted, well-meaning educator thrust into the classroom of 'at-risk' kids like a lamb led to the slaughter."[62] The film presents Johnson as pedagogically triumphant—indeed, she becomes "their light." Ironically, Johnson's very good-heartedness and her good intentions prevent her from actually hearing what her students are telling her about what their lives are all about.

More specifically, a theme running throughout Johnson's pedagogy is "choice." She tells her students that they have many choices in their lives and maintains that "choice" is the most powerful word in the English language. One grammar lesson begins with the sentence "I choose to die" and Johnson repeatedly insists that there are no victims in her classroom. While her good intentions may be to awaken her students' sense of agency and responsibility, the effect is to trivialize what choice means for her students. In effect, Johnson dismisses her students' real-life struggles by projecting the range of choice that she, a white middle-class woman, enjoys onto their lives, assuming that all they have to do is choose to work harder. Underlying this implicit "blame the victim" maneuver is a refusal to interrogate any complicity that Johnson herself might have in perpetuating a system of oppression that constructs the day-to-day reality of her students. Instead, she is allowed to think of herself as a savior, as doing something good *for them*. This heroic self-conception obscures Johnson's inability to recognize the restrictions of choice that circumscribe her students' lives. Such evasions of complicity do not result simply from personal and individual shortcomings; instead, they are grounded in powerful ideological structures that ensure that "nice" white people, those who have no prejudice or intention to harm, are innocent of any responsibility in sustaining systems that constitute and marginalize "Others."

White benevolence paradoxically provides an important site to search for signs of complicity that is obscured by white moral sensibilities. White benevolence often comes with implicit requisite demands, as Damien Riggs points out.[63] Riggs recounts how his white friend responded to a powerful quote on Riggs' refrigerator. The quote, by Lilla Watson, an Indigenous scholar, states, "If you have come to help me, you are wasting your time, but if you have come because your liberation is bound up with mine, let's work together." Riggs' white friend remarked quite indignantly, "Well, she's a rude bitch!" When Riggs asked what she meant, his friend said, "It was very ungrateful for the author to refuse help. Comments like that not only offend the people who want to help but will discourage them from helping in the future." In this illustration it becomes clear that the cost of a white person's benevolence is the silencing of the Other who might not find the white person's benevolence helpful and who may even believe that it usurps the Other's agency.

Whitely moral sensibilities often obscure complicity in other ways. In his study of "racism without racists," Eduardo Bonilla-Silva[64] explains how white people use the ideology of color-ignorance in ways that maintain systemic racial injustice without themselves appearing racist. In fact, the ideology of color-ignorance, the belief that race no longer matters in the United States and that racial inequality will disappear if we just stop referring to race, is often perceived by white people as a moral virtue. Amanda Lewis[65] explicates how color-ignorance is coded as moral and she demonstrates how the ideology of color-ignorance exists alongside color-conscious practices in schools in the United States. This refusal to take notice of color when color clearly matters consequently prevents racist patterns of practices from being recognized and interrogated.

Lewis[66] also contends that the discourse of color-ignorance encourages white people to dismiss what people of color are telling them through accusations such as "they are just playing the race card." In other words, if one believes it is a moral virtue not to take notice of color, then when color *is* relevant one will not have to notice it. One can, furthermore, dismiss what the victims of racism are saying as bringing in race where it does not belong. In his discussion of denials of white complicity, Tim Wise[67] suggests that "whatever 'card' claims of racism may prove to be for the black and brown, the denial card is far and away the trump, and whites play it regularly." White denials of complicity are an illustration of whitely ways of being. In other words, the claim that people of color "play the race card" is in itself a card being played—the white denial card. White denials of complicity will subsequently be taken up in more detail in the next chapter. Lewis adds that discourse that white people employ to protect their privilege from interrogation is often not conscious. White people instead seem to be saying just what they "believed to be true."[68]

Things become even more complex and thorny. Even when white people acknowledge their complicity, their white confessionals or public self-disclosures can serve to reinscribe privilege and offer redemption from complicity. Paraphrasing Foucault who equates confession with "whatever it is most difficult to tell,"[69] Robyn Wescott[70] argues that making one's whiteness visible is often like confession and that revealing what is "most difficult to tell" is rather like asking for penance. Judith Butler expresses a similar point when she writes,

> (T)aking account of race is thus equated with a reduction of the critic to a racial position. This willful act of self-reduction is sanctified as public self-declaration, and this culminates, paradoxically, in the production of the saintly white person, the responsible white person, the politically accountable white subject. In the place of a thoroughgoing analysis of race or racialization, we witness—obscenely, yet another self-glorification in which whiteness is equated with moral rectitude.[71]

Confessions of whiteness, therefore, constitute a form of pleasurable relief because what has produced the discomfort of learning about complicity is removed and one is purged of wrongdoing.

Thus, even the morality of the critic of whiteness must be interrogated for whitely ways. In her discussion of the declarations that white critics of whiteness pronounce, Sara Ahmed[72] explains how such utterances do something other than what they claim to do. Ahmed is not saying that in their declarations of whiteness, white people *do not mean* what they say. Instead, her point is that such assertions do not *do* what they say. For instance, in *declaring* "I am racist" or "I am complicit," the white critic of whiteness actually implies the opposite: "I am not racist" or "I am not complicit." Somewhat like the person who declares "I am modest" is clearly not a modest person, Ahmed cautions the white critic of whiteness that the assertion that "I am a bad white" can *indirectly* entail that "I am really a good white." Fiona Probyn contends that "a white studying whiteness trying not to reinscribe whiteness" is a paradox.[73] Whiteness is not only the object of the white critic's inquiry but also the subject and the obstacle to his/her project, especially when it obstructs the difficult task of being skeptical of the need to "have arrived somewhere."

What should be noticeably clear is that white privilege is something white people tend to assert even as they seek to challenge it. Fiona Probyn makes a piercing observation about the prevailing focus in critical whiteness studies on unmasking whiteness, unveiling, and then proclaiming "and now I see." In her discussion of the "shocks of revelation," she hopes that "it isn't just these shocks that keep the patient alive."[74] "Noble" declarations of whiteness, Probyn insists, must be probed for their desires for purity. Ahmed similarly cautions that the social conditions are not yet in place for white people to think that they can be non-racist[75] and she insists, "We need to consider the intimacy between privilege and the work we do, even in the work we do on privilege."[76]

Does this imply that whites cannot be ethically responsible when it comes to race and racism? It will be the aim of this book to refute such a conclusion. In fact, it will be argued that the white complicity claim does not reject the possibility of whites working to challenge racism. Instead, the white complicity claim calls for a specific type of vigilance that recognizes the dangers of presuming that one can transcend racist systems when one attempts to work to challenge racist systems. Ahmed hints at such a notion of vigilance when she notes,

> Surely the commitment to being against racism has "done things" and continues to "do things." What we might remember is that to be against something is precisely not to be in a position of transcendence: to be against something is, after all, to be in an intimate relations with that which one is against. To be anti "this" or anti "that" only makes sense if "this" or "that" exists. The messy work of 'againstness' might even help remind us that the work of critique does not mean the transcendence of the object of our critique; indeed, critique *might even be dependent on non-transcendence.*[77]

Even when white people think they are beyond race, race "sticks to us, or we become 'us' as an effect of how it sticks."[78] Ahmed exhorts whites to learn to live with this "stickiness" because it is the only way to effectively deal with racism.

According to white complicity in the second sense, being a good white is part of the problem rather than the solution to systemic racism. But then what can white moral responsibility consist of? This book addresses this crucial question. Traditional notions of moral responsibility that emphasize intentions and/or causal connections to harm tend to obscure white complicity rather than bring it to light. Moreover, such notions of responsibility encourage denials of complicity such as "I've never abused or insulted a black person" or "My parents came here thirty years ago from Croatia: my forebears were peasants not slaveowners."[79] As utterances, such statements might be true but they can also function as distancing strategies so that white people do not have to consider the subtle ways (subtle for white people) they are perpetuating a racist system and shielding the system from challenge.

One of the key points of the white complicity claim in the second sense described above is that it is problematic for white people to think that they can somehow stand outside of social contingencies. As Audrey Thompson cautions, "There is no such thing as racial innocence; there is only racial responsibility or irresponsibility."[80] This book takes seriously this second version of the white complicity claim because it encourages white people to grapple with racism perpetuated in the name of morality and with the best of intentions. Yet is there a model of moral responsibility that can reveal rather than conceal such white complicity? This question cannot be adequately addressed until we examine the conception of the subject that grounds the second version of the white complicity claim. Also required is an understanding of how discourse functions in our social world. First, however, we will take a closer look at the white complicity claim by examining two aspects of the claim that are illuminated when we complicate the notion of white privilege: systemic white ignorance and denials of complicity. With the connection between white ignorance and denials of complicity in mind, we can find a preliminary, although inadequate, way of explaining to students how "benefiting from a system" is connected to "contributing to its maintenance and perpetuation."

Three caveats before I continue. First, although systemic racism will provide the primary framework for the arguments subsequently developed, it is clear that racism is not the only type of social injustice nor does it stand alone. How and whether this framework of complicity can work for other axes of oppression is a question for future research. A second and related point is that although white complicity cannot but focus on whiteness, the dangers of using essentialist categories are acknowledged. While not claiming to circumvent these dangers, I invite feedback as to how this notion of complicity can be modified given the multiple ways that our identities intersect and especially the ways in which individuals can be simultaneously both systemically privileged and oppressed. Finally, in many parts of the paper I will use third-person pronouns to refer to white people even though I myself am white. The concern I have with using "we" is that it might imply that the arguments being advanced are exclusively addressed to white people. Although I use "they" or "them" to refer to white people, as a white person I include myself in everything I say here.

NOTES

1. Andrew Schaap, "Guilty Subjects and Political Responsibility: Arendt, Jaspers and the Resonance of the 'German Question' in Politics of Reconciliation," *Political Studies* 49, no. 4 (2001): 749–766. (Schaap is following Karl Jaspers in noting these posters.)

2. Hannah Arendt, *Eichmann in Jerusalem* (New York: Viking Press, 1964). Also see her "Personal Responsibility Under Dictatorship," in her *Responsibility and Judgment* (New York: Schocken Books, 2003), 17–48.

3. Arendt does not argue that all Germans are equally responsible. See her "Collective Responsibility" in her *Responsibility and Judgment*, 147–158, and "Organized Guilt and Universal Responsibility," in *Collective Responsibility: Decades of Debate in Theoretical and Applied Ethics*, ed. Larry May and Stacey Hoffman (Savage, Maryland: Rowman & Littlefield, 1991), 273–284.

4. Hannah Arendt, "Collective Responsibility," 147.

5. Karl Jaspers, *The Question of German Guilt* (Westport, Connecticut: Greenwood, 1948/1978).

6. Ibid., 32.

7. Ibid., 72.

8. See, for example, Mark McPhail, "(Re) Constructing the Color Line: Complicity and Black Conservativism," *Communication Theory* 7, no. 2 (1997): 162–175; Mae G. Henderson, "The Stories of O(Dessa): Stories of Complicity and Resistance," in *Female Subjects in Black and White: Race, Psychoanalysis, Feminism*, ed. Elizabeth Abel, Barbara Christian and Helen Moglen (Berkeley: University of California Press, 1997), 285–306.

9. Simone de Beauvoir, *The Second Sex*, translated by H. M. Parshley (New York: Penguin, 1949/1972); Sandra Lee Bartky, "On Psychological Oppression," in her *Femininity and Domination: Studies in the Phenomenology of Oppression* (New York: Routledge, 1990), 22–31; Susan James, "Complicity and Slavery in *The Second Sex*," in *The Cambridge Companion to Simone de Beauvoir*, ed. Claudia Card (Cambridge: Cambridge University Press, 2003), 149–167.

10. Jenny Gordon, "Inadvertent Complicity: Colorblindness in Teacher Education," *Educational Studies: A Journal of the American Educational Studies Association* 38, no. 2 (2005): 135–153.

11. Marilyn Frye, "On Being White: Thinking Toward a Feminist Understanding of Race and Race Supremacy," in her *The Politics of Reality: Essays in Feminist Theory* (Trumansburg, New York: Crossing Press, 1983), 113.

12. Linda Martin Alcoff, "What Should White People Do?" *Hypatia* 13, no. 3 (1998): 8.

13. Fiona Probyn, "Playing Chicken at the Intersection: The White Critic in/of Critical Whiteness Studies," *Borderlands* 13, no. 2 (2004) http://www.borderlandsejournal.adelaide.edu.au/vol3no2_2004/probyn_playing.htm (accessed July 19, 2009).

14. For some criticisms of white privilege pedagogy see Rosa Hernández Sheets, "Advancing the Field or Taking Center Stage: The White Movement in Multicultural Education," *Educational Researcher* 29, no. 9 (2000): 15–21; Maulana Karenga, "Whiteness Studies: Deceptive or Welcome Discourse?" Interview, *Black Issues in Higher Education* 16, no. 6 (May 13, 1999): 26; Sonia Kruks, "Simone de Beauvoir and the Politics of Privilege," *Hypatia* 20, no. 1 (2005): 178–205; Zeus Leonardo, "The Color of Supremacy: Beyond the Discourse of 'White Privilege'," *Educational Philosophy and Theory*, 36, no. 2 (2004): 137–152.

15. Sara Ahmed, "The Phenomenology of Whiteness," *Feminist Theory* 8, no. 2 (2007): 164–165.

16. Sara Ahmed, "Declarations of Whiteness: The Non-Performativity of Anti-Racism," *borderlands* e-journal 3, no. 2 (2004) http://www.borderlands.net.au/vol3no2_2004/ahmed_declarations.htm (accessed July 19, 2009).

17. Ibid.

18. Sara Ahmed, "The Phenomenology of Whiteness."

19. See David R. Roediger, ed., *Black Writers on What It Means to Be White* (New York: Schocken Books, 1998); Charles W. Mills, "White Right: The Idea of a Herrenvolk Ethics," in his *Blackness Visible: Essays on Philosophy and Race* (Ithaca: Cornell University Press, 1998), 139–166; W.E.B. Du Bois, *The Souls of Black Folk* (Boston: Bedford Books, 1920); bell hooks, *Black Looks: Race and Representation* (Boston: South End Press, 1992); Langston Hughes, *The Ways of White Folk* (New York: A.A. Knopf, 1969); and Toni Morrison, *Playing in the Dark: Whiteness and the Literary Imagination* (New York: Vintage Books, 1992).

20. Richard C. Lewontin, "The Apportionment of Human Diversity," *Evolutionary Biology* 6 (1972): 381–398; also see Kwame Anthony Appiah, *In My Father's House: Africa in the Philosophy of Culture* (New York: Oxford University Press, 1992) for an excellent review of the literature.

21. Michael Omi and Howard Winant, *Racial Formation in the United States: From the 1960s to the 1980s* (New York: Routledge, 1987).

22. Martha Minow, *Making All the Difference: Inclusion, Exclusion, and American Law* (Ithaca: Cornell University Press, 1990).

23. Toni Morrison, *Playing in the Dark*, 90.

24. Hazel V. Carby, "The Multicultural Wars," in *Black Popular Culture*, ed. Gina Dent (Seattle: Bay Press, 1992), 193.

25. Nelson M. Rodriguez, "Emptying the Content of Whiteness: Toward an Understanding of the Relation between Whiteness and Pedagogy," in *White Reign: Deploying Whiteness in America*, ed. Joe L. Kincheloe, Shirley R. Steinberg, Nelson M. Rodriguez, and Ronald E. Chennault (New York: MacMillan, 2000), 31–62; Howard Winant, "Behind Blue Eyes: Whiteness and Contemporary U.S. Racial Politics," in *Off White: Readings on Race, Power, and Society*, Michelle Fine, Lois Weis, L. C. Powell and L. M. Wong (New York: Routledge, 1991), 40–53; David R. Roediger, *The Wages of Whiteness: Race and the Making of the American Working Class* (New York: Verso, 1991).

26. Ruth Frankenberg, *White Women, Race Matters: The Social Construction of Whiteness* (Minneapolis: University of Minnesota Press, 1993), 1.

27. Cheryl Harris, "Whiteness as Property," *Harvard Law Review* 106, no. 8 (1993): 1707–1791.

28. Barbara Flagg, "Foreword: Whiteness as Metaprivilege," *Washington University Journal of Law and Policy* 18 (2005): 1.

29. Peggy McIntosh, "White Privilege and Male Privilege: A Personal Account of Coming to See Correspondences Between Work and Women's Studies," in *Critical*

White Studies: Looking Behind the Mirror, ed. Richard Delgado and Jean Stefancic (Philadelphia: Temple University Press, 1997), 291.

30. Ibid., 295.
31. Ibid.
32. Barbara Trepagnier, *Silent Racism: How Well-Meaning White People Perpetuate the Racial Divide* (Boulder: Paradigm Publishers, 2006), 15.
33. Ibid.
34. Ibid., 6.
35. Joyce E. King, "Dysconscious Racism: Ideology, Identity and Miseducation," in *Critical White Studies,* 128–132.
36. Ibid., 128.
37. Charles Lawrence III, "The Id, the Ego, and Equal Protection: Reckoning with Unconscious Racism," *Stanford Law Review* 39, no. 2 (1987): 317–388.
38. S. L. Gaertner and J.F. Dovidio, "The Aversive Form of Racism," in *Prejudice, Discrimination and Racism: Theory and Research,* ed. J.F. Dovidio and S.L. Gaertner (Orlando, FL: Academic Press), 61–89.
39. Larry May, *Sharing Responsibility* (Chicago: University of Chicago Press, 1992).
40. Dwight Boyd, "The Legacies of Liberalism and Oppressive Relations: Facing a Dilemma for the Subject of Moral Education," *Journal of Moral Education* 33, no. 1 (2004): 3–22.
41. Ibid., 10.
42. Ibid.
43. Peg O'Connor, *Oppression and Responsibility: A Wittgensteinian Approach to Social Practices and Moral Theory* (Pennsylvania State University Press, 2002).
44. Larry May, *Sharing Responsibility,* 44.
45. Dwight Boyd, "The Legacies of Liberalism," 13. Also see Dwight Boyd, "The Place of Locating Onself(Ves)/Myself(Ves) in Doing Philosophy of Education," *Philosophy of Education 1997,* Susan Laird, ed. (Urbana, Illinois: Philosophy of Education Society, 1998): 1–19.
46. Ibid., 16.
47. Ruth Frankenberg, *White Women, Race Matters: The Social Construction of Whiteness,* 16–17.
48. Dwight Boyd, "The Place of Locating," 17.
49. Stephanie M. Wildman with Adrienne D. Davis, "Language and Silence: Making Systems of Privilege Visible," in *Readings for Diversity and Social Justice,* ed. Maurianne Adams, Warren J. Blumenfeld, Rosie Castaneda, Heather W. Hackman, Madeline L. Peters and Ximena Zuniga (New York: Routledge, 2000), 56.
50. Sandra Lee Bartky, "In Defense of Guilt," in her *"Sympathy and Solidarity": And Other Essays* (Lanham: Rowman & Littlefield, 2002), 135–136.
51. Sandra Lee Bartky, "Race, Complicity, and Culpable Ignorance," in *"Sympathy and Solidarity,"* 154.
52. Ibid., 154.
53. Ibid., (emphasis added).
54. Ibid., 142.

55. Beverly Daniel Tatum, "*Why are All the Black Kids Sitting Together in the Cafeteria?*" *And Other Conversations About Race* (New York: Basic Books, 1997); Carol Brunson Phillips and Louise Derman-Sparks, *Teaching/Learning Anti-Racism: A Developmental Approach* (New York: Teachers College Press, 1997); Harlon L. Dalton, *Racial Healing: Confronting the Fear Between Blacks and Whites* (New York: Doubleday, 1995).

56. Marilyn Frye, "White Woman Feminist," in her *Willful Virgin: Essays in Feminism 1976–1992* (Freedom, CA: Crossing Press), 151.

57. Shannon Sullivan, *Revealing Whiteness: The Unconscious Habits of Racial Privilege* (Bloomington, Indiana: Indiana University Press, 2006), 4.

58. Ibid., 10.

59. Ibid.

60. Marilyn Frye, "White Woman Feminist," 154.

61. Henry Giroux, "Race, Pedagogy, and Whiteness in *Dangerous Minds*," *Cineaste* 22, no. 4 (1997): 46–49.

62. Ibid., 47.

63. Damien Riggs, "Benevolence and the Management of Stake: On Being 'Good White People'," *Philament* 4 (2004) http://www.arts.usyd.edu.au/publications/philament/issue4_Critique_Riggs.htm (accessed July 19, 2009).

64. Eduardo Bonilla-Silva, *Racism Without Racists: Color-Blind Racism and the Persistence of Racial Inequality in the United States* (Lanham: Rowman & Littlefield, 2003).

65. Amanda E. Lewis, "There is No 'Race' in the Schoolyard: Colorblind Ideology in An (Almost) All White School," *American Educational Research Journal* 38, no. 4 (2001): 781-812.

66. Amanda E. Lewis, "Whiteness Studies: Past Research and Future Directions," *African American Research Perspectives* 8, no. 1 (2002): 1–16.

67. Tim Wise, "What Kind of Card is Race? The Absurdity (and Consistency) of White Denial," http://www.zmag.org/content/showarticle.cfm?ItemID=10157 (accessed July 19, 2009).

68. Lewis, "Whiteness Studies," 9.

69. Michel Foucault, *The History of Sexuality: An Introduction* (New York: Vintage Books, 1978/1990), 59.

70. Robyn Westcott, "Witnessing Whiteness: Articulating Race and the 'Politics of Style'," *borderlands* e-journal 3, no. 2, (2004) http://www.borderlands.net.au/vol3no2_2004/westcott_witnessing.htm (accessed July 19, 2009).

71. Judith Butler, "Collected and Fractured: Response to Identities" in *Identities*, ed. K.A. Appiah and H.L. Gates (Chicago IL: University of Chicago Press, 1995), 443.

72. Sara Ahmed, "Declarations of Whiteness."

73. Fiona Probyn, "Playing Chicken at the Intersection."

74. Ibid.

75. Sara Ahmed, "Declarations of Whiteness."

76. Ibid.

77. Ibid.

78. Ibid.

79. Sandra Lee Bartky, "Race, Complicity," 141.

80. Audrey Thompson, "Not the Color Purple: Black Feminist Lessons for Educational Caring," *Harvard Educational Review* 68, no. 4 (1998): 524.

CHAPTER 2

White Ignorance
and Denials of Complicity

Linking "Benefiting From"
to "Contributing To"

WHITE COMPLICITY IN SYSTEMIC RACIAL INJUSTICE IS OFTEN ASSOCIATED WITH HAVING
white privilege. As Sandra Bartky puts it,

> . . . most people in this country are complicit in an unjust system of race relations
> that bestows unearned advantages on them while denying these advantages to
> racial Others.[1]

Those who take such a position envision racism as a system of group privilege
that white people benefit from and that simultaneously marginalizes people of
color. Racism so understood entails that all white people are racist or complicit
by virtue of benefiting from these privileges even though these privileges are
not something they can voluntarily renounce.[2]

After what I thought was a passionately engaged discussion of Peggy
McIntosh's[3] essay on white privilege, one of my white students asked, "I understand that I get these benefits and that other people don't. I also understand
that I get these benefits whether I am aware of it or not. How does that make
me complicit in systemic racism?" We had just discussed how white privilege
consists not only in the ability to walk through stores freely but also how privilege involves presumptions of white moral integrity when one is not followed.
Such privilege, I explained, was contingent upon the co-construction of Black
as morally suspect. I pointed to Lisa Delpit's[4] classic article, "The Silenced Dialogue," in which she demonstrates how unstated white norms in the classroom
privilege white students and more easily constitute them "as good students"
while those who do not conform to those norms are more readily labeled as
"problem students."

The white student's question also followed our discussion of Phillip, the
student in Kathy Hytten and John Warren's[5] study who recounts his efforts to
have the confederate flag removed from the mascot of his former high school.
Phillip's Black high school friend joined him in these efforts. Yet while both

he and his partner were equally active in this undertaking, people responded to and interpreted their endeavors very differently. Although Phillip was regarded as an individual who was engaged in laudable ethical work, his friend was considered as "another underprivileged black kid spending more time rebelling against authority than taking care of his grades, getting a job, and so on."[6] Phillip notes that prior to taking a course in diversity, he was aware that his friend was being treated in racist ways.

What he learns about this situation after taking the course, however, is that in this incident there were not only active, visible forms of oppression manifested but invisible ones as well. He offers, "prior to this reflection, I had failed to note that the racism in this experience came not just in the guise of individual acts of negative regard to my friend, but also in widespread and unthinking positive reaction to me."[7] My point in emphasizing Phillip's experience to the class was to complicate their understanding of white privilege and to underscore how systemic privilege protects white moral standing. In this way, I believed I could make it clear to my students how whites, sometimes without their volition, are implicated in the marginalization of Others.

Yet my student continued to demand explanations that would clarify why he was *personally* responsible for contributing to racism, especially since he insisted that he would want to renounce these privileges if he could. My white student's asking "Why am I responsible?" is a demand for a causal explanation that would elucidate why *he* is implicated in the maintenance of systemic racial injustice. It is a demand to know "why should *I* be blamed?" Given the conception of responsibility he has available to him that is connected to blame and fault, this does not seem like an unreasonable demand. Nevertheless, such conceptions of responsibility are not only inadequate to explain the type of white complicity that involves white ways of being but also can work to hide such complicity and make it impossible to consider.

In fact, my attempt to explain the link between "benefiting from" and "contributing to" that will subsequently be described was my effort at trying to provide my student with a causal link. In spite of this explanation, my student continued to resist any notion of responsibility in the sense of fault. What I realized is that what was needed was *not* a causal explanation between the individual and the system but a new conception of responsibility that did not rely so heavily on blame and causality.

Alternative notions of responsibility will be examined in subsequent chapters. In this chapter, I share my attempts to explain to my students how "benefiting from" is connected to "contributing to" because this explanation highlights the complex nature of systemic privilege. In order to make the link, I first had to challenge my students' simplistic understandings of white privilege and introduce a more complex notion of "benefit" that can account for the deep ways that white privilege is embedded in white ways of being and white moral sensibilities. With a more complex conception of systemic privilege and benefit, I believed I would be better equipped to move to a discussion of two manifestations of systemic white privilege that work hand in hand to protect white moral status and that shield systems of racial injustice from critique. The first of these manifestations of privilege is systemic white ignorance while the second involves white denials of privilege.

SYSTEMIC BENEFIT AND THE LIMITS OF WHITE PRIVILEGE PEDAGOGY

Currently, the leading approach in institutions of higher education across North America to teaching white students about their role in systemic racial injustice is "white privilege pedagogy." Although this approach has the advantage of exposing white students to the unrecognized benefits of whiteness, white privilege pedagogy has a number of serious shortcomings that require examination. I focus on the use of Peggy McIntosh's[8] essay because, although other scholars have published books and essays on white privilege, her essay has been enormously influential and has become a classic text in teaching about white privilege.

First of all, white privilege pedagogy often leads to a very superficial and simplistic analysis of privilege. White students who are first exposed to the idea that they have privilege (if they are not overtly resisting the idea that they have privilege) often perceive privilege as something individualistic, not systemic, and, thus, are able to ignore its relational dimension. McIntosh's claim that white privilege "confers dominance" clearly suggests the systemic aspect of privilege and also its relational effect but this aspect of her essay is often ignored or underemphasized in white privilege pedagogy.

That white people are not being followed around in stores because of their assumed moral standing, for example, is not *only* about the being able to walk through a store freely. Privilege also consists in the presumption of white moral integrity that is, in the larger picture, contingent upon the co-construction of Black as morally suspect. As Cynthia Kaufman succinctly explains,

> The image of the black thief helps stabilize the image of the average good citizen (who of course is coded as white). When I walk into a store and the clerks look at me with respect and assume that I am not going to steal anything, the trust that I receive is at least partially built upon the foundation of my distance from the image of the savage. When an African American walks into the store that unconscious material comes into play in the opposite way.[9]

White privilege protects and supports white moral standing and this protective shield depends on there being an "abject other" that constitutes white as "good." Whites, thus, benefit from white privilege in a very deep way. As Zeus

Leonardo[10] remarks, all whites are responsible for white dominance since their "very being depends on it."[11]

When I first began teaching about white privilege, I would ask my students to come up with three examples of how privilege in the sense that McIntosh articulates works on our own campus. Among the responses I received for what I thought was an exercise in recognizing dominant group privilege were:

> On Thursday night, females get free drinks in the bars while males have to pay all the time.
> Females get taken out on dates and the men pay for them.
> Students who work in the dining hall get free food.
> Blacks and other minorities get athletic scholarship and affirmative action benefits.

Not only did these white students fail to appreciate the relational aspect discussed above but they also entirely missed the systemic nature of dominant group privilege. Moreover, because of their individualistic focus they were also able to equate the benefits of affirmative action with the benefits of white privilege. "Whites as victim" discourse appears as a reasonable claim when white privilege is understood in individualist terms instead of relationally, collectively and macroscopically.[12] Such simplistic analyses of white privilege overlook the conditions that produce it.

The second line of critique of white privilege pedagogy targets how simplistic analyses of white privilege encourage naïve solutions in regard to having such privilege. It is not uncommon to hear white students claim that the remedy for racial injustice is just to ensure that all people have the privileges that white people enjoy. Laudable as this response initially seems (and, as I have been arguing, its laudability is part of its problem), it functions to relieve white students of considering any *direct* complicity they have in sustaining systems of racial oppression. Such solutions protect them from considering the unconscious habits and character traits that are manifestations of privileged experience and disregard how privilege is connected to one's very being constituted as white.

Privilege is not *only* a matter of receiving benefits but also consists in ways of being in the world. Sara Ahmed[13] discusses the phenomenology of whiteness that she illustrates by pointing to the tendency of white people to "take back the center" often without realizing it. Adrienne Rich makes a similar observation when she describes what she calls "white solipsism" or the penchant of whites "to speak, imagine and think as if whiteness described the world."[14] Shannon Sullivan[15] exemplifies white privilege as unconscious habits of whiteness when she highlights "white racial expansiveness" or the tendency of whites to think and act as if all spaces are or should be at their disposal, as they desire. These are all systemically privileged ways of being in the world.

McIntosh, quite correctly I believe, alludes to these negative ways of white being when she distinguishes between positive privileges that everyone should have and negative privileges that none should.

> We were given the cultural permission not to hear voices of people of other races, or to tepid cultural tolerance for hearing or acting on such voices . . . [16]

Some benefits of white privilege, McIntosh emphasizes, authorize white people to be ignorant, oblivious and arrogant *sometimes without realizing that that is what they are doing.* Yet white students (and teachers) so often overlook or de-emphasize this section of McIntosh's essay.

The "knapsack metaphor" particularly promotes this selective reading of McIntosh's essay. When the knapsack frames how one understands privilege, the implication is that privilege can be taken off or disowned at will and that there is a nonracial subject that will emerge if only one can divest oneself of white privilege. White students often walk away from reading McIntosh's article thinking that all there is to being anti-racist is "taking off the knapsack" without acknowledging that privilege is often ascribed even when one is not aware of it and even when one refuses it. The knapsack metaphor not only severely overlooks the unconscious habits and character traits[17] that are manifestations of privileged experiences but also allows white students to take no notice of privileged discourses of denial. In other words, white privilege pedagogy frequently ignores how the experience of systemic white privilege is constitutive of what it means to be white and how it infuses white moral ways of being.

Furthermore, white privilege pedagogy encourages a focus on white confessionals. Since white privilege pedagogy has developed based on the premise of the invisibility of white privilege, its prime objective is raising personal awareness of privilege. This leads to an individualistic psychologizing of privilege that white students assume can redeem them from complicity. The emphasis on personal awareness, therefore, overshadows the need for understanding and challenging the system of power that supports white privilege. White students often assume that responsibility begins and ends with the awareness of privilege. By admitting to or confessing privilege, however, white students are actually able *to avoid* owning up to their complicity in systemic racism. As Cynthia Levine-Rasky[18] argues,

> If the formula "education is transformation" drives a pedagogy inspired by liberalism, the mere hearing of white privilege may perform an educative function emancipating whites from participation in systems of domination. When learning about white privilege fulfills this redemptive function, the exercise becomes a confessional.[19]

Confessions of privilege, according to Levine-Rasky, serve as a "redemptive outlet" through which white students are able to perceive themselves as "good whites" in comparison to those "bad whites" who do not acknowledge privilege.

Similarly, by acknowledging their privilege white students might be led to believe that they have "arrived" and that they do not have to worry anymore about how they are implicated in systemic racial injustice. The assumption is "that confessing to the inner working of whiteness in their lives would redeem them from their complicity with racism."[20] Levine-Rasky further explains why this is so problematic.

> Emphases on white privilege often portray white social actors as author of social relations rather than inequitably interdependent upon the racialization of others through unjust social and historical processes. Teacher candidates may inhabit a whiteness normalized through its obliviousness to its effects, but they are also inscribed in the racist practices and discourses and history of their institutions and of the dominant culture in general. The contexts in which educators live and work are also white-dominated and the narratives they draw from to explain problems such as educational inequality are derived from this larger context.[21]

When white privilege is understood as a knapsack that one can take off at will, white students may too easily believe that by just confessing white privilege they are off the moral hook.

White privilege pedagogy fails to encourage white students to understand that "white domination is never settled once and for all; it is constantly re-established and reconstructed by whites from all walks of life."[22] While white privilege pedagogy acknowledges how good white people, who profess to be lovers of justice, perpetuate racism, it does not go far enough. The knapsack metaphor implies that privilege is separate from the constitution of white being and encourages the belief that once divested from privilege the white student is transformed to non-racist. The metaphor of the knapsack does not bring to attention the ways in which power works through white bodies and white discourses and that whites have to be continually vigilant of the ways in which whiteness preserves its invisibility.

Zeus Leonardo expands this critique of white privilege pedagogy when he advocates that white privilege must be studied not from a personal perspective but from the perspective of white supremacy because it is "the condition of white supremacy that makes white privilege possible."[23] Leonardo draws attention to the passivity assumed in white privilege pedagogy by responding to a seemingly innocent comment made by James Joseph Scheurich, a white educational researcher who has published many articles on whiteness and his own struggles to become aware of it. Scheurich equated white privilege to walking down the street and having money put in one's pocket without one's knowledge. Leonardo explains that this description of white privilege minimizes the active role that whites play in maintaining the system of racial oppression. "If money is being placed in white pockets," Leonardo wants to know, "who places it there?"[24]

Leonardo concedes that the description of white privilege that Scheurich works with has been of some value because it both encapsulates unearned privilege and also white people's obliviousness about it. He insists, however, that it is also dangerous because it

> downplay(s) the *active* role of whites who take resources from people of color all over the world, appropriate their labor, and construct policies that deny minorities full participation in society.[25]

White people do not only benefit from having money put in their pockets, Leonardo argues, they also take resources from people of color. Failing to pay attention to these processes perpetuates white innocence.

One of the ways that whites *actively* perpetuate systemic injustice is when they are privileged in ways that give them permission to be ignorant, oblivious, arrogant and destructive. Such negative white privilege is often manifested in discursive practices that deny complicity and that profess white innocence. To ignore such privilege is to disregard the injustice that good white people are perpetrating now, in the present and continually. White privilege pedagogy, thus, ironically works to protect white innocence rather than challenge white supremacy.

Ladelle McWhorter (although, like Leonardo, does not mean to be totally dismissive) wonders whether Whiteness Studies that focuses on white privilege "seeks not so much to destabilize race and end white supremacy as to find ways of being white (or of ceasing to be white) that purify individuals of racial complicity or guilt, that the movement *is more about innocence than about justice or transformation.*"[26] To be critical of white supremacy, as Leonardo contends, involves being less concerned about "the issue of unearned advantages, of the *state* of being dominant, and more around the direct processes that secure domination and the privileges associated with it."[27]

One of the consequences of white privilege pedagogy, as Leonardo takes pains to emphasize, is that my white students resist understanding the link between privileges that benefit white people and how such benefits *sustain* systems of oppression. It should come as no surprise that white students often assume that the remedy for having privilege is "giving it up" as if, like a knapsack, one can take up and take off systemic privilege at will when theorists and researchers have demonstrated not only that privilege is bestowed despite attempts by white people to denounce it[28] but also that privilege is deeply embedded in white ways of being.

When my students read McIntosh's article, they often come away understanding privilege as a sort of material gain and even psychological advantage. The term "privilege" pulls in this direction. But what they often fail to comprehend, although McIntosh clearly mentions this in her essay, is how white privilege also involves *protecting a type of moral certainty, arrogance and innocence.* My white students often remain trapped in an individualistic conceptualization of the benefits of white privilege and do not recognize such benefits' relational, collective and macroscopic[29] dimensions. To help them to understand how benefits need to be understood macroscopically, it is helpful to draw their attention to two ways that the meaning of harm can be determined. These different ways of understanding harm can be applied to understand different ways of comprehending benefits.

Surveys continue to find that there are large differences between the views of white and Black Americans on key measures of race relations in the United States such that in general whites minimize the effects of racism existing today.[30] One of the reasons that can explain why white people tend to minimize the effects of racism is, of course, that they do not have to experience the harms of racism. But even when the stories of such harms are made available, they still may be dismissed because harm is being perceived from the perpetrator's perspective. Critical Race Theorist Alan David Freeman[31] distinguishes between harm determined from the *perspective of the victim* and the *perspective of the perpetrator.* Understanding harm from the victim's perspective involves searching for

> those conditions of actual social existence as a member of a perpetual underclass
> . . . (and) include both the objective conditions of life . . . and the consciousness
> associated with those objective conditions . . . .[32]

Understanding harm from the victim's perspective involves more than just asking an individual victim what "harm" consists of. It involves understanding harm from the viewpoint of an unjust *system.*

Discrimination from the perpetrator's perspective, in contrast, is understood individualistically, not as systemic conditions but as individual actions, or series of actions, inflicted on the victim by the perpetrator. The focus is on *individual* fault and causality, on *what particular perpetrators have done or are doing to some victims* rather than on the overall life situation of the victim class.[33]

While there are dangers in using the term "victims" to describe the viewpoint of those who are marginalized, the central point to emphasize is that just as the harms of racism must be understood from a systemic viewpoint, so too the benefits of racism must be perceived *not individualistically* but *systemically.* In other words, the emphasis is on *the objective consequences of such benefits and how such benefits function systemically.* Only with this expanded notion of benefit can white students begin to appreciate how deeply white privilege is embedded in white ways of being and how white privilege functions systemically. Privilege is not only a matter of receiving benefits but also consists in traits of character or a certain outlook about the world and how people move around in the world that is sanctioned by dominant norms and work to keep systemic injustice in place.

With this expanded notion of privilege, harms and benefits, I move on to two manifestations of white privilege that require emphasis.

SYSTEMIC WHITE IGNORANCE

> Privilege . . . gives whites a way to not know that does not even fully recognize the extent to which they do not know that race matters or that their agency is closely connected with their status.[34]

Cris Mayo's provocative but discerning quote highlights the connection between privilege, ignorance and denials of complicity. It is Charles Mills, however, who has drawn special attention to the *epistemology* of ignorance[35] and, in particular, the dynamics of white ignorance. Mills' work is guided by the question, "How are white people able to consistently do the wrong thing while thinking that they are doing the right thing?"[36]

In his oft-cited book, *The Racial Contract*, Mills argues that a Racial Contract underwrites the modern Social Contract. The Racial Contract is a *covert* agreement or set of meta-agreements between white people to create and maintain a subperson class of non-whites. The purpose of the Racial Contract is to "secur(e) the privileges and advantages of the full white citizens and maint(ain) the subordination of nonwhites."[37] To achieve this purpose, there is a need to perpetuate ignorance and to misinterpret the world as it really is. The Racial Contract is an agreement to not know and *an assurance that this will count as a true version of reality* by those who benefit from the account. That such ignorance is socially sanctioned is of extreme significance. Mills refers to such lack of knowledge as an "inverted epistemology" and contends it is an

> officially sanctioned reality (that) is divergent from actual reality. . . . one has an agreement to *mis*interpret the world. One has to learn to see the world wrongly, but with the assurance that this set of mistaken perceptions will be validated by white epistemic authority, whether religious or secular.[38]

White ignorance, thus, will *feel* like knowledge to those who benefit from the system because it is supported by the social system as knowledge.

When I discussed Mills' work with one of my white colleagues, he charged Mills' arguments with promoting a type of "conspiracy theory." Thus, it is important to emphasize that Mills is not implying that an actual racial contract has taken place. Rather, the racial contract is a sort of imaginary device that can explain how systematic white ignorance remains unchallenged.

In his 2007 article titled "White Ignorance"[39] Mills further explains that white ignorance is distinguished from general patterns of ignorance "prevalent among people who are white but in whose doxastic states race has played no determining role."[40] Moreover, white ignorance is not exclusively focused on the type of ignorance prevalent in overtly racist white individuals who are uneducated but additionally covers the type of *not knowing* existing in even those who are well-intended and "educated" which "after the transition from de jure to de facto white supremacy, it is precisely this kind of white ignorance that is most important."[41]

White ignorance, accordingly, has a number of characteristic features among which are that it is intimately connected to racial positionality and works to protect white interests. Both these features of white ignorance need elucidation. First, white ignorance involves a "not knowing" that is *intimately* connected to racial positionality. As such, white ignorance is part of an epistemology of ignorance, "a particular pattern of localized and global cognitive dysfunctions (which are psychologically and socially functional), producing the ironic outcome that whites will in general be unable to understand the world they themselves have made."[42]

A good illustration of such white ignorance can be found in George Yancy's "Fragments of a Social Ontology of Whiteness."[43] Yancy describes how a white philosopher whom he deeply respected cautioned Yancy with deep concern and out of good intentions not to get pegged as someone who pursues issues in African-American philosophy. Yancy immediately thinks,

> "Pegged! I'm doing philosophy!" It immediately occurred to me that the introductory course in philosophy that I had taken with him some years back did not include a single person of color. Yet, *he did not see* his own philosophical performances—engagements with European and Anglo-American philosophy as "pegged"; he simply taught philosophy qua philosophy. Such a philosophy only masquerades as universal.[44]

In this illustration, race is a fundamental factor in the type of ignore-ance exhibited by the white philosopher.

As Mills underscores, such ignorance is connected to the conceptual framework that white people have at their disposal. Such ignorance is made possible because the conceptual framework from which one interprets one's social world "will not be neutral but oriented toward a certain understanding."[45] While Marxists refer to this as ideology, Mills notes that Foucault refers to this as discourse. In addition, Mills, enormously influenced by standpoint theorists, maintains that " . . . if the society is one structured by relations of domination and subordination . . . then in certain areas this conceptual apparatus is likely going to be shaped and inflected in various ways by the biases of the ruling group(s)."[46] Whatever one perceives, it is the "concept (that) is driving the perception."[47]

Mills, furthermore, insists, "whites (are) aprioristically intent on denying what is before them."[48] In other words, the exhibited ignorance is not merely a lack of knowledge that results from a cognitive flaw of a particular individual or, as Linda Alcoff explains, merely an individual's bad epistemic practice but rather is "a substantive epistemic practice itself."[49] White ignorance is a product of an *epistemology* of ignorance, a systemically supported, socially induced pattern of (mis)understanding the world that is connected to and works to sustain systemic oppression and privilege. White ignorance parallels what Joe Feagin and Henan Vera term as "sincere fictions" or the "personal ideological constructions that reproduce societal mythologies at the individual level."[50] Most significant, these white delusions about racism also function to protect white people from having to recognize their own racism.

Eve Sedgwick[51] brings to our attention how systemic ignorance is not a passive lacking, as the term "ignorance" implies, but is an activity. Extending Sedgwick's insights to the discourse of color-ignorance, Cris Mayo contends that such ignoring is not a "lack of knowledge" but "a particular kind of knowledge"[52] that does things. Mills argues that one's social positionality and the knowledge connected to it will influence what questions one believes are important to ask and the problems one believes are valuable to pursue. White ignorance involves not asking or not having to ask (i.e., having the privilege not to need to ask) certain questions. The Racial Contract, according to Mills, involves

> . . . simply a failure to ask certain questions, taking for granted as a status quo and baseline the existing color-coded configurations of wealth, poverty, property, and opportunities, the pretence that formal, juridical equality is sufficient to remedy inequities created on a foundation of several hundred years of racial privilege, and that foundation is a transgression of the terms of the social contract.[53]

Thus, white ignorance is a type of knowledge that protects systemic racial injustice from challenge.

In a distressing illustration of such habits of selective attention, Tyron Foreman and Amanda Lewis[54] underscore the intense surprise that many white Americans expressed after Hurricane Katrina about the social reality of racial inequality in New Orleans. Foreman and Lewis attribute this astonishment to a racial apathy that is a consequence of the white ignorance manifested in the

of color ignore-ance. White ignorance, therefore, generates specific
!elusions or wrong ways of perceiving the world that are socially
validated by the dominant norms and protect those norms from being interrogated.

Second, white ignorance is not only itself a type of white privilege (Who
has the privilege to be ignorant?) but also works to safeguard privilege. Mills
underscores that it is white group interest that is a "central causal factor in gen-
erating and sustaining white ignorance."[55] Such ignorance functions to mystify
the consequences of such unjust systems so that those who benefit from the
system do not have to consider their complicity in perpetuating it. There are
benefits for the dominant social group of such ignorance. In her analysis of
willful ignorance in literary characters, Vivian May writes, "there are many
things those in dominant groups are taught *not* to know, encouraged *not* to
see, *and the privileged are rewarded for this state of not-knowing.*"[56] Quoting
from Peggy McIntosh, May explicates that willful ignorance involves *a pattern
of assumptions* that privileges the dominant group and gives license to members of those groups "to be ignorant, oblivious, arrogant, and destructive"[57] all
the while thinking themselves "as good."

The connection between white privilege and white ignorance is intimated
when both Alcoff and May refer to white ignorance as *willful* ignorance. Although such ignorance may be willful in the sense of intended, it often appears
that white people are not even conscious of such ignorance, so in what sense
is it willful?

The term "willful ignorance" has often been employed to refer to a blatant
avoidance or disregard of facts or well-founded arguments because they oppose
one's personal beliefs, values or worldviews. Willful ignorance is customarily
used to refer to laziness or fear of critically examining one's personal point of
view. In other words, it is to intentionally remain ignorant of something that
one *should* know but one does not want to know. Willful seems to imply a level
of knowing, i.e., that one wants to ignore knowing and is aware of what one is
doing, as is evidenced in Thomas Green's description of such ignorance as

> that condition that I note from time to time in those who (1) are ignorant on
> some matter important to their lives, (2) *are aware of their ignorance,* but even
> more than that, are (3) resolved to remain in their ignorance, (4) not the least
> because it is such a source of enjoyment and pleasure to them. I suppose that
> each of us can recall someone who fits this description. It is a bit more difficult
> to admit what is probably no less true, that there are traces of this sort of thing
> in ourselves.[58]

White ignorance may be but is not always the result of a deliberate and conscious decision. Yet, as already noted, often such ignorance does not seem

willful in the sense of intentional but rather the product of a socially induced tendency to ignore that involves being *unaware that one does not know*. Why categorize white ignorance as willful?

I suggest that white ignorance might be understood to be a form of willful ignorance because willful ignorance is *culpable* ignorance. Interesting and complex questions about culpable ignorance can be found in the ethical debates around moral responsibility and will be addressed in Chapter 5. Briefly, involuntary ignorance is often thought to excuse one from moral culpability unless one knowingly contrives one's own ignorance. Then one is culpable even if one is ignorant.[59]

White ignorance may be a type of willful ignorance because there is a sense in which white people deliberately contrive their own ignorance. But white ignorance might also be willful not necessarily because the ignorance is consciously or deliberately manufactured but instead willful *because such ignorance benefits the person or the social group the person is a member of*. Members of the dominant group, for instance, have *a vested interest* in not knowing. Linda Alcoff[60] emphasizes that white people not only have less interest in understanding their complicity in social injustice than those who are victimized by such systems but also that white people have a *positive interest* in remaining ignorant. The point is that even if one does not deliberately manufacture such ignorance, white ignorance does not release one from moral responsibility and might be willful in the sense that it is something that someone *would* want. One of the types of vested interests that such ignorance serves is the sustaining of one's moral self-image.

Because of white ignorance, white people will be unable to understand the racial world they themselves have made. One of the significant features of white ignorance is that it involves not just "not knowing" but also "not knowing what one does not know and *believing that one knows*." *White ignorance is a form of white knowledge. It is a type of ignorance that arrogantly parades as knowledge.* Rather than an absence of knowledge, white ignorance is a particular way of everyday knowing or thinking that one knows how the social world works that is intimately related to what it means to be white.[61] Moreover, such "ignorance as knowledge" is socially sanctioned. Thus white people tend not to hesitate to dismiss and rebuff the knowledge of those who have been victims of systemic racial injustice rather than engaging with them, inquiring for more information and having the humility to acknowledge what they do not know.

What do white people know, what do they not know, and what can they know? Although I will not explore this conjecture here, the binaries knowledge/ignorance and knowing/not knowing not only seem inadequate but also misleading in terms of understanding the epistemological dynamics of whiteness. Further study of these binaries is required especially for those involved in helping white students acknowledge "white ignorance that is taken as knowledge."

What is significant is that white knowledge of the social world that is really white ignorance fuels *a refusal to consider* that one might be morally complicit and further promotes a resistance to knowing. Consequently, concepts "necessary for accurately mapping these realities will be absent."[62] In a provocative but evidently correct observation, Mills notes, "the crucial conceptual innovation necessary to map nonideal realities has *not* come from the dominant group."[63] All the more important for white people to acknowledge white ignorance so that they can hear what those who are not from the dominant group are telling them.

Although it is not only white people who are susceptible to white ignorance, white people are *particularly* susceptible because they are the ones who have the most to gain from remaining ignorant. As Sandra Harding argues, it is members of oppressed groups, those who have direct experience with oppression, who "have fewer interests in ignorance about the social order and fewer reasons to invest in maintaining or justifying the status quo than do dominant groups."[64] Again, this is not to imply that all members of oppressed groups automatically have such knowledge. Alcoff explains,

> identity does not determine one's interpretation of the facts, nor does it constitute fully formed perspectives, but rather, to use the hermeneutic terminology once again, identities operate as horizons from which certain aspects or layers of reality can be made visible. In stratified societies, differently identified individuals do not always have the same access to points of view or perceptual planes of observation. Two individuals may participate in the same event, but have perceptual access to different aspects of that event. Social identity is relevant to epistemic judgment, then, not because identity determines judgment but because identity can in some instances yield access to perceptual facts that themselves may be relevant to the formulation of various knowledge claims or theoretical analyses.[65]

What Alcoff underscores is that there is a greater tendency for those who experience the harms of systemic racism than those who benefit from it to be troubled by the normalization of white space and to be more affected by the white norms that are mystified as universal when they are not.

White people have a positive interest in remaining ignorant because such ignorance serves to sustain white moral innocence. White ignorance, however, simultaneously protects systems of privilege and oppression from being interrogated. Whiteness, according to Mills, requires certain "opacities in order to establish and maintain the white polity."[66] In her 1984 book, *The Politics of Reality*, Marilyn Frye similarly argues that ignorance is indispensable for the perpetuation of white power and privilege. She contends that ignorance is "not something simple; it is not a simple lack, absence or emptiness, and it is not a passive state."[67] In order to know one must pay attention, Frye contends. So too not knowing requires an *active* interest in ignoring or a *resistance* to knowing what is right in front of you. White people, Frye maintains, *actively refuse to pay attention to their complicity in racism.* Ignorance is "the condition that ensures its continuance."[68]

Systemic benefit works not only to keep ignorance in place but also to keep the status quo from being challenged. Mills cautions that it is crucial that white people take these "recognition problems"[69] seriously since, "(I)t becomes easier to do the right thing if one knows the wrong things that, to one's group, will typically *seem* like the right thing."[70] Yet it is not easy to get white people to consider their complicity. *Denials of complicity* are not understood to be "denials" but because of white ignorance masquerade as white racial common sense.

WHITE DENIALS OF COMPLICITY

A burgeoning body of research has developed around white denials of complicity. Such denials involve discursive ways in which white people reject any role in systemic racism and in which white people proclaim their white innocence. Sandra Bartky[71] delineates a typology of such denials in which is included the culpably ignorant or those who fail to know what they ought to know because such knowledge would morally implicate them. Since people generally want to see themselves as morally good, Bartky argues, any intimation that one plays a part in perpetuating unjust systems of oppression and privilege will be rebuffed.

Among the ways that white people protect their moral innocence, as already noted, is to maintain ideologies of color ignore-ance and meritocracy that, in effect, deny and dismiss how racism exists in the lives of the marginalized. Those who do not experience racism will more likely profess its non-existence or diminish its effects and, consequently, also relieve themselves of having to consider how they might be complicit in perpetuating a system that to them does not exist.

Peg O'Connor offers illustration of such white denial that may be familiar to those who teach courses that attempt to challenge systemic social injustice. O'Connor describes the response of her white student who resists engaging with the possibility that race and the ability to secure a mortgage are related. When shown statistics that support how people of color are refused a mortgage to a significant degree more than white people, the white student

... may seek out and then parade a variety of explanations for the refusal—the person may have bad credit history, the refusal does not have anything to do with the race of the person, but only with that person's financial history. Or the refusal may have nothing to do with the person but rather with the neighborhood. The neighborhood is the problem, not race. It just wouldn't make good business sense to give homeowners' loans for houses in certain neighborhoods. Banks have obligations to their customers.[72]

The point is not to reject the possibility that in isolated cases one of these explanations might be considered but instead to focus on how such discursive practices are a more global denial to contemplate the possibility that race and getting a mortgage might be related. No matter what one produces to try to engage this student with the possibility that financial history and race are systemically related, the student continues to refuse to even consider that race might be a factor. The student may even come back with the allegation that Black people are always "playing the race card."

As already noted in Chapter 1, the charge of "playing the race card" is often, ironically, the white denial card in play. Tim Wise[73] examines the "playing the race card" accusation and he calls into question why anyone would want to play this card especially since the card is often ineffective. Even if some people do play the "race card," Wise compellingly contends that white people play the white denial card even more frequently. White people have always doubted people of color when they claim that racism exists. In fact, this is why playing the race card is usually futile. White people, Wise notes, often continue to deny the racial aspects of incidents even when they are compelled to recognize the strong evidence that is produced before them. Wise concludes that "whatever 'card' claims of racism may prove to be for the black and brown, the denial card is far away the trump, and whites play it regularly."

Educational researchers, especially researchers who study how white students engage in social justice education, have given serious attention to such denials. At the present time, there are a plethora of studies[74] that have explored how white students use discursive maneuvers to resist knowledge of their complicity. Such resistance is expressed in multifarious ways from emotional oppositional outbursts in class to passivity and silence. Kim Case and Annette Hemmings[75] refer to "distancing strategies" to describe how white women preservice teachers avoid being positioned as racist or implicated in systemic oppression. They use these strategies to avoid acknowledging responsibility. Elizabeth Higgenbothan[76] underscores this very same point when she notes how it is not enough to explain different definitions of racism or to teach about the meaning of oppression. White students often resist this knowledge because the only message they can hear is "you are to blame."

Kathy Hytten and John Warren's outstanding ethnography of the rhetorical moves their white students performed in courses that attempt to teach about systemic oppression and privilege offers many examples of such tactics. Among the types of discursive strategies that Hytten and Warren discuss are:

remaining silent, evading questions, resorting to the rhetoric of ignoring color, focusing on progress, victim blaming and focusing on culture rather than race. Hytten and Warren emphasize that these discursive moves are culturally sanctioned discourses of evasion that "were not original—that is, they are already available, already common forms of asserting dominance."[77] These rhetorical strategies work to obstruct engagement so that deliberations about one's complicity in systemic oppression can be avoided.

Along similar lines, Alice McIntyre[78] coined the phrase "white talk" to name discourse that functions to "insulate White people from examining their/our individual and collective role(s) in the perpetuation of racism."[79] Sandra Bartky also explains how the unwillingness to acknowledge complicity in racism is more than just a personal lethargy or a private failure but rather a culturally sanctioned discourse of evasion that protects the interests of the privileged and their moral composure. What becomes apparent throughout this scholarship is that white ignorance is not only sustained by denials of complicity but white ignorance also authorizes such denials. In effect, "resisters" believe they are just disagreeing with the material. Consequently, their disagreement also functions as a "justified" reason to dismiss and to refuse to engage with what is not compatible with their beliefs.

One can disagree and remain engaged in the material, for example, by asking questions and searching for clarification and understanding. Denials, however, function as a way to distance oneself from the material and to dismiss *without engagement*. Hytten and Warren explain that such strategic denials are not only already available in the sense that they are socially authorized but also that they serve to protect the center, the location of privilege. Such discursive strategies of denial are an "implicit way of resisting critical engagements with whiteness."[80] When white students, for instance, refuse to acknowledge the depth of their privilege, their privilege is reflected in the very questioning of the social facts that are at odds with their experience. They have what Peggy McIntosh refers to as permission to escape[81] and what Alice McIntyre identifies as "privileged choice."[82] In other words, the mere fact that they can question the existence of systemic oppression is a function of their privilege to choose to ignore discussions of systemic oppression or not.

Color ignore-ance, as already noted, is a widespread position of moral belief but is also a strategy of denial.[83] A refusal on the part of white students to "see" color functions as a way in which to establish their moral, non-racist credentials. Moreover, they become defensive when such beliefs are challenged because to challenge such beliefs would entail challenging their moral innocence.[84] The students believe they are just expressing their belief but that belief also functions to shield them from any consideration of their own complicity. Nado Aveling contends, "These students firmly refused to 'see' colour as a means of establishing their *non-racist credentials* and became defensive when their assumptions were challenged."[85] To consider such challenges would implicate their moral innocence. There are a variety of socially sanctioned discursive practices available to systemically privileged students to avoid engaging with the fact of systemic oppression and their complicity in it. These discursive practices consist of a refusal to engage and involve a premature dismissal of whatever the student hears.

Ideologies of individualism also support white denials of complicity. In his discussion of the individualism that grounds color ignore-ance, Woody Doane explains that when whites claim that they do not notice race, they do not have to engage with the possibility that race matters or to see themselves in racial terms. This protects whites from having to consider the privileges they systemically enjoy. If they do not have to acknowledge their privilege, then they can rely exclusively on individualistic explanations for inequality.

> Whites also exhibit a *general inability* to perceive the persistence of discrimination and the effects of more subtle forms of institutional discrimination. In the context of color-blind racial ideology, whites are more likely to see the opportunity structure as open and institutions as impartial or objective in their functioning ... this combination supports an interpretive framework in which whites' explanations for inequality focus upon the cultural characteristics (e.g., motivation, values) of subordinate groups ... Politically, this blaming of subordinate groups for their lower economic position serves to neutralize demands for antidiscrimination initiatives or for a redistribution of resources.[86]

If white students believe that it is morally justified to refuse to consider race, they not only are authorized to ignore racial patterns of social injustice, they will also feel warranted in refusing to use racial labels to describe themselves. As a result, the unearned privilege that they are afforded because of their racial positionality can be disregarded or dismissed. Moreover, when they are confronted with marginalized voices recounting oppressive experience, they can easily interpret such narratives as "complaints" and dismiss them with the claim that this is an example of "being overly sensitive" or, as previously mentioned, of "playing the race card."[87]

Denials of complicity are not restricted to the classroom. Much has been written about the reactions of white feminists to the charge of racism from feminists of color. Sarita Srivastava,[88] for instance, highlights how white feminists who *as feminists* perceive themselves as committed to egalitarian principles find it incomprehensible that they, who are themselves so "progressive," can be accused of racism. White feminists understand themselves as challenging systemic oppression not contributing to it. Srivastava quotes from Ruth Frankenberg's class study, *White Women, Race Matters: The Social*

Construction of Whiteness, "Because we were basically well-meaning individuals, the idea of being part of the problem of racism was genuinely shocking to us."[89] Yet even in social movements that are organized around social justice, difference can be sacrificed in the name of unity and thus relations of power and inequity among women can be overlooked. It is this deep investment in their own moral innocence that often makes it difficult for white feminists to engage with the inequalities that occur within their own movements. Sherryl Kleinman[90] contends that

> . . . we become so invested in our beliefs as radicals or "good people" that we cannot see the reactionary or hurtful consequences of our behaviors.[91]

As Srivastava cautions, "an alternative moral identity can both foster and impede social change."[92]

A need for moral innocence can encourage a profound resistance to knowing that entrenches ignorance further. There is a *passion for ignorance,* as Deborah Britzman[93] puts it, when it comes to learning "difficult knowledge" that challenges one's moral integrity and that compels one to acknowledge one's role in the reproduction of social injustice. Britzman argues that such knowledge cannot be learned without emotional trauma. In our terminology, such trauma is required because white ignorance and denials of complicity mutually reinforce each other and support a refusal to engage in learning.

Barbara Flagg[94] explains that whiteness, "as an epistemological stance," is often "an exercise in denial" because whiteness controls the necessary discourse that might challenge how it works. In fact, as a metaprivilege white privilege consists of the very privilege not to have to be aware of one's privilege. According to Flagg, white privilege is not only a set of unearned privileges; it is also the "capacity to disguise those privileges behind structures of silence, obfuscation and denial."[95] Yet this talk of ignorance and denials often triggers indignant reactions on the part of white people. Why are white people responsible for ignorance? Is disagreement always resistance? Why are white denials not just expressions of disagreement? Does the charge of resistance undermine the possibility of criticism and legitimation altogether? Put differently, is there a danger that all disagreement will be labeled resistance and subsequently dismissed, leaving the position of those who argue for white ignorance beyond all challenge? Do the arguments that attempt to expose white ignorance function as a way to refuse to engage with the critic and are thus insulated against challenge? Moreover, if white ignorance is a product of ideology, how do those who argue for the actuality of such ignorance avoid ideology? These questions will be taken up later in this book. In the final section of this chapter, I want to briefly describe how I attempted to explain the complex nature of white privilege and its connection to systemic oppression by linking the benefits of white ignorance and denials of complicity to contributing to protecting an unjust system from being challenged.

LINKING "BENEFITING FROM" WITH "CONTRIBUTING TO"

Understanding white ignorance and white denials of complicity affords one way to illuminate the link between "benefiting from the system" and "contributing to its perpetuation" by highlighting how white people actively, even if unconsciously, protect their white innocence through denials of complicity and prevent white ignorance from being interrogated. White people resist learning/knowing. Shoshana Felman,[96] the eminent psychologist, explains that resistance to learning/knowing is a refusal to know that involves "not so much (a) lack of knowledge . . . (or) . . . simple lack of information but the incapacity—or refusal—to acknowledge one's own implication in the information."[97]

White people contribute to the perpetuation of systemic racism through benefiting from a perpetuating and systemically induced ignorance, a relentless readiness to deny, ignore and dismiss what victims who experience the effects of racism are saying in order that white people can maintain their moral innocence. Connecting systemic privilege to practices of ignorance helps us to understand how systems of oppression are protected from critique and how white people deny their complicity to safeguard self-understandings of moral goodness. In other words, "benefiting from" results in "contributing to."

Initially, I believed that this explanation linking "benefiting from" to "contributing to" would help my white students understand how they are complicit in systemic racism. Yet they continued to struggle with why they are responsible. What I realized is that they needed a concept of responsibility that differs from the blame/fault/causality model they were working with. They needed a model of responsibility that will help them to expose the subtle ways that whiteness works through them and that encourages a willingness to explore the blocks that inhibit the acknowledgement and thoughtful analysis of white complicity. A conception of responsibility is necessary that can explain how even those who are committed to acknowledging complicity are not absolved from complicity and that no white person is morally innocent, that no white person can stand outside of the system. Prior to articulating such a notion of responsibility, we must examine both the conception of the subject that grounds the white complicity claim and the understanding of language or discourse that is implied when we speak of the harms of denials of complicity.

NOTES

1. Sandra Lee Bartky, "Race, Complicity, and Culpable Ignorance," in her *"Sympathy and Solidarity": And Other Essays* (Lanham: Rowman & Littlefield, 2002), 154.

2. Beverly Daniel Tatum, "*Why are All the Black Kids Sitting Together in the Cafeteria?*" *And Other Conversations About Race* (New York: Basic Books, 1997); Carol Brunson Phillips and Louise Derman-Sparks, *Teaching/Learning Anti-Racism: A Developmental Approach* (New York: Teachers College Press, 1997); Harlon L. Dalton, *Racial Healing: Confronting the Fear Between Blacks and Whites* (New York: Doubleday, 1995).

3. Peggy McIntosh, "White Privilege and Male Privilege: A Personal Account of Coming to See Correspondences through Work in Women's Studies," in Richard Delgado and Jean Stefancic, eds., *Critical White Studies: Looking Behind the Mirror* (Philadelphia: Temple University Press, 1997), 291–299.

4. Lisa Delpit, "The Silenced Dialogue: Power and Pedagogy in Educating Other People's Children," *Harvard Educational Review* 58, no. 3 (1988): 289.

5. Kathy Hytten and John Warren, "Engaging Whiteness: How Racial Power Gets Reified in Education," *Qualitative Studies in Education* 16, no. 1 (2003): 65–89.

6. Ibid., 87.

7. Ibid.

8. Peggy McIntosh, "White Privilege and Male Privilege."

9. Cynthia Kaufman, "A User's Guide to White Privilege," *Radical Philosophy Review* 4, no. 1–2 (2002): 32.

10. Zeus Leonardo, "The Color of Supremacy: Beyond the Discourse of 'White Privilege'," *Educational Philosophy and Theory* 36, no. 2 (2004): 137–152.

11. Ibid., 144.

12. Marilyn Frye, "Oppression," in her *The Politics of Reality: Essays in Feminist Theory* (Trumansburg, NY: Crossing Press, 1983), 1–16.

13. Sara Ahmed, "A Phenomenology of Whiteness," *Feminist Theory* 8, no. 2 (2007): 148–168.

14. Adrienne Rich, "Disloyal to Civilization: Feminism, Racism, Gynephobia," in her *On Lies, Secrets, and Silence: Selected Prose 1966–1978*, (New York: W. W. Norton, 1979), 299.

15. Shannon Sullivan, *Revealing Whiteness: The Unconscious Habits of Racial Privilege* (Bloomington and Indianapolis: Indiana University Press, 2006).

16. Peggy McIntosh, "White Privilege and Male Privilege," 295.

17. Ibid.

18. Cynthia Levine-Rasky, "Framing Whiteness: Working through the Tensions of Introducing Whiteness to Educators," *Race, Ethnicity and Education* 3, no. 3 (2000): 271–292.

19. Ibid., 276.

20. Ibid., 277.

21. Ibid.

22. Zeus Leonardo, "The Color of Supremacy," 143.

23. Ibid., 137.

24. Ibid., 138.

25. Ibid., emphasis added.

26. Ladelle McWhorter, "Where Do White People Come From? A Foucaultian Critique of Whiteness Studies," *Philosophy & Social Criticism* 31, no. 5–6 (2005): 551, emphasis added.

27. Zeus Leonardo, "The Color of Supremacy," 137.

28. Dreama Moon and Lisa A. Flores, "Antiracism and the Abolition of Whiteness: Rhetorical Strategies of Domination among 'Race Traitors'," *Communication Studies* 51, no. 2 (2000): 97–115.

29. Marilyn Frye, "Oppression."

30. Jack Ludwig, "Perceptions of Black and White Americans Continue to Diverge Widely on Issues of Race Relations in the U.S." *Gallop Poll,* February 28, 2000, http://www.gallup.com/poll/3193/Perceptions-Black-White-Americans-Continue-Diverge-Widely.aspx (accessed July 19, 2009).

31. Alan David Freeman, "Legitimizing Racial Discrimination through Antidiscrimination Law: A Critical Review of Supreme Court Doctrine," in *Critical Race Theory: The Key Writing that Formed the Movement,* ed. Kimberle Crenshaw, Neil Gotanda, Gary Peller, and Kendall Thomas (New York: New Press, 1995), 29–45.

32. Ibid., 29.

33. Ibid. (emphasis added).

34. Cris Mayo, "Certain Privilege: Rethinking White Agency," *Philosophy of Education 2004,* ed. Chris Higgins (Urbana, Illinois: Philosophy of Education Society, 2005): 309.

35. Shannon Sullivan and Nancy Tuana, (eds.) *Race and Epistemologies of Ignorance* (Albany, New York: State University of New York Press, 2007).

36. Charles W. Mills, *The Racial Contract* (Ithaca, New York: Cornell University Press, 1997), 94.

37. Ibid., 14.

38. Ibid., 18.

39. Charles W. Mills, "White Ignorance," in *Race and Epistemologies of Ignorance,* ed. Shannon Sullivan and Nancy Tuana (Albany: State University of New York Press, 2007), 13–38.

40. Ibid., 20.

41. Ibid., 21.

42. Charles Mills, *The Racial Contract,* 18.

43. George Yancy, "Fragments of a Social Ontology of Whiteness," in his *What White Looks Like: African-American Philosophers on the Whiteness Question* (New York: Routledge, 2004), 1–24.

44. Ibid., 1, emphasis added.

45. Charles Mills, "White Ignorance," 24.

46. Ibid., 25.

47. Ibid., 27.

48. Ibid.

49. Linda Martin Alcoff, "Epistemologies of Ignorance: Three Types," in *Race and Epistemologies of Ignorance,* 39.

50. Joe Feagin and Henan Vera, *White Racism: The Basics* (New York: Routledge 2001), 186.

51. Eve Kosofsky Sedgwick, *Epistemology of the Closet* (New York: Oxford University Press, 1980), 225.

52. Cris Mayo, "Civility and Its Discontents: Sexuality, Race, and the Lure of Beautiful Manners," *Philosophy of Education 2001*, ed. Suzanne Rice (Urbana, Ill.: Philosophy of Education Society, 2002): 85.

53. Charles Mills, *The Racial Contract*, 73.

54. Tyrone Foreman and Amanda Lewis, "Racial Apathy and Hurricane Katrina: The Social Anatomy of Prejudice in the Post-Civil Rights Era," *DuBois Review* 3, no. 1 (2006): 175–202.

55. Charles Mills, "White Ignorance," 34.

56. Vivian M. May, "Trauma in Paradise: Willful and Strategic Ignorance in *Cereus Blooms at Night*," *Hypatia* 21, no. 3 (2006): 113, emphasis added.

57. Peggy McIntosh, "White Privilege and Male Privilege."

58. Thomas Green, "On the Illusion that We Can Choose to Believe," *Philosophy of Education Society 1994*, ed. Michael Katz (Urbana, Illinois: Philosophy of Education Society, 1995): 70, emphasis added.

59. Michael J. Zimmerman, "Moral Responsibility and Ignorance," *Ethics* 107, no. 3 (1997): 410–426; Holly Smith, "Culpable Ignorance," *Philosophical Review* 92 (1983): 543–571.

60. Linda Martin Alcoff, "Epistemologies of Ignorance," 47.

61. Zeus Leonardo, "Reading Whiteness: Antiracist Pedagogy Against White Racial Knowledge," *Handbook of Social Justice in Education*," ed. William C. Ayers, Therese Quinn and David Stovall (New York: Routledge), 231–248.

62. Charles Mills, "White Ignorance," 175.

63. Ibid.

64. Sandra Harding, *Whose Science? Whose Knowledge? Thinking From Women's Lives* (Ithaca, New York: Cornell University Press, 1991), 126.

65. Linda Martin Alcoff, *Visible Identities: Race, Gender, and the Self* (Oxford: Oxford University Press, 2006), 43.

66. Ibid., 19.

67. Marilyn Frye, "On Being White: Thinking Toward a Feminist Understanding of Race and Race Supremacy," in her *Politics of Reality*, 118.

68. Charles Mills, *The Racial Contract*, 120.

69. Ibid., 150.

70. Ibid., 149.

71. Sandra Bartky, "Race, Complicity and Culpable Ignorance."

72. Peg O'Connor, *Oppression and Responsibility: A Wittgensteinian Approach to Social Practices and Moral Theory* (University Park, Pennsylvania: Pennsylvania State University Press, 2002), 123–124.

73. Tim Wise, "What Kind of Card is Race? The Absurdity (and Consistency) of White Denial," http://www.lipmagazine.org/~timwise/whatcard.html (accessed July 19, 2009).

74. Estella Williams Chizhik and Alexander Williams Chizhik, "Are you Privileged or Oppressed? Students' Conceptions of Themselves and Others," *Urban Education* 40, no. 2 (2005): 116–143; Rudolfo Chavez Chavez and James O'Donnell,

Speaking the Unpleasant: The Politics of (non)Engagement in the Multicultural Education Terrain (Albany: State University Press, 1998); Ann Berlak, "Teaching and Testimony: Witnessing and Bearing Witness to Racisms in Culturally Diverse Classrooms," *Curriculum Inquiry* 29, no. 1 (1999): 99–127; Audrey Thompson, "Entertaining Doubts: Enjoyment and Ambiguity in White, Antiracist Classrooms," in *Passion and Pedagogy: Relation, Creation, and Transformation in Teaching,* ed. Elijah Mirochick and Debora C. Sherman (New York: Peter Lang, 2002), 431–452; Kevin Kumashiro, "Teaching and Learning through Desire, Crisis, and Difference: Perverted Reflections on Anti-Oppressive Education," *Radical Teacher* 58 (2000): 6–11; Kathy Hytten and Amee Adkins, "Thinking Through a Pedagogy of Whiteness," *Educational Theory* 51, no. 4, (2001): 433–450; Leslie G. Roman, "White is a Color! White Defensiveness, Postmodernism and Anti-racist Pedagogy," in *Race, Identity and Representation in Education,* ed. Cameron McCarthy and Warren Crinchlow (New York: Routledge, 1993), 71–88; Bonnie TuSmith, "Out on a Limb: Race and the Evaluation of Frontline Teaching," in *Race in the College Classroom,* ed. Bonnie TuSmith and Maureen T. Reddy (New Brunswick, New Jersey: Rutgers University Press, 2002), 112–125.

75. Kim Case and Annette Hemmings, "Distancing: White Women Preservice Teachers and Antiracist Curriculum," *Urban Education* 40, no. 6 (2005): 606–626.

76. Elizabeth Higginbotham, "Getting All Students to Listen," *American Behavioral Scientist* 40, no. 2 (November/December 1996): 203–211.

77. Kathy Hytten and John Warren, "Engaging Whiteness," 66.

78. Alice McIntyre, *Making Meaning of Whiteness: Exploring Racial Identity With White Teachers* (Albany, New York: State University of New York Press, 1997).

79. Ibid., 45.

80. Kathy Hytten and John Warren, "Engaging Whiteness," 65.

81. Peggy McIntosh, "White Privilege and Male Privilege," 295–296.

82. Alice McIntyre, "White Talk," 55.

83. Eduardo Bonilla-Silva, *Racism Without Racist: Color-Blind Racism and the Persistence of Racial Inequality in the United States* (New York: Rowman and Littlefield, 2003).

84. Nado Aveling, "Student Teachers' Resistance to Exploring Racism: Reflections on 'Doing' Border Pedagogy," *Asia-Pacific Journal of Teacher Education* 30, no. 2 (2002): 119–130.

85. Nado Aveling, "Student Teachers' Resistance," 120.

86. Woody Doane, "Rethinking Whiteness Studies," in *White Out: The Continuing Significance of Racism,* ed. Ashley W. Doane and Eduardo Bonilla-Silva (New York: Routledge, 2003), 13–14, emphasis added.

87. Amanda Lewis, "There is No Race in the School Yard: Color-Blind Ideology in an (Almost) All-White School," *American Educational Research Journal* 38, no. 4 (2001): 781–811; Tim Wise, "What Kind of Card is Race?"

88. Sarita Srivastava, "'You're Calling Me a Racist?' The Moral and Emotional Regulation of Antiracism and Feminism," *Signs* 31, no. 1 (2005): 29–62.

89. Ruth Frankenberg, *White Women, Race Matters: The Social Construction of Whiteness* (Minneapolis: University of Minnesota Press, 1993), 3.

90. Sherryl Kleinman, *Opposing Ambitions: Gender and Identity in an Alternative Organization* (Chicago: University of Chicago Press, 1996).
91. Ibid., p. 11.
92. Sarita Srivastava, "'You're Calling Me a Racist?'" 41.
93. Deborah Britzman, *Lost Subjects, Contested Objects: Toward a Psychoanalytic Inquiry of Learning* (Albany: State University of New York Press, 1998).
94. Barbara J. Flagg, "Foreword: Whiteness as Metaprivilege," *Washington University Journal of Law and Policy*, 16 (2005): 1–11.
95. Barbara Flagg, "Whiteness as Metaprivilege," 6.
96. Shoshanna Felman, "Psychoanalysis and Education: Teaching Terminable and Interminable," *Yale French Studies* 63 (1982): 21–44.
97. Ibid. p. 30.

CHAPTER 3

The Subject of White Complicity

OUTLINED IN CHAPTER 1 WAS A CONCEPTION OF WHITE COMPLICITY CONNECTED TO THE very ways of being white and characterized by the metaphor evoked by Dwight Boyd—"my mobs are always with me." A key to understanding the white complicity claim, then, is to explore the particular conception of the subject that it presumes. We need to look for a conception of the subject that explicates how complicity can be deeply involved in ways of being white. Moreover, since the white complicity claim presumes that white anti-racism begins with an acknowledgement of one's complicity, the notion of the subject that grounds white complicity must not be so determined as to foreclose the possibility of agency and responsibility.

In asking about the conception of the subject that grounds white complicity, it is no surprise that Judith Butler's conception of subject formation immediately comes to mind. Building on Michel Foucault's insight that the power that produces us is not just external to us but is also inherently part of our existence, Butler insists that there is no subjectivity outside of discursive regimes of power. Butler's conception of identity formation is rooted in a rejection of the model of the subject that is a product of "a metaphysics of presence" which is a fundamental feature of western thought. The myth of "presence" presumes that the self is the center of knowledge of the world and that such knowledge is a result of suppressing all contingency. Such knowledge is presumed to be exclusively an outcome of rationality, the crowning characteristic of persons. The rational subject is also assumed to be able to sufficiently transcend the social in order to be able to objectively and rationally reflect upon it and the world.

Postmodern/poststructuralist scholars, however, take issue with this view of the subject insisting that there is no "I" outside of particular linguistic frameworks. They contest the assumption of a humanist subject because of its exclusionary consequences. In its place, they speak of the subject as *an effect of power*. Butler's theory of subject formation contributes to this critique of the humanist subject by explicating how the fantasy of a stable self forms. Moreover, she exposes how presumptions of a prediscursive self can function to obscure the performative iterations of norms and the ways in which the subject is complicit in perpetuating truth regimes. Butler's work has also been exceptionally influential in its ability to bring to light the limitations of certain forms of seemingly progressive politics. Of particular interest is Butler's insistence that the constituted nature of the subject does not sacrifice agency.

A provocative figure in feminist theory, Butler offers an explanation for how the subject is completely entrenched in the social without succumbing to a determinism that precludes agency. Her work may help to facilitate two tasks that are necessary for understanding the subject of white complicity. First, Butler's notion of subject formation helps to explain how white complicity adheres to white subjects at the level of their very being constituted as white. Second, Butler suggests a conception of agency that is possible for subjects whose "mobs are always with us." While her work is clearly helpful for this first task whether her notion of agency is as helpful remains to be explored.

In what follows, the main tenets of Butler's theory of subject formation will be summarized and some of the criticisms that have been put forward against certain aspects of her work will be examined. Although a number of critiques will be explored, two critiques will be given particular attention. One critique that will be discussed is the charge that Butler is too focused on the discursive and ignores concrete life experiences. Another critique involves Butler's rejection of normative foundations. From both these critiques, a seeming inconsistency arises in Butler's work. On the one hand, Butler rejects identity categories as a basis for political action. On the other hand, she then concedes that identity categories are indispensable for political action. Moreover, while Butler rejects intentions, she also uses intentional terms in her writing. Ralph Sandland refers to this as Butler's "double moves."[1] By looking carefully at these "double moves," as well as her attempts to rearticulate an innovative notion of agency, we can discern the critical and ethical concerns that are a consistent mark of all her theorizing.

Butler's ethical concerns will come into sharper focus through a close examination of the reason she is so eager to reject any trace of a discursive core. Butler's critical concerns will be underscored through an alternate reading of her work. Ladelle McWhorter,[2] who defends Foucault against similar charges of inconsistency, influences my argument here. McWhorter contends that Foucault's analytics of power only appear inconsistent when one reads them as a model *about* power. In her alternate reading of Foucault, McWhorter interprets his claims about power *as a tool or a strategic move* that Foucault must make in order to do his genealogy of the subject, a move "designed to undermine some of the obstacles we face when we attempt to think in the absence of transcendental structures."[3] I take another cue from the work of Edwina Barvosa-Carter[4] who highlights Butler's ethical concerns. I submit that reading Butler's insights about subject formation *as a strategic tool* rather than about *the theory of subject formation* not only refutes the charge of inconsistency but also corroborates her ethical and critical concerns. Butler is consistently interested in opening up possibilities that are closed off by our "common" ways of thinking.

Emphasizing Butler's ethical and critical concerns allows me to do two things besides outlining the subject of white complicity. First, it allows me to open a space for others who have similar concerns and who have tried to accommodate some of the limitations of Butler's approach by taking her work in different directions. It is within this space that I believe putting Butler and Iris Marion Young's recent work on responsibility together promises to suggest productive insights both about the conception of the subject that is required for understanding white complicity and also for rearticulating the type of moral responsibility that underlies the white complicity claim.

Second, I argue that the types of ethical and critical concerns underlying Butler's work can help to illuminate the type of vigilance that is required for agency under complicity. Butler's work calls for critical reflection of what is "unthinkable" and in doing so often exposes even seemingly ethical practices as complicit. She challenges, for instance, what is considered politically progressive in feminism and seemingly progressive hate-speech legislation as, in fact, functioning to protect rather than to challenge power regimes.

Insights from Butler's work suggest that white complicity pedagogy pay serious attention to the danger in assuming a subject that can stand outside of power. She emphasizes the importance of opening up the "unthinkable" for consideration and highlights the necessity for uncertainty and humility. Butler's work, it is suggested, can be read more as *a cautionary tool* than *the theory of actual subject formation.* Her framework is like a pair of glasses that bring into sharper focus things that tend to remain blurred or invisible. Butler's work draws our attention to the need to always be open to questioning our certainties and to the significance of taking the position that nothing—neither our self nor our good intentions—is unaffected by power relations. These, I submit, are necessary to avoid the epistemic and ethical arrogance that is attached to white ways of being. As such, Butler's work offers important insights into the type of critical vigilance that is a crucial feature of the type of moral responsibility entailed by the white complicity claim.

JUDITH BUTLER, SUBJECT FORMATION AND COMPLICITY

> . . . if, following Foucault, we understand power as *forming* the subject as well as providing the very condition of its existence . . . then power is not simply what

we opposed but also, in a strong sense, what we depend on for our existence and what we harbor and preserve in the beings that we are.[5]

Butler's work is initially framed by a concern with the unproblematized identity category "women" that serves as the subject of feminism. Not only have white, straight feminists excluded women of color and lesbians from the universal concept of "women" but also they have not taken seriously Foucault's insights that all identities are *effects* of power regimes. What is required, Butler contends, is a critical analysis of the subject of feminism and how "the category of 'women' . . . is produced and restrained by the very structures of power through which emancipation is sought."[6] A genealogical critique of the concept "women" is thus necessary to expose who benefits and who is excluded when essentialist notions of identity are the basis of politics.

> A genealogical critique refuses to search for the origins of gender, the inner truth of female desire, a genuine or authentic sexual identity that repression has kept from view; rather genealogy *investigates the political stakes in designating as an origin and cause those identity categories that are in fact the effects of institutions, practices, discourses with multiple and diffuse points of origin.*[7]

In *Gender Trouble*, Butler embarks upon such a genealogy by exposing the political stakes that are hidden by the sex/gender distinction so crucial to second wave feminists in the United States.

The distinction between sex (being biologically male or female) and gender (culturally imposed roles of femininity and masculinity) played a major role in challenging biological determinism or the view that masculinity and femininity follow naturally from biological differences in the male and female body. Second wave feminists in the United States were able to fight for social change by arguing that gender roles and stereotypes were socially constructed and not biologically based. In doing so, however, the notion of sex as nature remained beyond interrogation. Butler deconstructs the distinction in order to uncover the heteronormative assumptions it preserves and perpetuates.

According to Butler, sex is already gendered since sex constrains subjects into one of only two sexed categories. In what becomes a prevailing theme of her work, Butler maintains that there is no prediscursive core that, in this case, is sex. The binary understanding of sex produced through the gender apparatus that supports the heterosexual matrix suggests that sex is already gendered. The heterosexual matrix involves a binary disjunction in which "one either identifies with a sex or desires it, but only those two relations are possible."[8] Drawing on discussions of hermaphroditism and the ambiguously sexed, Butler brings to light the arbitrary features of the heterosexual matrix by which one can only become male or female. Such a matrix produces a "domain of abjected beings, those who are not yet 'subject' but who form the constitutive outside to the domain of the subject."[9] Although sex is constructed so that it appears to precede gender, it is from the start a regulatory ideal that is exclusionary. Sex is not the origin of gender but rather it is gender that produces sex. Both gender and sex are constituted by and support the heterosexual matrix. By failing to interrogate the discourse of the sex/gender distinction, feminists unwittingly support heteronormativity through their seemingly liberatory project.

In *Bodies That Matter*, Butler further expands this claim by arguing that homosexuality is the constitutive outside of heterosexuality and is essential to the forming of the strict borders that police what lies within the norm. Bodies that matter are bodies that are intelligible and attributed worth or value but are also relationally contingent upon a domain of bodies that are unintelligible and "unlivable" within the matrix of hegemonic, heterosexual normativity. For Butler, the intelligible requires the abject. This applies not just to gender categories; *all* identity categories that presume to be stable or fixed and prediscursively "authentic" are "instruments of regulatory regimes."[10] All essentialist identity categories are not politically or ethically neutral; rather, they are ethically pernicious because they necessarily exclude and foreclose the possibility of certain identities. Butler argues that identity categories are never merely descriptive but instead are normative ideals.[11] Thus, she is led to conclude that identity categories, such as "women," must be rejected as a basis for politics, particularly feminist politics.

One of Butler's provocative claims is that feminism grounded in an essential female identity ends up being complicit in systemic oppression by promoting a falsely unified feminist subject that is exclusionary. More relevant to our topic of white complicity, Butler emphasizes the violence that constitutes us as subjects and how complicated it is to oppose such violence. She contends that such violence

> . . . cannot simply be opposed in the name of nonviolence, for when and where it is opposed, it is opposed from a position that *presupposes* this very violence . . . *The subject who would oppose violence, even violence to itself, is itself the effect of a prior violence without which the subject could not have emerged.*[12]

Butler argues that identity politics, although necessary for challenging systemic oppression, presumes a shared and unified identity that is exclusionary, especially when, in fact, members of such identity categories do not necessarily share a common experience. As she puts it,

> The minute that the category of women is invoked as *describing* the constituency for which feminism speaks, an internal debate invariably begins over what the

descriptive content of the term will be . . . (E)very time that specificity is articulated, there is resistance and factionalization within the very constituency that is supposed to be *unified* by the articulation of its common element.[13]

Butler concludes that "identity categories are never merely descriptive, but always normative, and as such, exclusionary."[14] Since social norms define the borders of what is thinkable, what is intelligible, these borders are established and strengthened by the constitutive outside, by that which is unintelligible and unacceptable or the realm of the abject.

Butler's argument is grounded in Foucault's contention that power is productive. Yet she expands this claim by elucidating *how* power works *through* exclusions. At the same time that power produces what is intelligible it also constructs what is unintelligible. While sex/gender norms, for example, produce subjects who are gendered, they simultaneously and violently exclude other types of bodies from the realm of the intelligible. While Foucault's work has been critiqued for presuming "docile" subjects, what is distinctive about Butler's account is that the subject is not inert but *actively* complicit in these exclusionary tactics of power through its constitution as a subject and through the way it is *compelled* to performatively reiterate these norms to maintain subject status.

In order to understand what Butler means by performativity, we must examine what Foucault means by power and what he means by discourse. The former issue will be taken up in this chapter but a more detailed discussion of the latter will have to wait for the next chapter.

Butler contends that as linguistic beings, our existence is unavoidably dependent on a "language we never made."[15] The subject is constituted through power. That is, we become subjects through the process of subjectivation or what Foucault referred to as *assujetissement*, the paradoxical process of becoming a subject through subjection. Power, in this sense, is not to be understood as primarily prohibitive and repressive, as an external force that only constrains behavior; instead, power is above all productive and provides the very conditions of the subject's existence. The linguistic act of naming, for instance, is a process of subject formation that interpellates (calls into being) the subject through socially sanctioned forms of address that "put us in our place even as they make us feel at home."[16]

Ascribed categories of identity, such as "girl," "homosexual" and "delinquent," Butler insists, establish not only a sense of what the body is but also "its 'location' in terms of prevailing cultural coordinates."[17] Just as naming a baby confers upon *him or her* (and it is important to underscore that to speak of such a subject as a subject is limited by those two options) the status of a recognizable and enduring social being, ascribed categories of identity provide us with *positions of subject status* from which we speak even though they are constraining and also not of our choosing. While social norms expressed in discursive formations constitute subject status, identity develops *an appearance* of stability through "a stylized repetition of acts."[18] As Butler puts it, gender is produced through

> a repeated stylization of the body, a set of repeated acts within a highly rigid regulatory frame that *congeal over time to produce the appearance of substance, of a natural sort of being.*[19]

This compelled repetition of norms, or what Butler refers to as performativity, implicates the subject in its own constitution. This repetition is crucial because gender is not achieved in one isolated moment of interpellation (the doctor's announcement at birth, "it is a girl") but rather is a repeated performance that is contingent upon dominant social norms and their concomitant regulatory force.

Regulatory norms, according to Butler, cannot reproduce or maintain themselves but instead require subjects whose existence depends on the reiteration of norms. As Butler explains, " . . . if conditions of power are to persist, they must be reiterated; the subject is precisely the site of such reiteration."[20] Since one's existence as a subject depends on a forced repetition of norms, one's "being" as a subject is necessarily complicit in the perpetuation of such norms. Butler's understanding of subject formation and her insistence on the compelled reiteration of norms as the essence of performativity clarify how subjects are *unwittingly* complicit in sustaining hegemonic social structures. Furthermore, she emphasizes that identity categories become fallaciously solidified through performative repetition and develop an appearance of "reality." Reliance on such identity categories for political action *reifies* power matrices rather than *destabilizes* them in a process that is so mystified that it does not seem that that is what is occurring.

In a statement that sums up Butler's argument, performativity can be understood "not as a singular or deliberate 'act', but, rather, as the reiterative and citational practice by which discourse produces the effects that it names."[21] Butler, however, takes pains to emphasize that these performative acts are not scripts executed by a detached actor. They are rather constitutive constraints without which we could not exist as subjects who think, live, and make sense of the world. *There is no subject that precedes the enactment of norms.* Since power is located in the norms and conventions that regulate discourse, this means that having subject status depends upon complying with and participating in dominant norms and conventions. One speaks and acts intelligibly (that is, one is a subject) only insofar as one is able to conform to the norms that regulate discourse. As such, social norms are both enabling and constraining: they enable a subject to speak insofar as they constrain the subject as a subject.

Consequently, Butler's notion of performativity or "doing" must not be equated with "acting" or a theatrical performance because theatrical performance presumes a prediscursive self who exists behind the performance. According to Butler, gender is not a noun but always a doing and there is no subject that transcends the expression of gender. As she emphasizes,

> ... gender is always a doing, though not a doing by a subject who might be said to preexist the deed ... *there is no gender identity behind the expression of gender; that identity is performatively constituted by the very 'expressions' that are said to be its results.*[22]

The extent of Butler's rejection of any presumption of a prediscursive subject becomes noticeably conspicuous in an exchange between Seyla Benhabib and Judith Butler.[23] While both Benhabib and Butler perceive the subject as socially constructed and embedded in discourse, Benhabib holds on to the belief that there is a nucleus of autonomy underlying the situated self from which agency springs and that makes feasible liberation from power structures that constitute its very being. Butler, in contrast, rejects all reference to an autonomous subject and draws attention to the dangers of presuming *any* prediscursive core.

The interchange between Benhabib and Butler around prediscursivity was triggered by Benhabib's review of the three basic theses of postmodernism as depicted by Jane Flax: the death of Man, the death of history and the death of metaphysics. According to Benhabib, there are two ways that these theses can be read: a strong and weak form. Benhabib rejects the former and acknowledges the latter in each case. It is, however, her discussion of the strong and weak versions of the death of Man thesis that raises issues of prediscursivity. Benhabib maintains that the strong version of postmodernism forfeits any notion of agency and the possibility of social change because the very resources required for agency, i.e., intention, reflexivity, autonomy and accountability, are renounced as fictions. Such a subject, Benhabib argues (making reference to Flax's terminology),

> ... thus dissolves into the chain of significations of which it was supposed to be the initiator. Along with the dissolution of the subject into yet "another position in language" disappear of course concepts of intentionality, accountability, self-reflexivity, and autonomy. The subject that is but another position in language can no longer master and create that distance between itself and the chain of signification in which it is immersed such that it can reflect upon them and creatively alter them.[24]

Benhabib cautions feminists not to embrace the thoroughly discursive subject because she insists that it sacrifices the possibility of agency and emancipation.

Instead, Benhabib advocates for the weaker form of the thesis that "would situate the subject in the context of various social, linguistic and discursive practices"[25] and remains capable of intentional action and autonomy. She argues for a *situated*, not *constituted*, subject that is not merely a passive product of regulatory norms but one in which autonomy, choice and self-determination are possible. Agency, for Benhabib, implies that we are "not merely extensions of our histories, that vis-à-vis our own stories we are in the position of author and character at once."[26] In other words, agency for Benhabib presumes that subjects are not constituted *all the way down*. While Benhabib concurs with the postmodern rejection of the transcendental subject and acknowledges that subjects are situated in the context of social and linguistic practices, she is adamant that at the core of this subject is a return to at least a token nugget of the ahistorical, transcendental subject from which agency can spring. According to Benhabib, a presdiscursive nucleus that can be autonomous of the social is indispensable for agency.

Butler, in contrast, steadfastly insists that the subject is not "situated" but rather "constituted" all the way down. As she puts it,

> It is clearly not the case that "I" preside over the positions that have constituted me, shuffling through them instrumentally . . . The "I" who would select between them is always already constituted by them. The "I" is the transfer point of that replay, but it is simply not a strong enough claim to say that the "I" is situated; the "I," this "I," is *constituted* by these positions.[27]

Butler rejects the possibility of the subject being "situated" because such a subject assumes a sovereign core that resurrects the *fantasy* of autonomy.

At one point in this exchange, Benhabib mistakenly equates Butler's notion of performativity with theatrical acting when she writes

> If we are no more than the sum total of the gendered expressions we perform, is there ever a chance to stop the performance for a while, to pull the curtain down, and let it rise only if one can have a say in the production of the play itself? Isn't this what the struggle over gender is about?[28]

Butler, however, insists that performativity is not merely about acting a role and she clearly spells this out.

> . . . if I were to argue that genders are performative, that could mean that I thought that one woke in the morning, perused the closet or some more open space for the gender of choice, donned that gender for the day, and then restored the garment to its place at night. Such a willful and instrumental subject, one who decides *on* its gender, is clearly not its gender from the start and fails to realize that its existence is already decided *by* its gender.[29]

Butler refuses the willful or volitional subject because such a subject would require a return to a prediscursive self that disregards how intentions are constituted. In her discussion of the limits of performativity, Lise Nelson specifically underscores that "'Intention' is not within the vocabulary of performativity."[30]

In Butler's account of agency, intention (or choice) does not play the role that it does in traditional accounts of agency. Since words that are recited always originate from language whose use is already regulated by norms and conventions, performative acts draw upon and recite linguistic conventions that are not simply the product of individual volition but are the effect of "historically sedimented linguistic intentions."[31] To cite, therefore, is to be able to carry out the norms and conventions that give meaning to the words cited. The force underlying such recitation, however, is attributed to those norms and not to individual intention (a point that will be taken up again and elucidated in the subsequent discussion of Butler's arguments in *Excitable Speech*).

Butler completely denounces any reference to a prediscursive self and contends that the subject is constructed *all the way down*. Paraphrasing Nietzsche who wrote, "there is no 'being' behind doing, effecting, becoming; 'the doer' is merely a fiction added to the deed,"[32] Butler argues "there need not be a 'doer behind the deed,' but that 'the doer' is variably constructed in and by the deed."[33] There is no transcendental, prediscursive doer behind the deed. Rather, the "doer" comes into being as a subject only through "doing" and by "doing" *sustains the very norms* that construct the subject as one who can "do." Edwina Barvosa-Carter gives emphasis to this point when she writes that

> The citational process *implicates* those who reiterate prevailing gender norms in the perpetuation of the existing gender order and its (differential) relations of power.[34]

In a quote reminiscent of the "mobs" that Boyd refers to, Butler writes, "power is not simply what we oppose but also, in a strong sense, what we depend on for our existence and what we harbor and preserve in the beings that we are."[35] One of the reasons that Butler's notion of subject formation is so helpful for understanding white complicity is because such a conception of the subject acknowledges that white subjects are implicated in perpetuating prevailing racial norms in their very constitution as, and recitations of, white norms and ways of being.

The notion of performativity precludes any return of a prediscursive, autonomous subject. Any hint of the humanist subject problematically presumes transcendence. Drawing upon Michel Foucault's pioneering interpretation of power, Butler argues that the subject is not some fixed essence but rather *an effect of and positioned by* patterns of discourse through which power works. According to Foucault, power is " . . . never localized here or there, never in anybody's hands, never appropriated as a commodity or a piece of wealth. Power is exercised through a net-like organization . . . "[36] Foucault maintains that it is a mistake

> to think of the individual as a sort of elementary nucleus, a primitive atom or some multiple, inert matter to which power is applied, or which is struck by a power that subordinates or destroys individuals. In actual fact, one of the first effects of power is that it allows bodies, gestures, discourses, and desires to be identified and constituted as something individual. The individual is not, in other words, power's opposite number; the individual is one of power's first effects. The individual is in fact a power-effect, and at the same time, to the extent that he is a power-effect, the individual is a relay: power passes through the individuals it has constituted.[37]

Like Foucault, Butler conceives the subject as constituted through discourses of power and she repeatedly asserts that there is no prediscursive subject that stands outside of power.

Discourse, for Butler as well as for Foucault, is not presumed to be some transparent means of communication nor is power something that is primarily repressive. Rather power works through discourse to produce subjects. How discourse works to constitute us as subjects will be further explained in the next chapter. More specifically, power does things through discursive regimes of truth. Foucault again,

> And not only do individuals circulate between its (power) threads; they are always in the position of simultaneously undergoing and exercising this power. They are not only its inert or consenting target; *they are always also the elements of its articulation.*[38]

Foucault explains that to conceive the subject as an effect of discourse is not to preclude agency. He leaves us with an aporia, however, when he claims but does not elucidate that

> Where there is power, there is resistance, and yet, or rather consequently, this resistance is never in a position of exteriority in relation to power.[39]

Resistance and the agency necessary to resist are not outside of power regimes. Butler fills in the gaps left by this aporia by explaining, first, how subjects are not only constituted through discursive power regimes *but also perpetuate them* and, second, how agency is to be found in the very occasion of perpetuating power.

AGENCY UNDER COMPLICITY

Butler's notion of the subject is deeply intertwined with regimes of power to the core of its very existence. Nevertheless, Butler insists that this does *not* preclude the possibility of agency. As Butler argues, "to claim that the subject is constituted is not to claim that it is determined."[40] She finds the opportunity for subversive agency in the *necessity* of repetition and, more specifically, in both the compulsion to reiterate and in the instability of such reiterations. According to Butler, the processes of reiteration that play such a crucial role in her conception of subject formation do not resolutely establish what may be said and done. Building on the insights of Jacques Derrida, she notes that recitation is not rigidly fixed. Change is possible because of the *instability* of symbolic and discursive norms.

Resignification is always possible because language is never the same thing twice. For example, citing the word "woman" in one context will signify different meanings from those it carries when recited in alternate contexts. The possibility of such shifts creates the opportunity for reiteration to be either stabilizing or destabilizing. Agency is to be found not in a denial of complicity but rather in the possibility to disrupt the repetition of social norms. As Butler puts it, "All signification takes place within the orbit of the compulsion to repeat; 'agency' then, is to be located in the possible variation on that repetition."[41] The compulsion to reiterate, according to Butler, opens a space to subvert citations. She emphasizes that a citation "will be at once an interpretation of the norm and an occasion to expose the norm itself as a privileged interpretation."[42] An "occasion," she underscores, but not a guarantee that subversive resignifications will achieve social change.

Regulative norms are never totally successful. If they were, they would not have to be repeatedly cited. Gender norms, Butler accentuates, are "continually haunted by their own inefficacy; hence, the anxiously repeated effort to install and augment their jurisdiction."[43] In addition, "to the extent that gender is an assignment, it is an assignment which is never quite carried out according to expectation, whose addressee never quite inhabits the ideal s/he is compelled to approximate."[44] Discursive formations, Butler argues, are prone to "misfire." It is because of this instability that subversive resignification becomes possible.

In an attempt to illuminate this ability of discursive formations to misfire, Butler points to a problem with Althusser's theory of interpellation that similarly understands subject formation as contingent on language. Butler critically notes the uni-directionality of Althusser's approach. In Althusser's famous example of the process of interpellation involving a call and a response, the police officer hails a person by uttering "hey, you!" and when the person turns around, the subject is called into existence.[45] Althusser explains that the authority of the officer is backed by ideology that gives his speech act power to constitute a subject. Butler, however, insists that Althusser does not acknowledge the role that the subject plays in its own subjection. For the hailing to evoke subjectivity, the subject has to be willing to be hailed, to be named, and to be presumed guilty by this naming.[46] Even if language attempts to name us, however, the call into the linguistic field may be received differently.

A more concrete albeit extremely complex illustration of Butler's conception of agency can be found in *Excitable Speech*. In this book, Butler offers a response to the anti-pornography debates and the controversy around hate speech legislation in the United States. These debates are centered on the conflict between the first amendment (free speech) and the 14th amendment (freedom from the harm of other's conduct). Advocates of legal regulations concentrate their arguments on the establishment of hate speech and pornography as *forms of conduct*. The rationale is that as conduct, government regulation is legitimate. If hate speech and pornography are considered merely matters of speech, then the laws that protect free speech would apply and restrictions would not be justified.

Given Butler's emphasis on the role of discourse in subject formation and her account of performativity, it would at first seem reasonable to assume that Butler would support the call to equate speech and conduct. Yet she rejects this approach both because of her insistence on agency and her interest in exposing the consequences of a reliance on state intervention. The reliance on sovereign power in legal interventions, Butler argues, results in both granting too much power to words that wound and sacrifices the agency of the subject. It is not that Butler denies the power of language to injure. Nor does she intend to minimize the pain of those injured. As Butler explains,

> I wish to question for the moment the presumption that hate speech always works, not to minimize the pain that is suffered as a consequence of hate speech, but to leave open the possibility that its failure is the condition of a critical response.[47]

Her main objective is to demonstrate that agency is not sacrificed when the sovereign subject is dissolved. On the contrary, she insists, "agency begins where sovereignty wanes."[48] While she acknowledges the power of language to injure and that there is a sense in which language always wounds, she denies that speech has the power that hate speech advocates attribute to it. To assume that speech has such power robs the subject of agency.

While we are vulnerable to language, Butler contends that language is itself vulnerable. This is crucial because it is within this vulnerability that agency can arise. About the vulnerability of language, Butler notes,

> Could language injure us if we were not, in some sense, linguistic beings, beings who require language in order to be? Is our vulnerability to language a consequence of our being constituted within its terms? If we are formed in language,

then that formative power precedes and conditions any decision we might make about it, insulting us from the start, as it were, by its prior power.[49]

By employing Derrida's critique of J. L. Austin's speech act theory, Butler brilliantly demonstrates that the power of speech to injure is not attributed *to words themselves* or *to the intentions of the speaker*, but rather *to the historicity upon which speech is authorized and its future effects of which the speaker has no control.*

To clarify what Butler means, it is important to notice that the arguments advocating legal restrictions against hate-speech or pornography presume that language or discursive practices *instantaneously and without mediation* cause harm. Words *themselves* can wound. Indeed, a number of hate-speech legislation advocates have contended that pornography and hate-speech are not just speech but assaultive conduct. Charles Lawrence III argues that

> The experience of being called a "nigger," "spic," "Jap," or "kike" is like receiving a slap in the face. The injury is instantaneous.[50]

Similarly Catherine MacKinnon's *Only Words*[51] and Mari Matsuda's *Words that Wound*[52] equate speech with action to argue that speech is performative. These scholars rely on J. L. Austin's[53] theory of performative speech acts and, more specifically, Austin's notion of illocutionary speech acts to support their argument.

Austin distinguishes between constative speech, speech that is merely descriptive and a tool for communication, and performative speech acts, which do something or bring something into existence. Within the category of performative speech acts, Austin distinguishes between illocutionary and perlocutionary speech acts. Illocutionary speech does something at the moment that the words are uttered. The minister's utterance, "And I now pronounce you man and wife," at a wedding ceremony is an example of such illocutionary speech in which the saying *is* the doing. Perlocutionary speech acts also do things but in contrast to illocutionary speech, there is a temporal gap between the speech and its consequences. The shouting "Fire!" in a theatre whose effect is that people rush to the exit is an instance of perlocutionary speech. Those who advocate for legal restrictions on speech contend that hate speech, for example, has illocutionary force (the harm is in the act of uttering) and thus is conduct that should be restricted.

Austin acknowledged that illocutionary speech acts derive their power from institutional norms and, thus, depend on "felicity" conditions. Austin recognized that only if the minister is authorized to marry people and if the people being married fulfilled the conventional conditions of being married (for example, in many states in the United States a couple must be male and female and not married to someone else) does *the speaker* then possess the sovereign power to make the utterance do what the words say. The force of speech is determined by ritual and convention that then bestow upon the speaker the authority to make the spoken words do something. Drawing on Jacques Derrida's critique of Austin, Butler challenges this assumption about the force behind illocutionary speech.

According to Derrida, speech act theory assumes a humanist subject who has the power to bring certain consequences into being under certain external conditions. The performative speech act, however, is not a founding act but rather *an instance of citationality*. As Derrida puts it,

> Could a performative utterance succeed if its formulation did not repeat a "coded" or iterable utterance, or in other words, if the formula I pronounce in order to open a meeting, launch a ship or a marriage were not identifiable as conforming with an iterable model, if it were not then identifiable in some way as a "citation"?[54]

Derrida argues that the binding power that Austin attributes to the speaker is more appropriately attributable to iterability or the citational force of the utterance and not to the sovereign subject who speaks.

Moreover, Austin makes it seem as if the effectiveness of the utterance is to be found in that one moment of speech. Derrida insists, and Butler concurs, that to the extent that the moment depends on ritualization, it is never merely a single moment but a condensed historicity "that exceeds itself in past and future directions, an effect of prior and future invocations that constitute and escape the instance of utterance."[55] This is to imply that the force of the speech act is *not* to be found in the authority or the intentions of the speaker. Speech and action are not necessarily the same. To assume so would be to give the words a magical power to harm.

Butler claims that Althusser similarly supposes that words have a magical power to bring into being that which the interpellation hails. Althusser, moreover, presumed that the sovereign's hailing is always successful. Butler, conversely, argues that there is no magical effect to the words of the one who hails. The force of interpellation originates in the citationality and historicity of the speech and *not* in the sovereign voice of the one who utters the words. When the police officer hails the pedestrian who in turning around comes into being, it is the historicity of the convention that enables the becoming of being at the moment of its enunciation.[56] And because any particular citation carries with it a linguistic vulnerability, it is always possible to restate or alter the response to being hailed in ways that destabilize rather than support regulatory norms.

In contrast to scholars like Delgado, Matsuda, and MacKinnon, Butler insists that injury is not inherent in the very utterance of words themselves. The analogy of "words that wound" to a physical slap in the face presumes that the perpetrators of hate speech are the originators of the ideas they convey with their speech. As Butler explains,

> Racist speech works through the invocation of convention; it circulates and though it requires the subject for its speaking, it neither begins nor ends with the subject who speaks or with the specific name that is used.[57]

In Butler's argument, the power of the racist speech is derived *not* from any particular speaker but from the iteration and reiteration of a linguistic field that already exists. The speaker, by uttering the racist speech, makes "linguistic community with a history of speakers" whose previous citations have invested it with the accumulated force that enables its injurious capacity.[58]

Why is this important? First of all, this is crucial because it is where Butler finds the space for agency. Second, Butler claims that presumptions of a sovereign subject who can wound with words draws attention to the individual who harms *at the risk of ignoring the broader system of norms that form the discursive practices that the individual repeats.* Third, Butler is apprehensive of legal regulations since legal restrictions have been used against those they were intended to protect.

What Butler underscores is that the power underlying words that wound does not originate in the individual speaker but from the historicity of norms behind the words. In this, the illocutionary speech act is no different from all performative speech acts. The success of all performatives is a function of "action (that) echoes prior actions, and accumulates the force of authority through the repetition or citation of prior and authoritative set of practices."[59] It is because of the vulnerability of reiterations and the possible failure of speech that agency in the sense of counter speech can spring.

Although Butler acknowledges that hate speech has the power to constitute subjects, she emphasizes that such interpellation is always vulnerable to resignification and destabilization. Both the historicity upon which the power of speech depends, as well as the lack of power that the speaker has to determine how the speech will be taken up, opens up an occasion for agency. To situate all the power in the utterance is to discount the complex relations of power upon which the force of the utterance depends as well as its vulnerability to failure and resignification. Moreover, as Butler skillfully argues, an account of hate speech that forecloses the possibility of agency is an account that "confirms the totalizing effects of such injury."[60]

Butler provides two illustrations of counter speech. First, she offers the way in which the term "queer" has been reappropriated to indicate positive identification rather than a means of interpellating abject others.[61] Second, Butler describes how she was once accosted by a child who asked her, "Are you a lesbian?" to which Butler replied, "Yes, I am a lesbian."[62] Such counter speech, according to Butler, is an example of reappropriation and subversion of the interpellative hailing. Legal restrictions, Butler contends, deprive the victim of the possibility of agency. Hate speech legislation constitutes its subjects as injured victims who are incapable of defending themselves, are unable to act for themselves, and in need of the law's protection.

Butler is also critical of relying on legal restrictions to speech because they allow us to focus on the individual speaker but ignore the norms that form the discursive practices that give the individual's words the power to harm. It is *the historicity that must be challenged*, not only *the individual speaker and his/her utterance*. Butler's concern is that legal restrictions target the utterance and the person who makes the utterance *but leaves the power of regulatory norms unaffected*. Focus on legal intervention diverts attention from the challenges to the root cause of the hateful speech.

Finally, legal restrictions have been used against those they were intended to protect. Legal restrictions allow the state to act as a seemingly neutral arbiter of speech when, in fact, the state uses similar arguments to censor the marginalized when it is in its interest. Butler discusses how the United States military's policy of "don't ask, don't tell" has assumed the identification of speech with action to declare that to profess "I am gay" constitutes homosexual conduct and a justified restriction.

It must be emphasized that the type of agency that Butler recovers does not presume a sovereign, masterful agent. It is not the traditional conception of agency that Benhabib presumes in which "a subject is endowed with a will, a freedom, an intentionality which is then subsequently 'expressed' in language, in action, in the public domain."[63] Butler avoids any such notion of agency since such a view protects notions like "freedom" and "will" from interrogation. She explain that when assuming a sovereign subject

> . . . "freedom" and "the will" are treated as universal resources to which all humans qua humans have access. The self who is composed of such faculties or capacities is thus thwarted by relations of power which are considered external to the subject itself. And those who break through such external barriers are considered heroic or bearers of a universal capacity which has been subdued by oppressive circumstances.[64]

Butler's attempts to separate the speech act from the sovereign subject facilitates the development of

> an alternative notion of agency and, ultimately, of responsibility, that more fully acknowledges the way in which the subject is constituted in language, how what it creates is also what it derives from elsewhere.[65]

Butler's point is always to emphasize that not only the subject but also agency should not be presumed to be outside of power regimes.

Clearly Butler and Benhabib work with different meanings of agency. For Benhabib, agency involves the capacity for choice and self-determination and presumes the possibility of self-generated and intentional actions. For Butler, such notions of agency suppose a sovereign subject and must be refused. Instead, agency involves resistance in the sense of "locating strategies of subversive repetition" that expose norms as social and hegemonic rather than neutral and natural. In addition, Butler insists that change occurs through *slippages* within the process of repetition that are provoked by what is repressed by dominant discourses.[66] In *Gender Trouble*, Butler refers to "the *inadvertent* reemergence of the repressed"[67] and she opposes agency that is based on "the capacity for reflexive mediation, that remains intact regardless of its cultural embeddedness."[68] Butler is resolute that such slippages remain accidental and unintentional. Agency, for Butler, is not about "choice" for choice is also a discursive formation; it is not grounded in the subject's distance from constituting discourses but rather in the subject's capacity to vary rather than repeat those discourses.

Butler rejects any return to prediscursivity and or allusions of being outside of power matrices. In doing so, she questions our understanding of agency and puts traditional notions of self-reflexivity, autonomy and accountability under interrogation. In her discussion of social and political consciousness, Teresa de Laurentis[69] notes that a woman who acknowledges her historical and social location but uses this politically has "agency (rather than 'choice')."[70] The distinction between agency and choice underscores the understanding that our identities are never "outside" social structures; power and privilege are not things we can give up "by an act of goodwill or a more humane ethics."[71] As we cannot escape our social location, we must *continually interrogate* our political practices for exclusions and omissions *even when, and especially when, we think we are doing good.* In her attempts to articulate agency within complicity, Butler also draws our attention to the limitations of hate speech legislation undertaken as an ethical project. Legal interventions succeed in censoring the harmful utterance but at the cost of the victim's agency and of stifling possible challenges to the larger system of power from within which hate speech injures. Butler's notion of agency has drawn much criticism, to some of which we now turn.

BUTLER'S TROUBLES

An enormous body of critical scholarship has developed around Butler's work. There have been especially interesting debates focused around her notion of agency. This scholarship has grown into almost a sub-discipline itself and continues to proliferate because Butler troubles and is also troubling. Much of the friendly critiques of Butler's work have not only pointed to some of the limitations of her account of subject formation and agency but have also generated a rich and intensely thoughtful dialogue around some of the extremely important issues that her work raises.

Two areas of concern regarding her work will be briefly addressed especially as they are related to her notion of agency. First, the extreme emphasis on discursive formations to the disregard of material life and experience will be examined. Then, second, Butler's refusal of normative foundations will be briefly taken up. It is the criticism about her rejection of normative foundations that leads to a discussion around another charge against Butler involving the seemingly inconsistency of her "double moves." I argue that these "double moves," in fact, demonstrate Butler's consistent *critical and ethical concerns.*

Butler, the Body and Lived Experience

A frequent criticism leveled against Butler's account of the subject involves its abstract nature and its disregard of the body and lived experience. Benhabib's skepticism in regards to Butler's subject "as yet another position in language" can be recognized as a harbinger of this concern. According to Lise Nelson, Butler is so overly concerned to reject "assumptions of foundational, pre-discursive moments and the concomitant notion of an autonomous masterful subject"[72] that she ends up exclusively focused on the "abstracted as a subject *position* in a given discourse."[73] Lois McNay similarly emphasizes Butler's tendency "to privilege a symbolic account of subjectification over an examination of its material dimensions."[74] McNay also contends that Butler's emphasis on subversive resignification as the means of resistance tends to "valorize the linguistic act of resignification per se as inherently subversive at the expense of a more sustained consideration of the extent to which attendant social relations are dislodged or reinforced by such an act."[75] The result is that Butler's strategy for change remains abstract rather than a concrete possibility.

Nelson, moreover, is highly critical of Butler's refusal to make any reference to intention. Why, she asks, is Butler so ready to associate "anything smacking of intentionality" with "a discursive 'god trick'" that "must be banished"?[76] Butler presents us with a false dichotomy, according to Nelson. The choice is between the masterful humanist subject that is exclusionary and perpetuates systems of oppression and the unthinking subject as a node in power/discourse matrices. Since the former must be renounced, there is nothing left but the discursive subject that allows for "no space for conscious reflexivity, negotiation or agency in the doing of identity"[77] and that "limits how we can conceptualize the linkages between emerging identities, social change and spatially-embedded, intentional human practice."[78]

To state this succinctly, Butler, at least in her early work, is charged with paying almost no attention to the personal lived experiences of concrete individuals and their historical and geographical embeddedness. In addition, Butler appears to discount the significance of reflexivity and intention that seem to be important aspects of daily living. Nelson concludes that it is Butler's exclusive preoccupation with discrediting the sovereign subject and the notion of unified identity that leads her to privilege the process of subjectivation from which only a negative sense of agency can arise. Nelson, in contrast, argues that reference to intentions does not require of necessity a return to prediscursivity and that intentions are crucial for understanding agency.

Kathy Dow Magnus[79] expands upon this point when she critically comments on the tight connection Butler draws between the subject and discourse, between the doer and the deed. Butler's notion of agency does not make clear, as Magnus puts it, "what, if anything, the subject actually 'does'."[80] Magnus writes,

> . . . it remains unclear whether the linguistic subject *performs* these acts of resistance or whether it is actually only the power of "language" that does the work and uses the subject as its instrument. Butler's theory of linguistic performance seems to allow that a subject can at least "do things with words," but, as she herself admits, there is no definitive way to distinguish a subject "doing" things with language from *language's* "doing things" with the subject.[81]

Magnus notes that Butler herself needs to make use of the very terms that presume the agency she claims to reject. Butler ends up vacillating between repudiating the sovereign subject and being haunted by it.

Of significance, Magnus emphasizes that Butler's abstract discussion of the subject conflates the *symbolic understanding* of oppression with the *concrete experience* of systemic oppression. The consequence of this move is that Butler implies *all* subjects are subjected or oppressed in ways that overlook the different real-life social and economic experiences that the marginalized and the privileged undergo. Magnus clearly articulates this point when she writes

> That is to say, she reduces social oppression to an abstract necessity embedded in the structure of a "discourse" whose speakers are all equally subjected and equally culpable. This has important consequences: the notion that all subjects are subjected makes the question of responsibility superfluous, and it vitiates the distinction between dominating and subordinated cultures and discourses.[82]

Magnus accurately points to a difficulty in Butler's work and she specifically highlights Butler's presumption that resistance always comes from the margins. Magnus wonders why those who lack the power to speak as subjects should have to bear the burden for change.[83] And from the perspective of the privileged subject one might wonder, as does Veronica Vasterling, why the systemically privileged Butlerian subject would seek "to rival the power in which we are implicated"?[84] Why would a subject attempt to turn power against itself?

Butler's response has been that the incentive to resist is to be found in the violence against and the dehumanization of the excluded and delegitimated. The destabilizing process of resignification is provoked by the violence and conflict suffered on the part of those who are degraded by the normative regime. Butler, however, does not adequately explain the motivation of those who are privileged by the hegemonic norms to subvert such a system. Why should one resist what provides them not only with systemic privileges but also with the privilege of subject status?

In *Psychic Life*, Butler reworks the Freudian concepts of mourning and melancholia to account for what draws the subject to resist, i.e., a loss of alterity that is foundational to the subject.[85] This seems compelling when framed in terms of "heterosexual melancholy." In other words, for heterosexuality to remain stable there must be an abjection of homosexuality and this produces mourning for a loss. Yet, it is not clear how this concretely works for race. Butler seems to connect racial concerns and sexuality when she turns to address issues of race and focuses on the love foreclosed in the history of miscegenation. In doing this, she regrettably reduces the reasons for the white privileged subject to resist (in the sense of challenging systemic racism) exclusively to issues of desires that are foreclosed.

Magnus, moreover, charges Butler's account of agency as being overly negative, disregarding the more positive and creative ways that real people affect the political realm. Magnus accuses Butler of "underestimate(ing) the power of subjects to work *together* to determine their lives and the social conditions that structure their existence."[86] In this, Magnus also highlights the excessively individualistic nature of Butler's subject. This is a point that I will return to in a subsequent chapter when addressing what Butler can learn from Iris Marion Young's conception of the Social Connections Model of Responsibility. Lois McNay[87] similarly underscores how Butler ignores the collective dimension required for social change, the relations between the private and the public and the economic and political conditions that support social change. As an instance of such disregard, McNay claims that Butler's concentration on the reappropriation of the term "queer" ignores the larger social and economic conditions within which such reappropriations have met with success.

Allison Weir,[88] as well, critiques Butler and other feminists who define identity as a function of normative violence for succumbing to "sacrificial logics." The fallacy of sacrifice presupposes that the subject *only* emerges in opposition to the constitution of other subjects. Weir insists that subjects also emerge in social relationships where sacrifice is not ontologically presumed. When identity is theorized solely on sacrificial logic and when the remedy is presumed to be the total abandonment of identity, Weir argues, the positive aspects of collective identity are ignored. Along similar lines, Moya Lloyd argues that if our social ties are constructed through "a disallowed dependence on those we unconsciously reject, then commonality—or identity—as the basis of our political affiliations is challenged."[89] In sum, because Butler's account relies so heavily on discursive formations she ends up with an individualistic and abstract conception of the subject as the source of political resistance. In doing so, Butler fails to seriously engage with the concrete and practical need to work collectively to challenge systemic injustice.

Butler and Normative Foundations

In her earlier work, Butler also clearly rejects any reference to normative foundations. Nancy Fraser argues that by equating all that is normative with being exclusionary, Butler's notion of resignification values resistance for the sake of resistance and does not provide any normative criteria for determining which resignifications are valuable and which reinscribe conservative political projects. There are no criteria upon which to rely in order to ascertain why, for example, Butler's theory of resistance is to be preferred. Why is it important to expose the false "naturalness" of the sex/gender binary? According to Fraser, Butler has "explicitly renounced the moral-theoretical resources necessary to account for her own explicit normative judgments."[90]

In response, Butler argues,

> To set the "norms" of political life in advance is to prefigure the kinds of practices which will qualify as the political and it is to seek to negotiate politics outside of a history which is always to a certain extent opaque to us in the moment of action. . . . To set norms, to affirm aspirations, to articulate the possibilities of a more fully democratic and participatory life is, nevertheless, a necessity.[91]

She questions,

> . . . who would set up those norms, and what contestation would they produce? To establish a normative foundation for settling the question of what are properly to be included in the description of women would be only and always to produce a new site of political contest. That foundation would settle nothing but of its own necessity founder on its own authoritarian ruse. *That is not to say there are no foundations, but rather, whenever there is one, there will also be a foundering, a contestation.*[92]

Butler, then, does not do away with foundations and, rather, claims that her objective is "to interrogate what the theoretical move that establishes foundations *authorizes*. And what precisely it excludes or forecloses."[93]

To some this may sound inconsistent (as having her deconstructive cake and eating it too), but I suggest that Butler is rather exceedingly consistent. By taking a cue from Bavorsa-Carter's defense of Butler's anti-normativity, Butler's critical and ethical objectives can be made clear. Barvosa-Carter writes that Butler's strident anti-normativity is

> . . . born out of her attempt to unmask the pretense, falsehood, and will to power behind attempts to declare socially constructed norms universal across space and time. To *reveal* the contours of normative precepts and activities of those who advance them is neither to dispense with the need for norms within political practice nor to eliminate their complex role in the formation and transformation of social relations and practices. . . . acknowledging the dynamics of normative contestation as Butler does may equip those who practice feminist politics to understand, plan, critique, and take responsibility for their actions as they strive to create, advance, and maintain norms of gender equality, universal human right, and so on.[94]

Barvosa-Carter's defense of Butler highlights the ways in which Butler's work provides tools for feminist practice and moves the debates around Butler's work to a focus on the ethical and critical concerns that Butler's arguments are attempting to address. These ethical and critical concerns specifically come to the forefront when we examine the charge of her "double moves."

THE SIGNIFICANCE OF BUTLER'S "DOUBLE MOVES"

Although Butler rejects references to critical consciousness, intentionality and reflexivity, as a real live person she does not shun using these concepts when she writes. In her discussion of drag as subversive resignification, for instance, she writes,

> the extent that it [drag] *reflects* on the imitative structure by which hegemonic gender is itself produced and *disputes* heterosexuality's claim on naturalness and originality.[95]

When Butler acknowledges the practical necessity for identity, in another instance, she refers to the need for

> *critical reflection* (of constitutive exclusions) . . . in order not to replicate at the level of identity politics the very exclusionary moves that initiated the turn to specific identities in the first place.[96]

And yet again,

> For one is, as it were, in power even as one opposes it, formed by it as one *reworks* it, and it is this simultaneity that is at once the condition of our partiality . . . and also the condition of action itself.[97]

In her discussion of queer politics, to bring one last example, Butler addresses " . . . the terms to which we do, nevertheless, lay claim, the terms through which we *insist* on politicizing identity and desire" and she refers to "a self-critical dimension within activism."[98]

Veronica Vasterling observes that terms such as "'reflection,' 'dispute,' 'laying claim to terms,' and 'self-criticism' require an intentional and reflective subject, capable of deliberate and purposive action."[99] These are exactly the concepts that Butler rejects. Lise Nelson also queries, "Who is the 'one' who 'reworks'?"[100] Although Butler's account of agency refuses to acknowledge that a viable notion of agency requires that "the subject is not only the carrier of the process of reiteration but also a possible participant in this process,"[101] in her actual texts there are clearly implications of such a participatory agent.

Vasterling argues that the concept of an intentional, reflexive subject that is capable of deliberate and purposive action does not have to be inconsistent with the discursive subject implicated in "relations of power that it cannot (fully) control."[102] She points out that Butler does not preclude the possibility that subjects intend to discursively subvert. Butler rather rejects the presumption that intention is prediscursive and is what controls or decides the consequences of speech acts. More specifically, Butler compels us to interrogate this presumption. Expanding on Butler's apparent rejection of intentions, Vasterling explains that intentional subversion does not need to assume the ability to control. All that is required for a viable understanding of agency is that intentional actions leave a trace.

> On the one hand, the subject always already finds itself in a language with more or less established signifying conventions. . . . yet . . . we can, intentionally, try to deflect or guide the signifying conventions or chains we are citing in a certain direction, aiming at the resignificiation, the shift of meaning, that is our goal. This initiative, on the other hand, does not imply that our intentions can control the future course of these signifying chains . . . But neither does it imply that the initiative or intervention on the part of the subject never leaves a trace. It does leave a trace, and it may be effective in the long run, when other subjects pick up and continue the deflecting course of the signifying chain.[103]

Nelson, in contrast, recommends a version of Benhabib's situated subject that is not fixed or unified but continually contested.

The subject that Nelson recommends allows for concrete subjects both individually and collectively to "do identity in relation to various discursive processes (e.g., those that constitute race, class, sexuality and gender), to other subjects, and to layers of institutions and practices."[104] Such a notion of agency is

> . . . never transparent because it is always inflected by the unconscious, by repressed desire and difference. Accepting that "conscious action" is not un-

mediated, that it is always encumbered with and influenced by (conscious or unconscious) constitutive discourses, is to truly accept the partiality of knowledge and to be rid of the autonomous, transparent subject of Enlightenment thought.[105]

Nelson suggests an account of agency that involves critical reflexivity without entailing presumptions that one can stand outside of power matrices.

Moreover, as we have seen, even when Butler eschews the possibility of stable identities categories, she also acknowledges their necessity. Butler claims that all identity categories are exclusionary fictions in that they are expressions of the metaphysics of substance. In other words, identity categories assume the illusionary belief that there is an internal essence that precedes the social and discursive. Yet Butler also contends that such categories are necessary for making political claims and she does not turn away from using such categories in her work. Lobbying efforts, she acknowledges, "are virtually impossible without recourse to identity politics."[106]

Her use of identity categories, however, is never merely strategic. Strategic uses of identity categories still presume "meanings that exceed the purposes for which they are intended."[107] Instead, any reference to identity categories must leave such terms open as a site of permanent openness and resignifiability. Butler contends that

> To deconstruct the subject of feminism is not, then, to censure its usage, but, on the contrary, to release the term into a future of multiple significations . . . and to give it play as a site where unanticipated meanings might come to bear.[108]

Thus, Butler is careful to insist that whenever it is necessary to use identity categories for political purposes, they must be employed vigilantly so that the categories remain open and a site for contestation.

In all these variations and extensions of Butler's work, what remains firmly secured is that the subject and agency are not outside of power matrices. This inability to get outside of the system requires one to continually interrogate, to be willing to be open to critique even the political and moral grounding from which one acts. It is this insight that permeates all of Butler's works. Once Butler's critical and ethical concerns are emphasized, conceptions of agency faithful to those concerns but that avoid the pitfalls of Butler's account are possible to articulate. Ralph Sandland[109] refers to "the double gesture" or the "double movement" that poststructuralist feminists often make. He points to Butler's contention that it is

> necessary to learn a double movement: to invoke the category and, hence, provisionally to institute an identity and at the same time to open the category as a site of permanent political contest. That the term (e.g. "Woman") is questionable

does not mean that we ought not to use it but neither does the necessity to use it mean that we ought not perpetually to interrogate the exclusions by which it proceeds.[110]

Similarly, Nelson notes that Butler's notions of agency should not be read as "a discrete, internalized quality" but instead as "a disturbance in self-certitude."[111]

I suggest that Butler should not be read as providing *the theory* of subject formation but rather an *account* that can help bring to light the ways in which complicity conceals its own working through discursive practices that naturalize its effects. Reading her main point less as rejecting what she deconstructs and more as a call for continual interrogation helps to highlight her critical and ethical concerns. As she emphasizes, "To call a presupposition into question is not the same as doing away with it."[112] Nancy Fraser recommends that feminists adopt a pragmatic view in which

there are a plurality of different angles from which sociocultural phenomena can be understood. Which is best will depend on one's purposes . . . In general, conceptions of discourse, like conceptions of subjectivity, *should be treated as tools,* not as the property of warring metaphysical sects.[113]

Similarly, in her discussion of Foucault's claim of the end of man, Amy Allen[114] argues this claim does not imply that Foucault wants to dispense with the "constituent subject." Rather, Allen contends, Foucault's aim is to be able to interrogate how we have arrived at such a conception of the subject.[115]

As Allen notes, Foucault explicitly says that

One has to dispense with the constituent subject, to get rid of the subject itself, that's to say, to arrive at an analysis which can account for the constitution of the subject within a historical framework. And this is what I would call genealogy, that is, a form of history which can account for the constitution of knowledges, discourses, domains of objects, etc., without having to make reference to a subject which is either transcendental in relation to the field of events or runs in its empty sameness throughout the course of history.[116]

Foucault's call for the end of man, according to Allen, is best read as a call for a critique of critique.[117] Allen notes that when asked in an interview if he forbids people to talk to him about the subject, Foucault responds,

No, I have not "forbidden" them. Perhaps I did not explain myself adequately. What I rejected was the idea of starting out with a theory of the subject—as is done, for example, in phenomenology and existentialism—and, on the basis of this theory, asking how a given form of knowledge was possible . . . I had to reject a priori theories of the subject in order to analyze the relationship that may exist between the constitution of the subject . . . and games of truth, practices of power, and so on.[118]

The end of man is not a rejection of subjectivity tout court but rather a call to interrogate the conditions of its possibility.

Along the same lines, Ladelle McWhorter argues that Foucault's analytics of power is often read as a description of what *power* really is and, thus, it is not surprising when certain criticisms are raised against his work. McWhorter, however, reads Foucault as not providing a descriptive account of some thing—power—but rather "a strategy, a movement"[119] that works "to erode a kind of barrier to its own project,"[120] that primary project being a genealogy of the subject. As McWhorter explains,

> . . . if subjectivity's historicity is what is to be thought, these traditional models of power are useless at best. And, in fact, in the absence of any alternative conceptualization of power, these models not only fail to accommodate; they actually hinder historical thinking in relation to subjectivity. Therefore, if historical thinking is to go on, it must find some *strategy* for loosing the grip of these traditional views of power on us. It must find a way to bypass the obstacles to the thought of historical occurrence presented by those traditional models of power.[121]

Thus, Foucault is not providing an *alternate* theory of power that is the *right* way to conceive of power but rather is deploying a strategy that allows for the possibility to open up questions that are unlikely to arise under traditional conceptions of power.

In the same way, I suggest that Butler's account of subject formation and agency can be read not as *the* theory about how the subject is constituted or how agency is possible. Rather her account can be understood as a tool to open up critical questions about politics when the sovereign subject is presumed. Indeed, Butler's refusal to return to any hint of a prediscursive self can be clearly understood to be ethically motivated. She contends that any assumption about a self that can be abstracted or be understood as "outside" power matrices is ethically pernicious and exclusionary. As David Stern[122] explains,

> If subjects are constituted by power, then to assume the existence of subjectivity and the possession of its capacities *would be to obscure the need to interrogate the political construction of the subject. It would thus close off questions about the ways in which the assignment of subjectivity and agency can work to include some and exclude others, authorizing some to speak and act in ways that bind others, while denying the same privileges to others. We must, then, interrogate how we are made into subjects, and what the consequences, both welcome and unwelcome, of such a making are.*[123]

Even in her critique of coherent identity position and the subject position "women" upon which feminist theory and politics is grounded, Butler's concern is who is being excluded and in whose interests.

Sara Salih further highlights Butler's ethical motivation when she explains how Butler's writing challenges the exclusionary normative assumptions about the subject that grounds ordinary language and notes that "To a greater or lesser extent, *this ethical impetus motivates all Butler's work.*"[124] Olson and Wosham underscore Butler's critical concerns when they come away from their interview with Butler concluding that

> For Butler, being a critical intellectual means constantly interrogating our assumptions, continually calling things into question, not necessarily to do away with what is being questioned but, rather, to discover, for example, how terms might assume new meanings in new contexts. Such a stance means learning to "live in the anxiety of that questioning without closing it down too quickly."[125]

At the heart of all Butler's theorizing, I submit, is an apprehension about the dangers of thinking that one can step outside systems of power and a willingness to consider the unthinkable. Her notion of subject formation and her understanding of agency have a strong ethical dimension and target feminist theorists and activists who see their projects as emancipatory in the sense of challenging oppressive norms. As Butler's work demonstrates, far from challenging such norms, such feminists are complicit in perpetuating them.

When Linda Nicholson expresses surprise concerning the "degree of intense feeling among feminists"[126] that Butler's writings have generated, it should really come as no surprise. Butler is exposing the complicity underlying the ethical and political work of feminist theorists and activists. Butler's work challenges not only the assumed conceptions of the subject and of agency underlying feminist theory. By exposing the ways in which feminist politics that is grounded in identity politics reifies rather than destabilizes gender norms, she also challenges feminist moral sensibilities. This charge goes to the heart of feminist theory and politics and as such has led to such an intense response to her work. Wendy Brown asks disdainfully,

> Why, then, is putting the subject in question—decentering its constitution, deconstructing its unity, denaturing its origins and components—such a lightning rod for feminist hostility to postfoundational thought?[127]

In response to Benhabib's accusation that poststructuralism puts feminist theory in danger of "losing its very reason for being,"[128] Brown maintains it poses an even greater risk by raising doubts about feminists' ability to know what is true.

In fact, postmodern decentering, disunifying, and denaturalizing of the subject is far more threatening to the status of feminism's well of truth than to feminism's raison d'etre.[129]

Poststructuralism in general (and Butler's theory more specifically) challenges long-established notions of radical critique and of the ethical, but in ways that promote rather than hinder feminist aims.

I have argued that Butler's critical and ethical spirit must be the framework from which we read her theory. Butler offers a cautionary tool to all who theorize that the political and moral grounding from which one theorizes must continually be open to interrogation. Even about poststructuralism itself, Butler remarks,

Inasmuch as poststructuralism offers a mode of critique that effects this contestation of the foundationalist move, it can be used as part of such a radical agenda. Note that I have said, "it can be used": I think there are no necessary political consequences for such a theory, but only a possible political deployment.[130]

If we keep Butler's critical and ethical concerns in clear sight, it may be possible to articulate a conception of agency (and responsibility) that is faithful to these concerns and yet avoid the problems that her particular notion of agency entails.

I resonate with a metaphor that Wendy Brown[131] employs to illustrate what she suggests should be the relationship between two prominent and compelling approaches in contemporary feminist thought which she reframes as the "radical instability of gender," on the one hand, and "the relentless power of gender," on the other hand. She asks,

at this moment, we appear to have two powerful, mutually canceling truths in feminism: on the one hand, there is no stable sex or gender and on the other, women too often find themselves unable to escape their gender and the sexual norms governing it. What to do with this double truth that does not even seem paradoxical in its operation? How to allow each to have a productive place in our theoretical and political work?[132]

The notion of counterpoint, Brown argues, suggests a framework in which truths can be enriched and informed by each other. Counterpoint, "is a deliberate practice of multiplicity that exceeds simple opposition."[133]

At once open-ended and tactical, counterpoint emanates from and promotes an antihegemonic sensibility and requires a modest and carefully styled embrace of multiplicity in which contrasting elements, featured simultaneously, do not simply war, harmonize, blend or compete but rather bring out the complexity that cannot emerge through a monolithic or single melody. This complexity does not add up to a whole but, rather, sets off a theme by providing an elsewhere to it; indeed, it can even highlight and thus contest dominance through its work of juxtaposition.[134]

It is in the spirit of counterpoint that I will attempt in a subsequent chapter to bring together insights from Butler's work and Iris Marion Young's recent work on responsibility in an attempt to reconstruct a notion of moral responsibility that can ground the white complicity claim. Young illuminates the limitations of applying a liability model of responsibility to issues of structural injustice. Butler draws our attention to the "I" who is accountable and the dangers of assuming that "I" can stand outside of power regimes. Butler underscores the significance of being willing to continually be open to critique, even to critique the political and moral grounds from which one acts. I close this chapter with some thoughts about the implications of Butler's work for the subject of white complicity.

IMPLICATIONS FOR THE SUBJECT OF WHITE COMPLICITY

. . . resistance and the subject who resists are fundamentally implicated within the relations of power they oppose. *This suggestion forms the crux of Judith Butler's recent work,* which is centrally concerned with the possibility of social transformation and resistance to regimes of power given that agency itself is an effect of power.[135]

Understanding agency under complicity forms the crux of Judith Butler's work. She can be read as attempting to explain how moral and political agency can be exclusionary even when such agency attempts to be progressive. Butler emphasizes that voluntarism must always be interrogated for its complicity with power, for what it forecloses. Nothing stands outside of power, or as I would put it, one can never assume that anything one does, and especially the moral and political position one takes, is innocent and does not need to be interrogated for complicity. The insight that "power pervades the very conceptual apparatus that seeks to negotiate its terms"[136] is the "very precondition of a politically engaged critique."[137] If the subject is constituted all the way down, then so are critical capacities.

This does not imply that critique is impossible but rather that uncertainty and humility must be an inherent part of critique. Butler is not announcing the death of the subject but is calling for the death of *arrogance.* As Barvosa-Carter puts it, poststructural tools "enable feminists to critique their own positions, to interrogate them for exclusions and omissions that may be part of their own theorizing and activism."[138]

Butler often intimates that her primary concern is not with "truth." Instead, she is interested in understanding or exposing the foundations upon which truth claims are made. She writes,

> For the question of whether or not a position is right, coherent, or interesting is, in this case, less informative than why it is we come to occupy and defend the territory that we do, what it promises us, from what it promises to protect us.[139]

In her discussion of Foucault's essay, "What is Critique?" Butler explains that

> the primary task of critique will not be to evaluate whether its objects—social conditions, practices, forms of knowledge, power, and discourse—are good or bad, valued highly or demeaned, but to bring into relief the very framework of evaluation itself. What is the relation of knowledge to power such that our epistemological certainties turn out to support a way of structuring the world that forecloses alternative possibilities of ordering?[140]

In *Giving an Account of Oneself*[141] Butler asks "Does the postulation of a subject who is not self-grounding, that is, whose conditions of emergence can never fully be accounted for, undermine the possibility of responsibility and, in practice, of giving an account of oneself?"[142] Butler explains that by rejecting a coherent account of the subject we are able to reconceive the conditions that make responsibility possible and a new sense of ethics can be articulated. In the "willingness to acknowledge the limits of acknowledgement itself,"[143] the very understanding of responsibility can be drawn around this "(self) limitation" and avoid the "*conceit* of a self fully transparent to itself."[144] Butler's understanding of responsibility will be elaborated in more detail in Chapter 6.

What is so radical about Butler's work is that she calls into question the nature of radical critique itself. As Cynthia Kaufman[145] writes of postmodernism,

> postmodernism begins with a radical reformulation of the nature of social criticism. . . . Postmodernism does in fact undermine any notion of critique that would supposedly offer the critic an objective position from which to analyze society. This should be seen as a virtue rather than a weakness . . . "[146]

Kaufman points to the value of postmodernism in providing a safety check to theorists who uncritically assume false universals. Similarly, Ellen T. Armour and Susan M. St. Ville[147] insist that

> More than identifying distinct truths about gender, Butler invites us into a mode of inquiry or process of thought, the character of which is captured well by the word trouble. Integral to it is a constant and thoroughgoing questioning

of received assumptions—a 'troubling' that allows new possibilities for thought and action to emerge.[148]

Magnus points out that in Butler's Adorno Lecture published as *Kritik der ethischen Gewalt*,[149] Butler begins by observing how moral issues arise only when ethical norms become violent impositions of unjust universality. Butler draws attention to how the subject can never tells its entire story.

> Since every "I" begins in and through others . . . every self-justification has to remain deficient . . . I can never fully explain who I am or how I came to act as I do. I cannot account for myself in any ultimate way.[150]

It is this unavailability that makes moral inquiry possible, a point that will be crucial for the rearticulated notion of white moral responsibility developed in Chapter 6. Further, Magnus explains,

> For Butler, the proper starting point of morality is not the self-transparent subject, but rather subjects who know they *cannot* fully account for themselves. With this claim, she does not deny the moral importance of "knowing oneself" to a certain degree, but she emphasizes that our *inability* to know ourselves completely *also* has moral value.[151]

Butler's understanding of ethics requires first and foremost an acknowledgement of one's own fallibility and lack of self-coherence. What Butler and her postmodern leanings offer us is a radical critique of radical criticality, the rejection of epistemic arrogance and an endorsement of epistemic humility.[152]

White complicity requires a conception of the subject that is sensitive to the way that power works through our very being and the ways in which subjects are implicated in sustaining or subverting the system. John Warren[153] maintains that Butler's theory of performativity provides a "heuristic lens for considering the reproduction of whiteness and racial power."[154] Through the notion of performativity, Warren explores the everyday discursive reiterations of whiteness and how white bodies are produced and reproduced. Whiteness, Warren argues, is a reiterative performance and "an identity that is maintained and naturalized through our everyday communication."[155] Whiteness needs to be constantly cited because it is both unachievable but also continuously sought. Rather than reading race as something with a biological essence, Butler is able to explicate how race is constituted through the repetition of discursive regimes of truth. Thus, race, and whiteness in particular, always invoke a reiteration of norms.

Butler's theory of subject formation therefore helps us to understand how the white subject is complicit in maintaining systems of privilege and oppression. Not only does the white subject cite white norms in order to maintain its status as a body that matters, in doing so the subject is implicated in perpetuating exclusions. Race is relational and only exists inasmuch as it exists as "different" from something else.

Moreover, Warren points to the reproduction of "whiteness as purity." Citing and reciting of the white discourses of purity constitutes whites as good. This point will be of particular importance and will be further examined in the next chapter when the topic of white denials of complicity is addressed in more detail. Yet what Butler's theory of subject formation and agency provide the critical whiteness scholar is the caution that even when white people act against the norm of whiteness, one does not become innocent and removed from power matrices because privilege is reproduced regardless of intent. Even when whiteness is disavowed, whiteness is reiterated.

Conceptions of agency (and especially agency that grounds ethical and political action) must be interrogated for what they foreclose. Nothing stands outside of power/discursive matrices. Similarly, the practice of critique always takes place "immanent to the regime of discourse/power whose claims it seek to adjudicate, which is to say that the practice of 'critique' is implicated in the very power-relations it seeks to adjudicate."[156] While her notion of agency may be still be open to critique (and I believe Butler would encourage such critique if it exposed her own complicity in systemic exclusions), the merit of Butler's account for understanding white complicity lies in her insistence of the fallibility and humility that are required even for, and especially for, moral and political agency.

One of Butler's insights is that a performance can enact something other than what the subject intends it to do. In the next chapter, we will examine what is meant by "doing something other than what one thinks one is doing" and "not knowing what one is doing." This is important for explicating systemic white ignorance and white denials of complicity, on the one hand, and for rearticulating the type of agency that can ground white moral responsibility, on the other.

NOTES

1. Ralph Sandland, "Seeing Double? Or, Why 'To Be or Not to Be' is (Not) the Question for Feminist Legal Studies," *Social and Legal Studies* 7, no. 3 (1998): 307–338.
2. Ladelle McWhorter, "Foucault's Analytics of Power," in *Crisis in Continental Philosophy (Selected Studies in Phenomenology and Existential Philosophy, 16)*, ed. Charles E. Scott, Arleen B. Dallery and P. Holly Roberts (Albany: State University of New York Press, 1990), 119–126.
3. Ibid., 120.
4. Edwina Barvosa-Carter, "Strange Tempest: Agency, Poststructuralism, and the Shape of Feminist Politics to Come," *International Journal of Sexuality and Gender Studies* 6, nos. 1–2 (2001): 123–137.

5. Judith Butler, *Psychic Life of Power: Theories in Subjugation* (Stanford: Stanford University Press, 1997), 2, emphasis in the original.

6. Judith Butler, *Gender Trouble: Feminism and the Subversion of Identity* (New York: Routledge, 1990), 2.

7. Ibid., x–xi, emphasis added.

8. Ibid., 22.

9. Judith Butler, *Bodies That Matter: On the Discursive Limits of Sex* (New York: Routledge, 1993), 3.

10. Judith Butler, "Imitation and Gender Subordination," in *Inside/Out: Lesbian Theories, Gay Theories*, ed. Diana Fuss (New York: Routledge, 1991), 13.

11. Judith Butler, *Gender Trouble*, 16.

12. Judith Butler, *The Psychic Life*, 64, emphasis added.

13. Judith Butler, "Contingent Foundations,'" in *Feminist Contentions: A Philosophical Exchange*, Seyla Benhabib, Judith Butler, Drucilla Cornell and Nancy Fraser (New York: Routledge, 1995), 49, italics in original.

14. Ibid., 50.

15. Judith Butler, *Excitable Speech: A Politics of the Performative* (New York: Routledge, 1997), 26.

16. Ibid., 5.

17. Judith Butler, *Excitable Speech*, 159–160.

18. Judith Butler, *Gender Trouble*, 140.

19. Ibid., 33, emphasis added.

20. Judith Butler, *The Psychic Life of Power*, 16.

21. Judith Butler, *Bodies That Matter*, 2.

22. Judith Butler, *Gender Trouble*, 25, emphasis added.

23. Seyla Benhabib, Judith Butler, Drucilla Cornell and Nancy Fraser, *Feminist Contentions*. The discussion takes place among Seyla Benhabib, Judith Butler, Drucilla Cornell and Nancy Fraser. I focus, however, on the essays by Benhabib and Butler as they forefront the question of subjectivity and agency that establish the contours of the debate.

24. Seyla Benhabib, "Feminism and Postmodernism: An Uneasy Alliance," in *Feminist Contentions*, 20.

25. Ibid., 20.

26. Ibid., 21.

27. Judith Butler, "Contingent Foundations," 42.

28. Seyla Benhabib, "Feminism and Postmodernism," 29.

29. Judith Butler, *Bodies That Matter*, x.

30. Lise Nelson, "Bodies (and Spaces) Do Matter: The Limits of Performativity," *Gender, Place and Culture* 6, no. 4 (1999): 331–353.

31. Judith Butler, "For a Careful Reading," in *Feminist Contentions*, 134.

32. Friedrich Nietzche, *The Basic Writings of Nietzsche*, edited and translated by Walter Kaufmann (New York: Modern Library, 1992), 481.

33. Judith Butler, *Gender Trouble*, 142.

34. Edwina Barvosa-Carter, "Strange Tempest," 125, emphasis added.

35. Judith Butler, *Psychic Life of Power*, 2.

36. Michel Foucault, *Power/Knowledge: Selected Interviews and Other Writings* (New York: Pantheon, 1980), 98.
37. Michel Foucault, *"Society Must Be Defended": Lectures at the College de France, 1975–76*, ed. Mauro Bertani and Alessandro Fontana (NewYork: Picador, 2003), 29–30.
38. Foucault, *Power/Knowledge*, 98, emphasis added.
39. Michel Foucault, *The History of Sexuality Volume 1: An Introduction* (New York: Vintage, 1978/1990), 95.
40. Judith Butler, "Contingent Foundation," 46.
41. Judith Butler, *Gender Trouble*, 145.
42. Judith Butler, *Bodies That Matter*, 108.
43. Ibid., 237.
44. Ibid., 231.
45. Louis Althusser, "Ideology and Ideological State Apparatuses (Notes Toward an Investigation)" in his *Lenin and Philosophy and Other Essays* (New York: Monthly Review Press, 1971), 163.
46. Judith Butler, *Bodies That Matter*, 121–122.
47. Judith Butler, *Excitable Speech*, 19.
48. Ibid., 16.
49. Ibid., 1–2.
50. Charles Lawrence III, "If He Hollers Let Him Go: Regulating Hate Speech," in *Hate Speech on Campus: Cases, Case Studies and Commentary*, ed. Milton Heumann and Thomas W. Church (Boston: Northeastern University Press, 1997), 278.
51. Catharine A. MacKinnon, *Only Words* (London: HarperCollins, 1994).
52. Mari J. Matsuda, Charles R. Lawrence III, Richard Delgado and Kimberle Williams Crenshaw, ed., *Words that Wound: Critical Race Theory, Assaultive Speech and the First Amendment* (Boulder, CO: Westview, 1993).
53. J. L. Austin, *How to Do Things with Words*, 2nd Edition (Oxford: Oxford University Press, 1962).
54. Jacques Derrida, "Signature Even Context," in *Limited, Inc.*, ed. Gerald Graff (Evanston: North Western University Press, 1988), 18.
55. Judith Butler, *Excitable Speech*, 3.
56. Ibid., 33.
57. Ibid., 34.
58. Ibid., 52.
59. Judith Butler, *Bodies That Matter*, 227.
60. Judith Butler, *Excitable Speech*, 19.
61. Judith Butler, *Bodies That Matter*, 228.
62. Gary A. Olson and Lynn Worsham, "Changing the Subject: Judith Butler's Politics of Radical Resignification," *JAC: A Journal of Composition Theory* 20, no. 4 (2000): 759.
63. Judith Butler, "For a Careful Reading," 136.
64. Ibid.
65. Judith Butler, *Excitable Speech*, 15–16.
66. Judith Butler, *Gender Trouble*, 30.

67. Ibid., 28, emphasis added.
68. Ibid., 143.
69. Teresa de Laurentes, "Eccentric Subjects: Feminist Theory and Historical Consciousness," *Feminist Studies* 16, no. 1 (1990): 115–150.
70. Ibid., 129.
71. Ibid.
72. Lise Nelson, "Bodies (and Spaces) Do Matter: The Limits of Performativity," *Gender, Place and Culture* 6, no. 4 (1999): 331.
73. Ibid., 332, emphasis in original.
74. Lois McNay, *Gender and Agency: Reconfiguring the Subject in Feminist and Social Theory* (Polity Press, 2000), 47.
75. Lois McNay, "Subject, Psyche, and Agency," *Theory, Culture and Society* 16, no. 2 (1999): 181.
76. Lise Nelson, "Bodies (and Spaces)," 347.
77. Ibid., 332.
78. Ibid., 331.
79. Kathy Dow Magnus, "The Unaccountable Subject: Judith Butler and the Social Conditions of Intersubjective Agency," *Hypatia* 21, no. 2 (2006): 81–103.
80. Ibid., 87.
81. Ibid., 88, emphasis in original.
82. Ibid., 85.
83. Ibid., 90.
84. Veronica Vasterling, "Butler's Sophisticated Constructivism: A Critical Assessment," *Hypatia* 14, no. 3 (1999): 31.
85. Judith Butler, *The Psychic Life of Power*, 9.
86. Kathy Dow Magnus, "The Unaccountable Subject," 83.
87. Lois McNay, "Subject, Psyche, and Agency."
88. Allison Weir, *Sacrificial Logics: Feminist Theory and the Critique of Identity* (New York: Routledge, 1996).
89. Moya Lloyd, "Politics and Melancholia," *Women's Philosophical Review* 20 (Winter 1998–1999), 38.
90. Nancy Fraser, *Justice Interruptus: Critical Reflections on the "Postsocialist" Condition* (New York: Routledge, 1997), 216.
91. Judith Butler, "For a Careful Reading," 129.
92. Judith Butler, "Contingent Foundations," 50–51, emphasis added.
93. Ibid., 39.
94. Barvosa-Carter, "Strange Tempest," 133, emphasis in original.
95. Judith Butler, *Bodies That Matter*, 125.
96. Ibid., 118, emphasis added.
97. Ibid., 241, emphasis added.
98. Ibid., 227.
99. Vernica Vasterling, "Butler's Sophisticated Constructivism," 26.
100. Lise Nelson, "Bodies (and Spaces)," 340.
101. Veronica Vasterling, "Butler's Sophisticated Constructivism," 28.
102. Ibid., 27.

103. Ibid., 29.

104. Lise Nelson, "Bodies (and Spaces)," 331.

105. Ibid., 348.

106. Judith Butler, "Contingent Foundations," 49.

107. Judith Butler, *Gender Trouble*, 8.

108. Judith Butler, "Contingent Foundations," 49–50.

109. Ralph Sandland, "Seeing Double?"

110. Judith Butler, *Bodies That Matter*, 221–222.

111. Lise Nelson, "Bodies (and Spaces)," 348.

112. Judith Butler, *Bodies That Matter*, 30.

113. Nancy Fraser, "Pragmatism, Feminism, and the Linguistic Turn," in *Feminist Contentions*, 166–167.

114. Amy Allen, *The Politics of Our Selves: Power, Autonomy, and Gender in Contemporary Critical Theory* (New York: Columbia University Press, 2007), 21.

115. Ibid., 36–37.

116. Michel Foucault, "Truth and Power," in *Power/Knowledge: Selected Interviews and Other Writings 1972–1977*, ed. Colin Gordon (New York: Pantheon, 1980), 117.

117. Amy Allen, *The Politics of Our Selves*, 42.

118. Michel Foucault, "The Ethics of Concern for the Self as a Practice of Freedom," in *Ethics, Subjectivity, and Truth Volume 1 of the Essential Works of Michel Foucault*, ed. Paul Rabinow (New York: The New Press, 1997), 290.

119. Ladelle McWhorter, "Foucault's Analytics of Power," 121.

120. Ibid., 122.

121. Ibid., 123, emphasis added.

122. David Stern, "The Return of the Subject? Power, Reflexivity and Agency," *Philosophy and Social Criticism* 26, no. 5 (2000): 109–122.

123. Ibid., 113, emphasis added.

124. Sara Salih, "Judith Butler and the Ethics of 'Difficulty'," *Critical Quarterly* 45, no. 3 (2003): 46, emphasis added.

125. Gary A. Olson and Lynn Worsham, "Changing the Subject," 729.

126. Linda Nicholson, "Feminism and the Politics of Postmodernism," *boundary 2*, 19, no. 2 (1992): 53.

127. Wendy Brown, *States of Injury: Power and Freedom in Late Modernity* (Princeton, New Jersey: Princeton University Press, 1995), 40.

128. Seyla Benhabib, "On Contemporary Feminist Theory," *Dissent* 36 (1989): 369.

129. Wendy Brown, *States of Injury*, 40.

130. Judith Butler, "Contingent Foundations," 41.

131. Wendy Brown, "Gender in Counterpoint," *Feminist Theory* 4, no. 3 (2003): 365–368.

132. Ibid., 366.

133. Ibid., 367.

134. Ibid.

135. Catherine Mills, "Efficacy and Vulnerability: Judith Butler on Reiteration and Resistance," *Australian Feminist Studies* 15, no. 32 (2000): 265, emphasis added.

136. Judith Butler, "Contingent Foundations," 39.

137. Ibid.

138. Barvosa-Carter, "Strange Tempest," 134.

139. Judith Butler, "For a Careful Reading," 127–128.

140. Judith Butler, "What is Critique? An Essay on Foucault's Virtue," in *The Political*, ed. David Ingram (Boston, Blackwell, 2002), 212–228.

141. Judith Butler, *Giving an Account of Oneself* (New York: Fordham University Press, 2005).

142. Ibid., 19.

143. Ibid., 42.

144. Ibid., 83, emphasis added.

145. Cynthia Kaufman, "Postmodernism and Praxis: Waving Radical Theory from Threads of Desire and Discourse," *Socialist Review* 24, no. 3 (1994): 57–80.

146. Ibid., 57–58.

147. Ellen T. Armour and Susan M. St. Ville, "Judith Butler—in Theory" in *Bodily Citations: Religion and Judith Butler*, ed. Ellen T. Armour and Susan M. St. Ville (New York: Columbia University Press, 2006), 1–15.

148. Ibid., 2.

149. Judith Butler, *Kritik der ethischen Gewalt Adorno Lectures, 2002* (Frankfurt am Main: Institute fur Sozialforschung an der Johann Wolfgang Goethe-Universitat, 2002).

150. Ibid., 92.

151. Ibid., 93.

152. Linda Nicholson, "Feminism and the Politics of Postmodernism," 68–69.

153. John T. Warren, *Performing Purity: Whiteness, Pedagogy, and the Reconstitution of Power* (New York: Peter Lang, 2003).

154. Ibid., 8.

155. Ibid.

156. Judith Butler, "For a Careful Reading," 138–139.

CHAPTER 4

The Epistemology of Complicity

The Discourse of Not Knowing
and Refusing to Know

Discourse transmits and produces power.[1]

IN CHAPTER 2 SOME OF THE EPISTEMOLOGICAL FEATURES OF WHITE COMPLICITY WERE EX-
plored. In particular, the meaning of white ignorance and the role that denials
of complicity play in maintaining white ignorance were examined. In addition,
how white ignorance protects moral innocence and simultaneously shields
power regimes from possible challenge was addressed. In the first part of this
chapter, I argue that in order to understand what white denials of complicity
do, one has to make a shift in one's understanding of language from language
as representation to language as discourse. The second part of the chapter
focuses on a question entailed by such a shift: Does such an understanding of
discourse preclude the possibility of disagreement? While this question can be
understood as an instance of white denial, I maintain that it is a question that
must be taken seriously because without the possibility of disagreement the
white complicity claim insulates itself against refutation.

As a reminder of what white denials refer to, some cases and the scholarship around them are briefly reviewed. In her discussion of the limitations of
cross-cultural dialogue, Alison Jones[2] contends that the dialogue between her
white students and students of color that seemed to the white students to express a empathetic desire to know the Other in effect functioned to maintain
the white students' self-image as "good." When the students of color snubbed
the white students' well-intended desires for integrated discussion, the white
students expressed indignation instead of working to understand their role
in the students' of color preference for separate classes. The white students
were unaware but also *unwilling* to recognize that what they perceived as an
empathetic desire functioned as a type of absolution. Jones attributes the white
students' indignation to their interpretation of the students of color as standing in their way of being "good whites." The white students' "cannibal desire
to know the other through being taught or fed by her," according to Jones,

is at the same time "*a refusal* to know."[3] Jones underscores that white desire for knowledge that is based on empathy works to save oneself from having to consider one's complicity in racial injustice. The white students thought their talk reflected empathy. Their talk, instead, served to reproduce and maintain the culture of power in their classroom.

In their ethnographic study of how discourses of whiteness operate in the classroom, John Warren and Kathy Hytten[4] describe similar *culturally sanctioned* discursive practices that white students *inadvertently* use to *evade* consideration of their complicity. Some of the discursive moves that Hytten and Warren discuss are: remaining silent, evading questions, resorting to the rhetoric of ignoring color, focusing on progress, victim blaming and focusing on culture rather than race. Warren and Hytten group these practices of whiteness into four categories: appeals to self, appeals to progress, appeals to authenticity and appeals to extremes, and they provide illustrations of each. Kim Case and Annette Hemmings[5] refer to such discursive moves as "distancing strategies" and also maintain that the effect of such discourse is that white students can avoid being positioned as racist or implicated in systemic oppression. Alice McIntyre[6] examines parallel discursive moves. She coined the phrase "white talk" to name discourse that functions to "insulate White people from examining their/our individual and collective role(s) in the perpetuation of racism."[7] In all these cases, such discursive practices reinscribe and protect whiteness *even within attempts to disrupt its normative influence.*

Underlying all these examples of white denials of complicity is an insinuation that discourse can function in ways that the social actor does not consciously intend. Moreover, these examples emphasize the point that white people cannot rely on their good intentions in order to know how their discourse affects others.

A classroom experience illustrates the significance of understanding what discourse does. A former student sent me a comic entitled "White Lies: The Top Ten List"[8] that I thought would make a great discussion piece to accompany the reading of Warren and Hytten's essay assigned in my course. Examples of the "white lies" on the list:

"Race doesn't matter to me!"
"We're liberals, so we can't be racist!"
"Whatever I achieved, I achieved on my own!"
"As long as no one consciously intends to be racist, that's what really matters!"
"To be fair, we should be talking about racism against whites, too."
"I hate the KKK. I admire MLK. I'm kind to non-whites I meet. So I can't be racist!"
"Our ancestors got here after slavery, so racism has nothing to do with us!"

What I asked my students to consider was how these comments were distancing strategies. In response, one of my white students exclaimed, "How can you even think these were distancing strategies? Weren't these people just stating their opinion?"

I could read my student's question as a "distancing strategy." By defending these remarks as opinions, he could protect his racial innocence in case he too had at some point in the course made similar comments. This, however, is exactly what my student was having difficulty contemplating. Hytten and Warren explain that such utterances are socially sanctioned, they "were not original—that is, they are already available, already common forms of asserting dominance."[9] As I tried to better understand how to respond to my student, I realized that my student's belief that "discursive strategies" are merely "opinions" rests in part on a particular and deeply rooted understanding of the relationship between the subject and language. Picking up on Hytten and Warren's claim that such discourses of evasion are not original, I asked what foundational framework supports my student's question.

FROM LANGUAGE AS REPRESENTATION TO LANGUAGE AS DISCOURSE

My student's question about reading these utterances not as distancing strategies but merely as "opinions" depends on a specific and common understanding of the relationship between the subject and language. Traditional accounts of the self that are inherited from the Enlightenment conceive of persons as beings with an essential core whose authentic qualities can be found underneath a contingent surface. If you dig deeply enough into this subjectivity and peel away its contingent aspects, you will find who that person *really* "is." Autonomy and rationality are the hallmarks of such a notion of the person. As a unified, coherent and rational agent, the person is the author or originator of the meaning of subjective experience. As free, the subject can represent its internal world to others through the use of language. The subject, thus, first exists in the world and then uses language as a tool to communicate one's inner world with others.

Traditionally, language is understood to be a transparent representation of reality, a tool or instrument that mirrors reality and that people use without their selves being affected by it. Such a position about language involves a number of assumptions. First and foremost, that the main function of language is representational, i.e., that language functions as a picture of reality and can be studied for the truth or accuracy of its portrayal of a mind independent of reality. The second and related assumption involves a sharp distinction between the world, language and people. These are distinct entities with language mediating between the world and people. The relationship between the external world and language is considered *passive*. Language adds nothing to the world and is merely a medium through which ideas about the world are conveyed from one mind to the next. According to this position, "language . . . is the neutral servant of the people."[10] Third, there is an assumption that because language is an unmediated tool that people use language to communicate what the speaker *intends* to communicate. In his discussion of the role played by language as representation in the debates around the value of cross-cultural dialogue in education, Charles Bingham explains,

> In this take on dialogue, language between communicants is conceptualized as a way to reveal who one is, to reveal how one thinks and experiences the world.[11]

Language as representation presumes that words are transparent instruments by which people transmit the ideas that they *want* to communicate to others. We always understand ourselves because we are the source of meaning of our own speech.[12]

Some scholars (as already intimated in the previous chapter) have contested this model of the language. In contrast to accounts of language as representation and notions of autonomous, rational selves, these scholars have been concerned with exposing how language or utterances are related to larger social patterns of power and the ways in which language may do things *through us* without our knowledge or consent. In this scholarship, attention is drawn to the linguistic space within which statements are uttered in order to uncover what our utterances do. According to these scholars, focusing on the intentions of the speaker can *actually hide* how power works through discourse. In a complete reversal of traditional and common sense accounts of language, words are not merely labels we use in our attempts to describe our internal states such as thoughts and feelings. Language does things. What exactly does language do?

First, language *constitutes our reality* by providing the conceptual framework from which meaning is given. Language, according to this view, structures how we understand ourselves, others and the social world around us. Ferdinand de Saussure,[13] the Swiss linguist who played an important role in modern conceptions of language use, maintained words are signs in a system that structures the possible ways in which we understand ourselves, others and the world around us. Language is a system of signs consisting of signifiers (words, the *spoken sound*) and what they signify (concepts or *the idea* of a thing in the mind of the language user). The link between signifier and signified, Saussure explains, is arbitrary. By this Saussure means not just that the words we use to describe things are a product of conventions but also that the *concepts themselves* are a product of arbitrary divisions and ways to categorize experience. Drawing attention to the relationship between signs allows us to highlight how language organizes our experiences. How we give meaning to our experiences is made possible (and is limited) by the concepts we have available to us.

Challenging the representational account of language as signs related to objects in some pre-linguistic space, Saussure argued that signs only have meaning in relationship to other signs whose entire system is part of a particular worldview. The word "dog," for instance, only has meaning as it can be distinguished from other signs like "cat" or "wall." The concepts that are available to us (or not available to us) provide the horizons that give meaning to our interpretation of our experiences. Language, thus, is not a tool or a medium but a system of signs that constitute meaning and constrain what is intelligible.

This is a complete reversal of traditional and common sense accounts of language. On the traditional account, words are the tools used to express thoughts, ideas, feelings and experiences that predate and exist independently of the words we use to describe them. Words, according to the traditional view, are merely labels we employ in our attempts to describe our internal states. Words are presumed to be a carrier of meaning, a transparent medium of inner states and passive in the sense of adding nothing to meaning itself. Language is understood as a device to convey internal states to other people; words are merely vessels for the containment of ideas. In this traditional understanding of language, however, power is understood to be entirely outside of language. Yet, as Sally Haslanger claims, "how we represent the world is both a constitutive part of that enactment and *keeps it going*."[14] It is mistaken to understand language as passive and distinct from power because language does things, and, more specifically, language plays a role in the production and reproduction of power systems.

Language is also performative. An early analysis of language as performative can be found in J. L. Austin's *How To Do Things With Words*.[15] Austin distinguished between those utterances that merely describe the world (constatives) and that do something (performatives). The minister's recitation, "I now pronounce you man and wife," in a marriage ceremony does not merely describe the world but actually does something at the time of its utterance. Austin recognizes that there are conditions that must be considered in order for this linguistic performance to successfully do what it says. For example, the minister must be a recognized authority who is licensed to marry the couple and the couple must not already be married to someone else and (at least in most states in the United States) must not be of the same sex. When those conditions are filled, however, Austin maintained that it is the intention of the minister that makes the performative utterance do what it says. In this, Austin's insight, however, was limited. He remained steeped in the analytic tradition that presumes the force of the speech act is to be found in the intentions of the sovereign subject.

As noted in the previous chapter, Jacques Derrida critiques Austin exactly on this point insisting that the force of performative utterances is not derived from the speaker's intentions but instead from the citationality of conventions that pre-exist the speaker who utters them. All language, according to Derrida, depends of the repetition of linguistic signs and conventions. In *On Grammatology*, Derrida writes, "there is nothing outside of the text."[16] By this Derrida does not mean to deny the existence of a non-discursive reality but rather to emphasize that our engagement with the world is contingent on the meanings that discourses make possible.

For Derrida, discourse is not a founding act by an originating subject but rather a derivative citation. Derrida does not deny that intentions exist but rather his point is that intentions are not the foundations of *the force of utterances*. Judith Butler puts this succinctly when she argues that even as one uses discourse to affect certain intentional ends, one is also used by the history of that discourse because discourse forecloses the field of what can be intended or said. As Butler puts it,

> So the difference we find in Derrida, over and against (J. L.) Austin, is that Derrida asks us how we are to locate intention within the field of discourse, which is not the same as doing away with it altogether.[17]

As one moves away from language as representation, therefore, the role of intention shifts as well. Our intentions too are discursively formed. This is not to imply that we do not mean what we say or that we do not have intentions when we speak but rather that discourse might have effects that are not consonant with our intentions. Moreover, the concern is to expose how utterances are related to a larger social pattern that may do things *through us* without our knowledge or consent.

In contrast to accounts of language as representation that look to intention as the determinant of the meaning of our utterances, Derrida and Butler draw our attention to the linguistic space within which a statement is uttered in order to bring to light what our utterances do. What Austin, therefore, fails to adequately consider is the *system* of discourse within which the speech act takes place. More specifically, exclusively focusing on the intentions of the speaker obscures the system within which the utterance functions and mystifies the ways in which power works through discourse.

Another way of getting at this same point is to follow Linda Martin Alcoff's[18] use of Foucault's notion of "rituals of speaking" in her analysis of the problem of speaking for others. Feminists have been acutely aware that speaking for others is unethical and imperialistic. Yet there are times when it seems appropriate and even morally responsible to speak for others. Alcoff asks whether speaking for others is ever a legitimate practice and if so, when?

Specifically, is it ever legitimate for someone who is systemically privileged to speak for the marginalized? One of the responses to the problem of speaking for others that has become popular in feminist circles has been to speak only for oneself. Joyce Trebilcot articulates such a position in an oft-cited paper, "Dyke Methods."[19]

Alcoff explains that "rituals of speaking" are *constitutive of meaning*. By this Alcoff wants to draw our attention to the "discursive practices of speaking or writing that involve not only the text or utterance but their position within a social space including the persons involved in, acting upon, and/or affected by the words."[20] In other words, rituals of speaking imply that both the social location of the speaker, *as well as* the discursive context, bear on the meaning and truth of what is being said. Discursive context, Alcoff clarifies, refers to "the connections and relations of involvement between the utterance/text and other utterances and texts as well as the material practices in the relevant environment . . . ."[21] Rituals of speaking make it clear that one can never transcend one's social location because " . . . there is no neutral place to stand free and clear in which one's words do not prescriptively affect or mediate the experience of others."[22] Moreover, every action one takes is part of an "intricate, delicate web" and "pulls on, breaks off, or maintains the tension in many strands of a web in which others find themselves moving also."[23]

Of particular significance is the way that Alcoff illuminates the limitations of the retreat position as advocated by Trebilcot and taken up by others. Alcoff highlights how language *as well as absence of language* must always be understood as embedded in social space that is not devoid of historicity. Even if one retreats to the position where one only speaks for oneself, one's speech is still not neutral and still reinforces the continuance of dominant discourses by omission. Even when one speaks only for oneself, one still constitutes a possible way of being in the world whether or not one intends to do so. In fact, as Alcoff concludes, speaking for oneself may serve as a way of avoiding responsibility, of avoiding criticism, of avoiding being wrong and at the same time reinscribing the status quo. "If I speak only for myself it may appear that I am immune from criticism because I am not making any claims that describe others or prescribe action for them."[24] Alcoff highlights that even silence or absence of speech is not unaffected by the discursive context in which such retreats are performed.

Derrida and Alcoff hint at another aspect of language as discourse that focuses on how discourse constitutes the subject and is informed by the work of Michel Foucault. Not only is discourse the prism through which reality is given meaning but also power works through discourse to constitute subjects. Discourses, thus, are not only the framework from which meaning is made. Discourses also serve the purposes of power. Power works through the subject via discursive practices. Discourse, as Foucault puts it, involves "practices that systematically form the objects of which they speak."[25] Although different scholars use the term discourse in a variety of ways, for our purposes, discourse is broadly construed as including language, texts, social practices, and the effects of these.

Discourse actively functions to construct and maintain particular versions of social reality and also constitutes who we can understand ourselves to be. One way to highlight this is to note that there are many ways to describe things and events and one description often competes with a variety of alternatives. Those who reject language as representation are interested in interrogating *why one version can be uttered but another is unthinkable*. Why this version or this utterance? What does it do? What does it accomplish and in whose interests? What does it tell us about the "wider discursive economy or the politics of representation which influence what is available to be said and what can be heard?"[26]

In *The Heart of Whiteness: Confronting Race, Racism and White Privilege*,[27] Robert Jensen provides an excellent illustration of how particular stories we tell about ourselves constitute particular understandings of who we are and obscure rather than reveal our complicity in systems of social injustice. In one biographical story, Jensen describes his life without any reference to his whiteness or his white privilege. It is the "color ignored" story.

> I was born in a small city in North Dakota, to parents in the lower middle-class who eventually scratched their way to a comfortable middle-class life through hard work. I never went hungry and always had a roof over my head, but I was expected to work, and I did. From the time I started shoveling snow as a kid, to part-time and summer jobs, through my professional career, I worked hard. From the time I was old enough to hold a steady job, I have held one. I was a conscientious student who studied hard and took school seriously. I went to college and did fairly well, taking a year off in the middle to work full-time. After graduation I worked as a journalist, in non-glamorous jobs for modest wages, working hard to learn a craft. I went on to get a master's degree and returned to work before eventually pursuing a doctorate so I could teach at the university level. I got a job at a major university and worked hard to get tenure. I'm still there today, still working hard.[28]

In a second story of the same life, Jensen highlights how whiteness and white privilege has influenced it. The city Jensen grew up in was almost entirely white and racist towards the indigenous people who originally lived on that land. He was educated in a school system that prepared him for a white world, a school system that celebrated the history of people who looked like him, and one in which his efforts were encouraged and in which he was made to feel at home. Always employed by other white people, Jensen recalls how one of his first jobs was in the warehouse of a white man with whom his father did business. He graduated a predominantly white university and continued to notice that in almost all the jobs he was hired for, it was a white person that hired him. Almost all his bosses were white. And so on . . .

While both stories are true, the first story recites and repeats the discourse of meritocracy and constitutes him as innocent. The second story that is told through an awareness of whiteness and white privilege illuminates rather than hides the ways in which merit alone is not a determinant of success in the United States today.

Integral to the understanding of how discourse works is the Foucaultian notion of power. Foucault challenged the customary conception of power as something someone "has" or as a possession that can be seized from someone else. Foucault argued that power is not only repressive, something that is applied to a pre-linguistic being, but is also productive of the beings that we are. Power, according to Foucault, is not only about limiting freedom or a negative infringement on someone's rights. Rather power enables the subject as it constrains the subject. In addition, power is not static but constantly circulates through society and through the subjects it constitutes. Power, Foucault argues, "is everywhere, not because it embraces everything but because it comes from everywhere."[29] In *The History of Sexuality: An Introduction,* Foucault explicates how "discourse transmits and produces power."[30] Such a notion of power forces us to rethink the role of discourse and its relationship to power because power, according to Foucault, is not necessarily manifest but rather is exercised through its invisibility.

Foucault contends that modern forms of governmentality moved *from* a grounding in sovereign power which is characteristically blatantly overt and visible *to* disciplinary forms of power that are exercised invisibly through normalization and technologies of self. As Foucault puts it,

> Traditionally, power was what was seen, what was shown and what was manifested. . . . Disciplinary power, on the other hand, is exercised through its invisibility; at the same time it imposes on those whom it subjects a principle of compulsory visibility.[31]

Foucault underscores that discourses transmit power because discourses limit who people can be and what can be thought. Power works through us and in invisible ways because discourses work through normalization to mask power relations operating in society. Foucault again,

> Power is tolerable only on condition that it masks a substantial part of itself. Its success is proportional to its ability to hide its own mechanisms.[32]

It is because of this invisibility, that Foucault maintains that everything is dangerous.

> My point is not that everything is bad, but that everything is dangerous, which is not exactly the same as bad. If everything is dangerous, then we always have something to do. So my position leads not to apathy but to a hyper- and pessimistic activism.[33]

This notion of discourse implies that the statements we make are not issued from an originating opinion, some place inside the person immune from power. Instead, power works through the person. There is no inner world independent of discourse or power from which opinions or beliefs spring. Our statements are always manifestations of discourses that have their origins in the discursive space and its historicity that people inhabit.

In a provocative and fascinating critique of language as representation, Foucault contends that assuming that people have "real" identities somewhere to be found internally is just a story told about the self. It is itself a discourse. For Foucault, the model of language of representation is "only another discourse already in operation."[34] Subjects do not pre-exist language because it is language that brings the person into being in the first place. Our existence *as beings that are intelligible,* that have meaning, is dependent on discourse. Charles Bingham explains this point succinctly.

> Representation is not only another way of thinking about language. It is a way of thinking about language that hides the fact that language works in other, less innocuous, discursive ways. Existing linguistic practices must be analyzed according the power invested in them by various forms of power. Language is itself is a site of power. Dialogue is not as innocent as a representational understanding indicates.[35]

Bingham argues that speech, even when it comes from the heart, in cross-cultural dialogue is not always beneficial to all. Speaking from the heart provides an innocent patina but such "conversational innocence may be an ill-founded feeling."[36]

Acknowledging how discourse exceeds intention can lead to a heightened vigilance and reflection about the "things going on other than representation when one speaks and listens."[37] Bingham demonstrates such vigilance about his own speech.

> While I, as a white man, ask simple questions while listening to, and trying to understand, an African American student's point of view, the *effect* of my questioning and listening may be on another plane altogether than representation. It is very possible that the social act of dialogue is itself a stage for racist hierar-

chies to be played out, for example. If the *effect* of speech is oppression, then a genealogical skepticism toward dialogue causes me to wonder if representation really took place at all. Let us say that my questioning and listening enacted racist codes that I do not condone, but that were in the air nonetheless. . . . At such a point, it is not so useful to make up a convoluted description of the limits of representational dialogue. It is more useful to follow Foucault's linguistic pragmatism and admit that what just happened was a discursive act. And that act was oppressive.[38]

Bingham advocates the development of skepticism that eschews confidence about language as representation and a willingness to be open to non-representational models of language.

Such critical skepticism is integral to education, according to Kevin McDonough.[39] McDonough notes that Foucault's main concern has always been to critically interrogate what is taken as ordinary. Such an inquiry, McDonough explains, requires us to interrogate how we have come to accept certain things as authoritative, how we have come to consent to them, to regard them as legitimate, and therefore to value them. McDonough reads Foucault's hyper and pessimistic activism as referring to a specific type of critique that those who presume language as representation and the sovereign subject fail to take into account and that has important educational implications.

If we take Foucault seriously, then, the purpose of education gets turned on its head. Instead of making the uncertain certain, the unfamiliar familiar, McDonough reads the implication of Foucault's work for education as "primarily a matter of making the certain uncertain, the familiar unfamiliar, the given contingent."[40] We will return to the significance of this particular type of critical reflection for white moral responsibility in the last chapter.

Constructivism, deconstruction and language as discourse are ideas that have incited passionate and interesting debates about relativism and also around the possibility of agency, debates that should not be neglected but neither have they been resolved. These debates are too expansive and complicated to review here and, besides, that is not the central point of this chapter.[41] Without seriously engaging with challenges to language as representation, the claims about white denials of complicity will not make any sense. In fact, traditional accounts of language as representation, because they do not expose denials of complicity for consideration (they are merely opinions), may end up supporting and encouraging such denials.

I have been arguing that it is important to expose students to the problem of language as representation and to have them engage with the idea that discourse is a site of power. Only then can it make any sense that "distancing strategies" are not merely individual opinions but part of a pattern of beliefs and practices that benefit certain groups of people and are socially sanctioned.

Couldn't any disagreement be labeled a "distancing strategy" and thus dismissed? In the next half of this chapter, we will explore a common concern that white students express about not being able to disagree with the content material of courses that teach with commitments to social justice.

DISAGREEMENT, DENIALS, AND DISTANCING STRATEGIES

After presenting some of my work on white complicity to a philosophy of education reading group of which I am a member, a colleague queried whether my arguments leave open the possibility of disagreement. She was concerned that the white complicity claim was shielded from critique because if anyone disagreed with the claim they could be just labeled "denying their complicity." This astute question raises the issue of the conditions of disagreement and deserves particular attention given that students in courses that make systemic injustice explicit often complain in teacher evaluations that they have not been allowed to disagree in the course. Students often maintain that such courses indoctrinate a particular view about racism that they are not willing to accept.

In November of 2007, for instance, the University of Delaware was charged with indoctrination and bias because in the mandatory resident life program the claim that "all whites are racist" was addressed. According to the *Foundation for Individual Rights in Education* (FIRE), the Office of Residence Life and Diversity Education Training included in its documents the following definition of a racist.

> A RACIST: A racist is one who is both privileged and socialized on the basis of race by a white supremacist (racist) system. The term applies to all white people (i.e., people of European descent) living in the United States, regardless of class, gender, religion, culture or sexuality. By this definition, people of color cannot be racists, because as people within the U.S. system, they do not have the power to back up their prejudices, hostilities, or acts of discrimination . . . [42]

In addition, FIRE complained that the program teaches that "reverse racism" is "a term created and used by white people to deny their white privilege" and that there is no such thing as a white non-racist because the term was

> created by whites to deny responsibility for systemic racism, to maintain an aura of innocence in the face of racial oppression, and to shift the responsibility for that oppression from whites to people of color (called "blaming the victim").[43]

FIRE objected to what they interpreted as a demand *without possibility of disagreement* for University of Delaware students "to adopt highly specific university-approved views on issues ranging from politics to race, sexuality, sociology, moral philosophy and environmentalism."[44]

Similarly, in her discussion of some of her student evaluations, Nado Aveling[45] describes how some of her white students protested that her class is "Not a safe, comfortable environment to explore and discuss ideas for fear of censorship." Others maintain that "I felt I was forced to take on her views—otherwise I would not get anywhere with my marks." One student insisted that a lot of students "didn't say what they really thought" and that the course was especially hostile towards white males.[46] Examining a controversy around course guidelines that asked students to take systemic injustice seriously helps to shift the focus of concern from agreement/disagreement to the issue of what it means to engage in learning about one's complicity in social injustice.

LYNN WEBER'S COURSE GUIDELINES: FORECLOSING DISAGREEMENT?

While it is not uncommon to find discussion guidelines on course syllabi and in first class introductions on university campuses throughout North America, in 2002 the rules for classroom discourse that Lynn Weber has used for over 18 years in teaching courses in women's studies at University of South Carolina at Columbia sparked a ferocious controversy involving charges of "bias" and "indoctrination." In these guidelines Weber asked students *for this class* "to acknowledge that racism, classism, sexism, heterosexism, and other institutionalized forms of oppression exist" and "to agree to combat actively the myths and stereotypes about our own groups and other groups so that we can break down the walls that prohibit group cooperation and group gain."[47]

One of the students in Weber's class objected to "being told to think that way."[48] She argued that the guidelines are inappropriate because they could be viewed as requiring her to agree with the professor's beliefs as they were expressed in the guidelines. Somehow the guidelines were sent to FIRE. As in the more recent case against the University of Delaware mentioned above, this time FIRE sent a letter to Weber's university president and publicly denounced the guidelines as "thought control" and "a threat to freedom of both speech and conscience" because it "require(d) students to hold certain arguments as unquestionable truth in order to participate in class without penalty." Charles Duncan, chairman of the university's College Republicans chapter, added his support to the letter by declaring that the guidelines represented a "closed mind to conservative opinions" and to those who have beliefs that conflict with the professor. Duncan said he personally would take issue with guidelines that asked students to acknowledge heterosexism because "My personal opinion is that homosexuality is wrong."[49]

To many, these guidelines epitomized a "liberal bias" pervasive on university campuses and exemplified the imposition of a particular ideology on students and intimidated and silenced students who may disagree with this political orthodoxy. Weber (and others who defend similar guidelines) maintained that the guidelines were necessary to encourage a safe classroom environment where not only full and open but also sensitive and respectful dialogue can occur. In addition, the guidelines, according to Weber, were required for discussion that has a high level of participation and where students could be exposed to multiple realities in respectful and enlightening ways. The guidelines, then, were understood by Weber as necessary for creating a classroom where race, class, gender, and other power dynamics do not inhibit learning. To the objection that her guidelines tell students what to believe, Weber responded that her guidelines require only that students maintain an open mind. According to Weber, "It's not about agreeing . . . (but about) promoting respect while recognizing difference."[50]

Whether Weber's guidelines are necessary for social justice education will not be the main issue here. Nor will I discuss the pedagogical efficacy of Weber's exercise. I am also not necessarily endorsing this particular method. Instead, I want to try to tease out what Weber means when she claims that the guidelines *are not about agreeing but rather respect*. At this juncture, it might seem of philosophical interest to jump into the extensive debate around freedom of speech that some philosophers of education have so competently addressed[51] and to defend (or at least explain) Weber's guidelines on the basis of this scholarship. Prematurely framing the issue as one that involves questions of freedom of speech, however, risks underemphasizing the interesting and unique conditions regarding learning and teaching that Weber's guidelines are a response to and ignores the type of engagement that Weber insists is a prerequisite of learning about our roles in maintaining systems of oppression.

I use the incident about Weber's guidelines to underscore the complexities of student engagement and disengagement that are unique to courses that teach with commitments to social justice. I want to understand why it is so common to hear social justice educators inform their students that what they are concerned with is their students' engagement with the issues rather than their agreement[52] and what they might mean when they say this. In order to do this, it will also be important to examine the type of resistance to learning/knowing so rampant in such courses. Shoshana Felman,[53] the eminent psychologist, explains that resistance to learning/knowing is a refusal to know that involves "not so much (a) lack of knowledge . . . (or) . . . simple lack of information but the incapacity—or refusal—to acknowledge one's own implication in the information."[54]

Resistance to learning/knowledge is very prevalent in courses that address systemic oppression and privilege. Unlike courses that do not make race, gender, class and sexuality explicit, courses that address systemic oppression have to consider that the classroom dynamics *are* an essential part of the course content. Highlighting the unique challenges that might be overlooked by those who do not have such classroom experiences requires emphasis in order to better understand the distinction between disagreement and resistance to learning. I will argue that resistance to learning/knowing in such courses is not to be equated with mere disagreement. While one can engage with course material and disagree, what often takes place in courses that teach about systemic injustice involves a premature disengagement and refusal to engage. I will discuss the unique challenges of engagement that social justice educators face and then, employing Kelly Oliver's[55] notion of "witnessing," I flesh out the type of engagement that I believe Weber's guidelines attempt to encourage. I maintain that Weber's guidelines can only be understood within the context and complexities of this unique type of student engagement and disengagement.

THE UNIQUE CHALLENGES OF TEACHING
WITH COMMITMENTS TO SOCIAL JUSTICE

In the last two decades, scholarship on race and racism in education has recognized that "the failure of equity education initiatives is attributable to a misidentification of change object."[56] The need to focus not only on the victims of systemic injustice but also to "turn the gaze inward"[57] on those who perpetuate and sustain such systems has, in many circles in higher education, become routine. Many universities now include in their curriculum courses whose primary objective is to understand, analyze and challenge oppressive social systems, courses that aim to critically examine dominant norms (such as, for example, whiteness and heteronormativity) on the basis of which "difference" is constructed. In schools of education, where a predominantly white student body is expected to go out into schools to teach children from diverse backgrounds and social positionalities, courses that encourage students to critically examine systemic privilege and oppression have often become a fundamental part of the curriculum. These courses aim not only to empower marginalized students but also to stimulate systemically privileged students to reflect on their status as privileged and how such privilege impacts what they do in the classroom.

Concomitantly, and as has already been noted, another body of scholarship has developed around students' resistance to courses that unleash "unpopular ideas."[58] The unique challenges that educators face in classrooms where systemically privileged[59] students are encouraged to engage with learning about systemic oppression have become the focus of academic study. Because they do not experience systemic oppression and because the frameworks through which they interpret their experience support their beliefs, systemically privileged students often enter such courses believing that systemic oppression is a relic of the past, or if it does exist they are not responsible for it. Just as they deny systemic oppression, they also disagree and sometimes refuse to consider that they are systemically privileged. Often such students insist that any advantage they enjoy is merited or "normal" and "natural." In terms of race, for instance, since whiteness is traditionally the unmarked category that confers privilege on those who are ascribed whiteness, white students often resist interrogating what it means to be white.

Moreover, such students do not perceive themselves as resisting but rather often maintain that they are just expressing their disagreement with the political nature of the course. University courses should be ideologically neutral, they maintain, not biased and imposing of particular viewpoints. As Roberta Ahlquist[60] notes (but does not endorse), resistance can be perceived as "a healthy response to controversial material, as critical questioning, and as a lack of willingness by students to conform blindly to the expectations of others."[61] To teach these students about systemic oppression and privilege, then, is a distinctively demanding task.

It is important to emphasize that not all systemically privileged students tenaciously resist. Some might resist at first but then welcome engagement and become willing to explore the sources of systemic oppression even when this means they must consider their own accountability and complicity. Yet others are so certain that their viewpoint is correct and are so convinced of their own moral innocence that they are reluctant to even consider a critical exploration of their view. For social justice educators, the challenge is how to get *all* students to engage in a context in which *a concern for the comfort and safety to learn of systemically privileged students often comes at the expense of the comfort and safety to learn of those systemically marginalized.* If the aim of social justice pedagogy is to encourage students to examine and bring to awareness the power dynamics supporting systems of oppression and privilege, then social justice pedagogy itself must strive to avoid reproducing such systems of oppression and privilege in the classroom, at least as much as possible.

Unlike courses that do not explicitly deal with issues of systemic oppression, for social justice educators, dealing with classroom dynamics *is* part of the course content.[62] Elizabeth Higginbotham[63] explains,

> . . . Teaching to a diverse student population requires attention to classroom interactions. Our classrooms are part of the larger social world, thus structural inequalities in the larger society are reproduced in the classroom in terms of power and privilege.[64]

Following Weber, Higginbotham notes how in the classroom, "members of privileged groups are more likely to talk, have their ideas validated, and be perceived as making significant contributions to group tasks."[65]

While it is important to help all students to recognize the racial effects of practices and discourse, often the needs of systemically privileged students are tended to without consideration of the needs of marginalized students who have the right to be able to be educated in a safe environment free from overt and covert forms of discrimination. Marginalized students must often listen to their privileged peers who either, in the best case, are in the process of learning or, in the worse, become further entrenched in their own privilege. The point is that the education of white students becomes the educator's focal point. An incident that Karen Elias, a white educator who teaches with commitments to social justice, recalls in her writing seminar illustrates this pedagogical dilemma. She notes how

> . . . some white students began vigorously denying the existence of racial profiling. I tried using these comments as springboards for further analysis, but I noticed that a young Afro-Caribbean woman was obviously disturbed. She met with me in private to say that she was having a hard time sitting through the class. "I hear enough of this in my daily life," she said. "I shouldn't have to put up with it here . . . " . . . One of my biggest fears is that despite my best intentions, the racist dynamics of the larger society will get replicated in the classroom. Her words had a profound impact on me.[66]

Often white students not only refuse to acknowledge their privilege, *their privilege is reflected in the very questioning of the social facts that are at odds with their experiences.*[67] They have what Peggy McIntosh refers to as "permission to escape"[68] and what Alice McIntyre calls "privileged choice."[69] The mere fact that they can question the existence of systemic oppression is a function of their privilege to choose to ignore discussions of systemic oppression or not.

Systemically marginalized students may be offended, hurt and feel unsafe (and feel that their humanity is denied) in classrooms where such systemically privileged students are allowed to recenter their privilege. In my own class, after showing students statistics about the gender/race wage gap, one white male student dismissed the data with the claim that this has not been *his* experience and that where he works women are paid more than him. This student forcefully insisted that even if the gap were true, women should not complain because they are still better off than women in Third World countries. Some white women in the class supported his claims and it is not clear if they did so to maintain some type of "fictive kinship." Chizhik[70] notes that some of their white preservice teachers established a classroom atmosphere in which "students felt pressure to share in their opposition to the course or keep silent." Consequently, "(t)he silence of some fostered the misconception that many people had similar dissenting views. . . ."[71]

In the aforementioned case, it is the white student's experience that counts and his arguments seem to him to make perfect sense because, as Higginbotham explains, "his sense of entitlement gives him the liberty to challenge the validity of those data, even when they are supported by government statistics."[72] Allowing him to express his disagreement and spending time trying to challenge his beliefs often comes at a cost to marginalized students whose experiences are (even if indirectly) dismissed by his claims, even when the marginalized student is willing to challenge such discourse.

For educators who are committed to social justice managing a diverse classroom discussion involves balancing the needs and perspectives of all students and not just centering attention on the pedagogical needs of white students. One of the most intractable challenges for those who educate with commitments to social justice is getting systemically privileged students to engage while at the same time avoiding (or at least minimizing) recentering their privilege. Weber's guidelines can only be understood within this pedagogical challenge. Educators with commitments to social justice must find ways to " . . . reach white students to teach them about race—especially accountability and white privilege—without simply recentering them (and whiteness) to the exclusion and detriment of students of color."[73]

As many of us who teach such courses know, this is not easy. The class is traditionally imbalanced to benefit systemically privileged students as their issues and their concerns are usually the center of the educator's interest. When balance is established in the classroom by seriously considering the needs of systemically marginalized students, the group that has usually been routinely centered will often complain of "imbalance" and even challenge the professor's authority to change the classroom status quo. (Indeed, this challenge to authority is often greater when the professor is a person of color who is assumed to have an "agenda."[74])

RESISTANCE NOT DISAGREEMENT

Systemically privileged students' resistance to learning/knowing is more than merely one's individual personal disagreement with the course content. Rather, it is an exhibition of a culturally sponsored defensiveness and refusal to engage that is not only offensive to the systemically marginalized but that also reproduces systems of oppression and privilege in the classroom. Such resistance can take many forms but it is most insidious when it is manifest in a refusal to explore or attribute credibility to the existence of systemic oppression.[75] Denials of systemic injustice are fueled by culturally supported moral sensibilities. For instance, in terms of race, students might argue that they do not "see color" and consider this morally virtuous. As Nado Aveling contends, "These students firmly refused to 'see' colour as a means of establishing their *non-racist credentials* and became defensive when their assumptions were challenged."[76] To consider such challenges would implicate their moral innocence.

Yet if students believe they are morally justified in refusing to see race, they not only will reject the acknowledgement of racial patterns of social injustice, they also will not use racial labels to describe themselves. As a result, the unearned privilege that they are afforded because of their racial positionality need not be explored. Such "moral sensibilities" are often manifest in the classroom when privileged students describe marginalized students as "just too sensitive" or that "they complain too much" or they are "playing the race card," i.e., we ought all just ignore race. Resistance to learning is also ironically encouraged by conceptions of moral responsibility and moral agency that forefront individual intention, as is implicit in one of the student evaluations Alhquist reports receiving.

> This course was an assault of horrors . . . every class some new injustice was presented . . . students were not sure what these had to do with them. (The teacher) went overboard in her concerns. Things aren't all that bad. And even if they were, one person couldn't do that much to change them. Some of them just didn't want to deal with this order of things . . . *(they shouldn't be blamed because) they were nice people and not participating in these injustices.*[77]

In Chapter 6 we will examine the need to rearticulate our conceptions of moral responsibility and moral agency not only to expose complicity but also to guide the systemically privileged in their attempts to challenge social injustice. For now, the point is to consider the discursive practices available to systemically privileged students and what they protect. Such discursive practices encourage a refusal to engage with any material that challenges the student's worldview and such practices also support a premature dismissal of anything such material can teach.

In Hytten and Warren's study, for instance, some systemically privileged students asserted their ethnic identity to demonstrate that they are victims, too. While bringing up one's ethnic identity is important to highlight how identity is multiple and complex, in some cases highlighting connections to ethnic identity functions to recenter the attention on oneself and to divert attention from considering one's own accountability in racial injustice. Another tactic is to insist that people of color are racist, too, or to complain about reverse discrimination, again, to demonstrate that white people are the real victims. In all these cases, although it may appear the student is just stating an opinion, the discourse also works to redirect the conversation away from having to consider how systemically privileged students might be complicit in systemic injustice. It is important to note how such students often do not realize how dismissive their discourse is of the experiences of marginalized students and so they are totally bewildered when marginalized students retreat in frustration.[78]

Kim Case and Annette Hemmings[79] describe a white student in their class who expressed the belief that Black people just have to take more personal responsibility for their own progress in the face of racism. This student told the class of how her Black friend dropped out of college because he felt that in many ways the environment was cold and hostile. It was not that she actually denied that he was having experiences that never happened to her. However, she felt the best response was "Just ignore those people. Just go back and deal with it." While her intentions are undeniably good, what her discourse *does* is minimize and dismiss the systematic dimension of her friend's experiences and places the burden on her friend rather than on the need for real institutional change. In the end, her good intentions contribute to the perpetuation of the status quo. To explain this to her would require that she consider her own complicity in systemic oppression when she may not as yet have the tools to do so.

I understand the objective of Weber's guidelines, controversial as they may be, is to address such classroom complexities. They attempt to balance the playing field in the classroom as much as possible by strongly conveying the message that certain types of engagement will be required for learning to occur in her class.

WHAT TYPE OF ENGAGEMENT AND DOES IT DEMAND AGREEMENT?

To be engaged is to be willing to participate, to take part in and to give attention to something. Yet what type of student engagement is a prerequisite for learning in courses that focus on systemic oppression and privilege? To reply that students must be open-minded and willing to critically examine their taken-for-granted cultural beliefs seems trite. I find Marilyn Frye's[80] suggestion more helpful. Frye contends that in our relations with the Other we must take care to avoid relating as an "arrogant perceiver." Arrogant perception involves relating in a way in which everything one hears is viewed with reference to oneself and one's interests.

In her 1998 Philosophy of Education Society Presidential Address, Ann Diller offers another valuable suggestion (that I use in the introduction to my courses) when she argues that in order to be a philosopher of one's own education, one must be willing to be torpified. The capacity to be torpified involves an

> . . . ability to be awed, to be surprised, to be astonished, to be moved in a deeply moral or ethical, or aesthetical, or epistemological or ontological way. It takes considerable courage, self-knowledge, a brave heart, and honest openness to face one's own ignorance and to stay present in the concomitant experience of discomfort.[81]

I have found that Kelly Oliver's distinction between eyewitness testimony and bearing witness extends Diller's recommendations and is extremely effective to help flesh out the type of engagement required in courses that make systemic injustice visible. I believe something along the lines of this type of engagement is implicit in Weber's discussion guidelines. Although demanding such engagement, of course, does not ensure students will so engage, discussing what such engagement requires is, I submit, an important component of social justice pedagogy.

Oliver critiques the politics of recognition so popular in discourses around multiculturalism and multicultural education on the grounds that such "recognition" perpetuates rather than challenges systemic oppression. Recognition as a condition of positive identity formation assumes that there is one invested with power to grant such recognition and, thus, keeps relationships of dominance and subordination in place. Instead of recognition, Oliver advances the metaphor of witnessing, and more specifically "bearing witness," as a more fruitful method of social relation. Witnessing is more than just an issue of eyewitness reporting but also suggests an almost religious sense of "bearing witness" to that which cannot be seen, what is considered impossible to think of, to that which is "beyond recognition."[82] What victims of oppression seek is not only visibility and recognition from someone who has the power to recognize. Rather, according to Oliver, what they seek is witnessing to the horrors of what is beyond recognition.[83]

In order to explicate how subjects can avoid assimilating difference into what is familiar to them and, instead, to encourage the type of listening that can hear what is beyond one's recognition, Oliver distinguishes between eyewitnessing and bearing witness to what cannot be seen. She makes this distinction concrete through a provocative story based on the work of Dori Laub, a psychoanalyst who does research on Holocaust survivors. Laub reports a debate between historians and psychoanalysts involving a woman who claims to be an eyewitness to the Auschwitz uprising. The woman describes the fires set by the Jewish prisoners noting in her description that four chimneys were destroyed. Laub observes how this woman's testimony was dismissed and discredited by the historians because while the woman reported that four chimneys were set ablaze, historical evidence indicates that there was only one chimney destroyed. In contrast, the psychoanalysts responded differently to the woman, understanding that she was not reporting on historical facts but rather about another level of truth involving something so radical and unimaginable, something beyond recognition, i.e., the occurrence of resistance at Auschwitz. Such experiences cannot be captured by the facts and figures. Oliver writes quoting Laub that "what the historians could not hear, listening for empirical facts, was the 'very secret of survival and of resistance to extermination.'"[84]

While there are many fascinating questions that can be raised, the relevance of this story for the discussion of student engagement in social justice education is illuminating. Oliver explains that while the historians were listening for confirmation of something that they already knew, the psychoanalysts were listening "to hear something new, something yet beyond comprehension."[85] It is not that Oliver implies that historical accuracy does not count. Rather, she is drawing our attention to a type of listening that does not require prior agreement and in fact is a response in which agreement or disagreement is (like in Weber's guidelines) tentatively suspended. Such an address and response, rather than recognition, according to Oliver, is the lynchpin of subjectivity because it is not the recognizer's approval but rather an acknowledgment of one's humanity that is paramount.

Michalinos Zembylas succinctly articulates this type of engagement with others when he writes, "bearing witness to the other means opening oneself to creative affective connections with the Other."[86] That the marginalized are bearing witness that requires this type of engagement has been powerfully expressed by the quote from Gayle Jones with which Hazel Carby opens her oft-quoted article, "White Woman Listen! Black Feminism and the Boundaries of Sisterhood."

> I'm leaving evidence. And you got to leave evidence too. And your children got to leave evidence . . . They burned all the documents . . . We got to burn out what they put in our minds, like you burn out a wound. Except we got to keep what we need to bear witness. That scar that's left to bear witness. We got to keep it as visible as our blood.[87]

I read Weber's discussion guidelines as laying out the necessary condition for learning in her course: the type of engagement that involves bearing witness. Her guidelines do not demand agreement with her viewpoint but rather an engagement with the course material and with the experiences of marginalized others. This might require students to sometimes tentatively suspend their beliefs about the nonexistence of systemic oppression but also leaves open the possibility that silence can be a distancing strategy, which Weber would address and not ignore. Her guidelines also convey a strong message to those who might resist knowing/learning. Resistance will not be allowed to derail the class discussions! Of course, those who refuse to engage might mistakenly perceive this as a declaration that they will not be allowed to express their disagreement but that is only precisely *because* they are resisting engagement.

Weber's guidelines also convey a powerful message to marginalized students that the learning of the systemically privileged will not be recentered at the expense of the learning and growth of the marginalized. Her guidelines I believe do not foreclose disagreement but insist that one must engage before one can disagree. Although this remains unsubstantiated at this moment, I would argue that systemically marginalized students would be more likely and willing to invest energy and time, and be more willing to engage with the systemically privileged, when the latter acknowledge their complicity and are willing to listen rather than dismiss the struggles and the experiences of the systemically marginalized.[88]

Given the unique challenges that educators with commitments to social justice face, Weber's guidelines can be understood as exemplifying not a "liberal bias" or the "imposition of a particular ideology" but rather emphasizing the necessary condition for full and open dialogue across difference that is necessary for critical reflection and learning to occur, and that is engagement. Weber's discussion guidelines are not a panacea as she herself acknowledges (and certainly not the only way of implementing what Megan Boler refers to as "affirmative action pedagogy"[89]). Yet unless we fully appreciate the conditions under which Weber's guidelines are employed and that these guidelines are "not about agreeing . . . (but about) promoting respect while recognizing difference," questions about freedom of speech cannot be equitably raised.

In the next chapter, we will turn from questions about discourse and what one knows/does not know to questions involving complicity and moral responsibility. What notion of moral responsibility can help the white person who wants to understand his/her complicity in and to challenge systemic social injustice? Which notions of responsibility obstruct such understanding? In the following chapter, I review many of the philosophical accounts of complicity and responsibility and will find them inadequate because of their strong emphasis on causality and individual choice/control. In other words, these accounts are focused too much on questions of whether or not this particular individual is guilty or to blame. Not only can these accounts not capture white complicity, they also support denials of complicity that have been the focus of this chapter.

NOTES

1. Michel Foucault, *History of Sexuality: An Introduction Volume I* (New York: Vintage Books, 1990), 101.
2. Alison Jones, "The Limits of Cross-Cultural Dialogue: Pedagogy, Desire, and Absolution in the Classroom," *Educational Theory* 49, no. 3 (1999): 299–316.
3. Ibid., 313.
4. Kathy Hytten and John Warren, "Engaging Whiteness: How Racial Power Gets Reified in Education," *Qualitative Studies in Education* 16, no. 1 (2003): 65–89.
5. Kim Case and Annette Hemmings, "Distancing: White Women Preservice Teachers and Antiracist Curriculum," *Urban Education* 40/6 (November 2005): 606–626.

6. Alice McIntyre, *Making Meaning of Whiteness: Exploring Racial Identity With White Teachers* (Albany, New York: State University of New York Press, 1997).

7. Ibid., 45.

8. "White Lies: A Top Ten List," http://www.amren.com/mtnews/archives/2007/08/white_lies_a_to.php (accessed November 25, 2009).

9. Kathy Hytten and John Warren, "Engaging Whiteness," 66.

10. Margaret Wetherell, "Themes in Discourse Research: The Case of Diana," in *Discourse Theory and Practice: A Reader,* ed. Margaret Wetherell, Stephanie Taylor, and Simeon Yates (London: Sage, 2001), 15.

11. Charles W. Bingham, "A Dangerous Benefit: Dialogue, Discourse, and Michel Foucault's Critique of Representation," *Interchange* 33, no. 4 (2002): 354.

12. Stuart Hall, "Foucault: Power, Knowledge and Discourse," in *Discourse Theory and Practice: A Reader,* 72–81, 79.

13. Ferdinand de Saussure, *Course in General Linguistics* (London: Fountana, 1974).

14. Sally Haslanger, "'But Mom, Crop-Tops *Are* Cute!': Social Knowledge, Social Structure and Ideology Critique," *Philosophical Issues* 17, no. 1 (2007): 75.

15. J. L. Austin, *How to Do Things with Words,* 2nd Edition (Oxford: Oxford University Press, 1962).

16. Jacques Derrida, *On Grammatology* (Baltimore: Johns Hopkins University Press, 1976), 158.

17. Judith Butler, "Conversation with Judith Butler IV," in *Judith Butler in Conversation: Analyzing the Texts and Talk of Everyday Life,* ed. Bronwyn Davies (New York: Routledge, 2008), 187–216.

18. Linda Martin Alcoff, "The Problem of Speaking for Others," *Cultural Critique* 20 (Winter 1991): 5–32.

19. Joyce Trebilcot, "Dyke Methods," *Hypatia* 3, no. 2 (1988): 1–13.

20. Linda Martin Alcoff, "The Problem of Speaking for Others," 12.

21. Ibid.

22. Ibid., 20.

23. Ibid., 21.

24. Ibid., 22.

25. Michel Foucault, *The Archaeology of Knowledge,* trans. Sheridan Smith (London: Travistock, first pub. 1969/1972), 49.

26. Margaret Wetherell, "Themes in Discourse Research," 17.

27. Robert Jensen, *The Heart of Whiteness: Confronting Race, Racism and White Privilege* (San Francisco: City Light Publishers, 2005), 23.

28. Ibid.

29. Michel Foucault, *The History of Sexuality,* 93.

30. Ibid., 101.

31. Michel Foucault, *Discipline and Punish: The Birth of the Prison* (New York: Pantheon Books, 1977), 187.

32. Michel Foucault, *History of Sexuality,* 86.

33. Michel Foucault, "On the Genealogy of Ethics," in *Michel Foucault: Beyond Structuralism and Hermeneutics,* ed. Hubert L. Dreyfus and Paul Rabinow, 2nd ed. (Chicago: The University of Chicago Press, 1983), 231–232. Also in *Ethics,*

Subjectivity and Truth: Essential Works of Foucault 1954–1984, Volume 1, ed. Paul Rabinow (New York: The New Press, 1994), 253–280, 256.

34. Michel Foucault, *The Archaeology Knowledge and the Discourse on Language*, 228.
35. Charles Bingham, "A Dangerous Benefit," 362.
36. Ibid., 363.
37. Ibid., 366.
38. Ibid.
39. Kevin McDonough, "Overcoming Ambivalence about Foucault's Relevance for Education," *Philosophy of Education Society 1993*, ed. Clive Beck (Urbana, Illinois: Philosophy of Education Society, 1994): 86–90.
40. Ibid., 88.
41. See Sara Mills' *Discourse* for a review of some of the debates.
42. "Excerpts from the University of Delaware Office of Residence Life Diversity Facilitation Training," http://www.thefire.org/index.php/article/8552.html (accessed November 25, 2009)
43. Ibid.
44. Ibid.
45. Nado Averling, "'Hacking at Our Very Roots': Rearticulating White Racial Identity Within the Context of Teacher Education," *Race, Ethnicity and Education* 9, no. 3 (2006): 261–274.
46. Ibid., 271.
47. Lynn Weber Cannon, "Fostering Positive Race, Class, Gender Dynamics in the Classroom," *Women's Studies Quarterly* 18 (Spring/Summer 1990): 126–134; "Classroom Discussion Guidelines: Promoting Understanding Across Race, Class, Gender and Sexuality," in *Teaching Sociological Concepts and the Sociology of Gender, Racism and Racial Inequality: Implications for Teacher Education*, 2nd Edition, ed. Marybeth Stalp and Julie Childers (Washington, DC: American Sociological Association Teaching Resource Center, 2005), 182–186.
48. Thomas Bartlett, "Guidelines for Discussion, or Thought Control?" *The Chronicle of Higher Education* 45, no. 9 (September 27, 2002): A10–A11.
49. Ibid.
50. As quoted in Thomas Bartlett.
51. Megan Boler "All Speech Is Not Free: The Ethics of 'Affirmative Action Pedagogy,'" in *Philosophy of Education 2000*, ed. Lynda Stone (Urbana, IL: Philosophy of Education Society, 2001): 321–29; Claudia Ruitenberg,, "Check Your Language! Political Correctness, Censorship, and Performativity in Education," *Philosophy of Education 2004*, ed. C. Higgins (Urbana, IL: Philosophy of Education Society, 2005): 37–45; Audrey Thompson, "Anti-Racist Pedagogy—Art or Propaganda?" in *Philosophy of Education 1995*, ed. Alven Neiman (Urbana, IL: Philosophy of Education Society, 1996): 130–141.
52. Ann Berlak, "Confrontation and Pedagogy: Cultural Secrets, Trauma, and Emotion in Antioppressive Pedagogies," in *Democratic Dialogue in Education: Troubling Speech, Disturbing Silence*, ed. Megan Boler (New York: Peter Lang, 2004), 125.
53. Shoshanna Felman, "Psychoanalysis and Education: Teaching Terminable and Interminable," *Yale French Studies* 63, 1982: 21–44.

54. Ibid., 30.
55. Kelly Oliver, *Witnessing: Beyond Recognition* (Minneapolis: University of Minnesota Press, 2001).
56. Cynthia Levine-Rasky, "The Practice of Whiteness Among Teacher Candidates," *International Studies in Sociology of Education* 10, no. 3 (2000): 263.
57. Nado Aveling, "Student Teachers' Resistance to Exploring Racism: Reflections on 'Doing' Border Pedagogy," *Asia-Pacific Journal of Teacher Education,* 30, no. 2 (2002): 119–130.
58. Deborah P. Britzman, "Decentering Discourses in Teacher Education: Or, The Unleashing of Unpopular Things," *Journal of Education* 173, no. 3 (1991): 60–80.
59. By systemically privileged students I mean to refer to students who are afforded privileges that they take for granted because they are in one way or another ascribed membership to a dominant social group.
60. Roberta Ahlquist, "Position and Imposition: Power Relations in a Multicultural Foundations Class," *Journal of Negro Education* 60, No. 2 (Spring, 1991): 158–169.
61. Ibid., 166.
62. Bonnie TuSmith, "Out on a Limb: Race and the Evaluation of Frontline Teaching," in *Race in the College Classroom,* ed. Bonnie TuSmith and Maureen T. Reddy (New Brunswick, New Jersey: Rutgers University Press, 2002): 120.
63. Elizabeth Higginbotham, "Getting All Students to Listen," *American Behavioral Scientist* 40/2 (November/December 1996): 203-211.
64. Ibid., 205.
65. Ibid.
66. Karen Elias and Judith C. Jones, "Two Voices from the Front Lines: A Conversation about Race in the Classroom," in *Race in the College Classroom,* 11.
67. Elizabeth Higginbotham, "Getting All Students to Listen," 209.
68. Peggy McIntosh, "White Privilege and Male Privilege: A Personal Account of Coming to See Correspondences through Work in Women's Studies," in *Critical White Studies: Looking Behind the Mirror,* ed. R. Delgado and J. Stefancic (Philadelphia: Temple University Press, 1997), 295–296.
69. Alice McIntyre, *Making Meaning of Whiteness* (Albany, New York: State University of New York Press, 1997), 55.
70. Estella Williams Chizhik, "Reflecting on the Challenge of Preparing Suburban Teachers for Urban Schools," *Education and Urban Society* 35, vol. 4 (2003): 443–461.
71. Ibid., 452.
72. Elizabeth Higginbotham, "Getting All Students to Listen," 209.
73. Patti Duncan, "Decentering Whiteness: Resisting Racism in the Women's Studies Classroom," in *Race in the College Classroom,* 45–56.
74. Gloria Ladson-Billings, "Silences as Weapons: Challenges of a Black Professor Teaching White Students," *Theory and Practice* 35, no. 2 (Spring, 1996): 80–85; Kendra Hamilton, "'Race in the College Classroom': Minority Faculty Often Face Student Resistance When Teaching about Race," *Black Issues in Higher Education* 19, no. 1 (March 14, 2002): 32–37.

75. Pat Griffin, "Facilitating Social Justice Education Courses," in *Teaching for Diversity and Social Justice: A Sourcebook,* ed. Maurianne Adams, Lee Anne Bell and Pat Griffin (New York: Routledge, 1997): 292.

76. Nado Aveling, "Student Teachers' Resistance," 120.

77. Roberta Ahlquist, "Position and Imposition," 163, emphasis mine.

78. Alison Jones, "The Limits of Cross-Cultural Dialogue."

79. Kim Case and Annette Hemmings, "Distancing Strategies," 616–617.

80. Marilyn Frye, "In and Out of Harm's Way: Arrogance and Love," in her *The Politics of Reality: Essays in Feminist Theory* (Trumansburg, New York: The Crossing Press, 1983), 67.

81. Ann Diller, "Facing the Torpedo Fish: Becoming a Philosopher of One's Own Education," *Philosophy of Education 1998*, ed. Steven Tozer (Urbana, IL.: Philosophy of Education Society, 1999): 8.

82. Kelly Oliver, *Witnessing*, 16.

83. Ibid., 8.

84. Shoshana Felman and Dori Laub, *Testimony: Crisis of Witnessing in Literature, Psychoanalysis, and History* (New York: Routledge, 1992), 62.

85. Kelly Oliver, *Witnessing*, 42.

86. Michalinos Zembylas, "Witnessing in the Classroom: The Ethics and Politics of Affect," *Educational Theory* 56, vol. 3 (2006): 313.

87. Gayle Jones, *Corregidora* (Random House, 1975), 14 and 72 as quoted in Hazel V. Carby, "White Woman Listen! Black Feminism and the Boundaries of Sisterhood," in *Theories of Race and Racism: A Reader,* ed. Les Back and John Solomos (London: Routledge, 2000): 389.

88. See also Amanda E. Lewis, Mark Chesler, and Tyrone A. Forman, "The Impact of 'Colorblind' Ideologies on Students of Color: Intergroup Relations at a Predominantly White University," *The Journal of Negro Education* 69, no. 1–2 (2000): 74–91.

89. Megan Boler, "All Speech is Not Free."

CHAPTER 5

Moral Responsibility and Complicity in Philosophical Scholarship

In the philosophical scholarship one can find debates around complicity in discussions of legal and moral responsibility for actions one did not do. Specific and extensive attention has been given to complicity in philosophy of law under the topic of accessorial liability. An accessory is an individual who assists in the commission of crime but does not participate as a co-principal. This body of scholarship is exclusively focused on the justification of punishment. Philosophers in the field of ethics have given complicity considerably less attention, having traditionally been more concerned with those who directly commit a wrong. Nevertheless, there are stimulating discussions about complicity that arise in the debates around the moral responsibility of those who are indirectly connected to the wrong that other people do that might have relevance to understanding responsibility for white complicity.

Three debates within the scholarship on moral responsibility that directly or indirectly relate to complicity will be explored. The first focuses on the presumed relationship between causal connections to the wrong and attributions of complicity. What it could mean for individuals to be responsible for *non-causally* participating in the collective harms perpetrated by their group is examined. The second debate concentrates on individual responsibility for wrongs that are part of a system of socially accepted practices that impede one's ability to understand the wrongness of one's actions. Finally, discussions around that claim that *all* group members are responsible for wrongs committed by their group will be examined.

Recall that a unique feature of the white complicity claim is that *well-intentioned* white people are responsible for the perpetuation of systemic racism. Moreover, white complicity assumes a sense of responsibility that can capture how "our mobs are always with us." Conditions of systemic ignorance, moreover, must be considered when addressing responsibility for white complicity. What understanding of moral responsibility can be attributed to white individuals who may have no clear causal connection to a wrong and who might not even recognize the wrong because it is so normalized that its moral relevance is obscured? In addition, I am looking for a conception of moral responsibility that can ground the claim that *all* white people are complicit in sustaining systemic injustice not because they have a direct causal link to the harms of racial injustice, not because they have particular bad intentions or bad attitudes against those who are not white, but by virtue of being a member of a social group that benefits from such systemic injustices. Finally, what conception of moral responsibility can be appealed to pedagogically that has the potential to facilitate and not obstruct acknowledging white complicity?

I will argue that conceptions of moral responsibility that are focused on blame and liability cannot capture the ways in which individual white people are complicit by virtue of their social group membership. Moreover, I contend that such conceptions may also encourage and support denials of complicity.

The chapter concludes with the contention that while there are interesting insights that can be derived from the philosophical scholarship on complicity and responsibility, ultimately, these discussions are limited by a conception of moral responsibility that is unable to name white complicity and may even obscure considering its possibility. The need for a rearticulated conception of moral responsibility to ground white complicity is introduced but taken up in the following chapter.

COMPLICITY: CAUSALITY, PARTICIPATION, AND COLLECTIVE HARMS

"I did not cause racism, so why am I responsible?" my white student asks. Traditionally, causality is one of the hallmarks of responsibility; one is responsible only if one caused something to come about, *if one made or could have made a difference in the world.* If one does not make or cannot make a difference, ascriptions of responsibility seem out of place. John Gardner[1] highlights the role of causal responsibility in situations where one *cannot* make a difference to a harm coming into the world by quoting from Alexander Solzhenitsyn.

> And the simple step of a simple courageous man is not to take part in the lie, not to support the deceit. Let the lie come into the world, even dominate the world, but not through me.[2]

Moral integrity, according to Gardner's reading of Solzhenitsyn, requires that one must avoid being implicated in a clear moral wrong—a lie, deceit—even when the wrong would happen with or without one's participation. Complicity is a moral taint that one must avoid; wrongs must not "come through me." Gardner attributes the position to Solzhenitsyn that one is not only responsible for what one brings into the world but one can be complicit if one participates in the wrongs that others cause even if one does not make any causal difference to whether or not the wrong comes into being.

Yet complicity without causality troubles Gardner. He insists that accomplices, not unlike principals, do make a causal contribution to the harm and he goes about fleshing out this causal connection. Accomplices make a difference, i.e., they have a causal connection to the wrong, except the causal connection is distinguished from the causal connection that principals have to the harm. Unlike the principal, the causal connection of the accomplice to the harm is mediated rather than direct. One is complicit when one makes "a difference to the difference that the principal makes."[3] Complicity arises, according to Gardner, because I am not only responsible for my own actions (as a principal) but I am also responsible for how my actions causally contribute to your actions even when it appears as if I am not directly making a difference to the final outcome. If, for example, one lends a tool that picks locks to a thief who then uses it to rob a house, although the thief would have been able to enter the house by other means, one is still complicit in the theft because one makes "a difference to the difference that the principal makes." The wrongdoing still comes "through me"—I am *part of the chain of events* that leads to the wrong. Both accomplices and principals bring wrongdoing into the world, but the place one is situated within the causal chain that leads to the wrong is different.

Why should this matter? Although it is not always clear whether Gardner is referring to moral or legal responsibility, the underlying assumption is that responsibility involves some sort of fault that justifies punishment. Therefore, an individual should not be held accountable without some type of causal link to the wrong.

This account of complicity with its tight connection to causality, however, has been criticized as too individualistic. Complicity, Lindsay Farmer[4] contends, can involve *non-causal* connections to a harm that other people perpetrate. The harm brought about by a mob in which individuals are simultaneously principals *and* accomplices is an example of non-causal connection because it is the *collective* nature of their actions, and not the individual, that brings the harm into the world. Gardner's strong emphasis on both causality and his individualistic conception of complicity, according to Farmer, overlooks the type of complicity that involves collective participation. As Farmer insists, there are a " . . . variety of forms of collective involvement in wrongdoing that cannot easily be reduced to the model of one person causing another to act."[5]

Farmer maintains that Gardner overlooks "the social and legal structures within which our actions are already embedded"[6] and thus cannot account for the type of non-causal complicity when one's government, for instance, commits wrong and one's passivity or failing to do something can be a non-causal contribution to that wrong coming into being. These are cases of complicity in which the individual *does not actively do something that stands in the causal change that results in the wrong coming into existence.* If one fails to protest, it is not a matter of *allowing a wrong not to come through me* in a causal sense but rather a matter of *allowing a wrong to be done in my name* (non-causally). In fact, Farmer's reading of Solzhenitsyn's quote underscores this.

> . . . let me not be complicit in sustaining the political legitimacy of the lying or deceptive regime. Let me not participate in sustaining the lie by whatever forms of political resistance are available to me. Let it not be done in my name.[7]

There are all sorts of non-causal contributions that one can make to sustain or legitimate a wrong that one does not directly bring into the world. While some may feel the need to force these into a causal chain, Farmer insists that "it would seem both artificial and unduly constraining to do so."[8]

The discussion around the relationship between causality and complicity highlights some crucial characteristics about responsibility for white complicity. As Farmer notes, an overly individualistic conception of complicity and a notion of moral responsibility that is excessively tied to causality tend to allow a variety of forms of collective participation in wrongdoing to escape attention. Since white complicity is not exclusively concerned with individuals qua individuals causally contributing to racist acts that other people do but involves the ways in which individuals as members of a social group are involved in sustaining systemic racial oppression and privilege, the shift to non-causal connections and responsibility for collective harms is helpful. White complicity is not necessarily about individuals qua individuals bringing something into the world (causally) but more about ways of being that participate in and sustain systemic injustice.

Christopher Kutz's[9] thought-provoking book, *Complicity: Ethics and Law for a Collective Age,* offers a complex philosophical examination of complicity in collective harms that also shifts our attention from causality to participation. Kutz opens the book with the observation that complicity in collective harms is remarkably widespread.

> We live in a morally flawed world, one full of regrets and reproaches. Some of the things we regret, or for which we are reproached, we bring about intentionally and on our own. But our lives are increasingly complicated by regrettable things brought about through our associations with other people or with the social, economic, and political institutions in which we live our lives and make our livings. Try as we might to live well, we find ourselves connected to harms and wrongs, albeit by relations that fall outside the paradigm of individual, intentional wrongdoing.[10]

Like Farmer, Kutz highlights the problems of the individualist focus in traditional notions of moral responsibility. Kutz maintains that such notions are evaluatively solipsistic and, as such, allow for participation in collective harms to go unnoticed.

Such solipsism is manifested in the two related principles that are fundamentally basic to traditional accounts of moral responsibility and that Kutz labels the "Individual Difference Principle" and the "Control Principle." Both principles focus on the individual to the extent that they ignore the significance of our collective relations with others. The "Individual Difference Principle" involves the assumption that one is only accountable for harm if something one does makes a difference to the harm's occurrence. The "Control Principle" presumes that one is accountable only if one could control the occurrence of the harm by producing or preventing it.[11]

Initially it seems quite plausible to build the source of responsibility tightly to the individual's causal relationship to the harm because "our sense of ourselves as agents emerges from the experience of making changes in our environment."[12] Yet, contra Gardner, Kutz rejects complicity as causality and instead, like Farmer, accentuates participation, not causality. Causality fails to explain complicity when many of the most egregious harms are the product of collective action in which each member makes no difference to the outcome and could not control what happens. In such cases, the causal link between such harms and the individual dissolves.

> The most important and far-reaching harms and wrongs of contemporary life are the products of collective actions, mediated by social and institutional structures. These harms and wrongs are essentially collective products, and individual agents rarely make a difference to their occurrence. So long as individuals are only responsible for the effects they produce, then the result of this disparity between collective harm and individual effect is the *disappearance of individual accountability*.[13]

Kutz contends that the plausibility of "solipsistic" conceptions of accountability derives from the perpetrator's perspective. For the individual agent, the "Individual Difference Principle" and the "Control Principle" seem most natural and persuasive.[14] Kutz explains that the tight connection between traditional conceptions of moral responsibility and notions of praise or blame draws our attention to what the agent deserves and, thus, the solipsism that emphasizes facts *about the agent* rather than the *agent's collective relations to others*.[15]

In light of this, Kutz suggests a contrasting principle that highlights what one is accountable for even when one could not have made a difference to the resulting harm. The "Complicity Principle" emphasizes that one is accountable for what others do when one *intentionally participates* in a collective that causes the harm together. One is accountable for the harm *we* do together, independently of the actual difference an individual who intentionally participates in such group action makes.[16] *Participatory intention* is intention to act as part of a group in collective action of agents who orient themselves around *a joint project.* The Allied pilots who firebombed Dresden, Kutz's paradigm case, were individually complicit, even when the particular pilot did not cause civilian devastation (even if the pilot missed his target). Kutz notes that in interviews many people who were indirectly involved with the Dresden bombing expressed emotions implying that they shared some kind of responsibility. Kutz argues it is important to capture this sense of *feeling* responsible.

When the Complicity Principle is emphasized and brought to the forefront, a different conception of individual moral responsibility results. Kutz explains,

> Where the individualistic principles (of accountability) exculpate, the principle of complicity implicates. It specifies an individualistic basis (participation) that grounds, rather than precludes, accountability for collective harms.[17]

The "Complicity Principle" is aptly summed up in Kutz's slogan, "No participation without implication."[18]

Kutz, however, does not relinquish the individualist perspective. He insists that it is individuals who "are the ultimate loci of normative motivation and deliberation . . . only forms of accountability aimed at and sensitive to what individuals do can succeed in controlling the emergence of collective harms."[19] As he succinctly puts it, "The oughts of morality and politics apply to *me*."[20] What he attempts to accomplish is to move the intentional aspect of action from causality to participation. And this helps to explain the feelings of responsibility that those indirectly involved in the Dresden bombing express.

Both Farmer and Kutz shift our attention to how wrongs are perpetuated by individuals participating in collective harms. These arguments initially appear promising for naming white complicity. Yet Farmer does not clearly address the relationship between the individual and the group as Kutz does. In addition, Farmer is concerned with blatant wrongs. The moral dimension of telling a lie, killing, stealing, the recurrent types of moral wrongs involved in the cases generally discussed, are not open to dispute. In considering white complicity, however, the practices under consideration are often so normalized that their status as morally wrong is exactly what is being contested. White complicity involves practices that white people often consider "harmless" and even "benevolent."

Kutz's work, although underscoring a particular type of participation in a collective action, is still focused exclusively on individuals qua individuals and *not individuals qua members of social groups, like race or gender.* Kutz acknowledges that he is primarily concerned to salvage the individualist perspective by making it "more at home in a collective world."[21] In spite of his attempts to transfer attributions of responsibility away from the causal effects of individual actions, Kutz's "Complicity Principle" with its strong focus on *intentional participation* also cannot capture white complicity that is distinctly characterized by its *unintentional* participation in the perpetuation of injustice that is, as we explained in previous chapters, fundamentally connected to ways of being white, something one may not choose (remember Butler's claim that subjects are *compelled* to reiterate norms) or have control over. Kutz's notion of complicity assumes that individuals choose to participate in the groups whose collective harms they participate in. Even when he discusses participation in the harms that groups cause, Kutz presumes the subject of complicity is an individual qua individual. White complicity involves a subject that *as white* participates in the perpetuation of systemic injustice.

In addition, Kutz's Complicity Principle does not specifically address the type of complicity that involves participation in wrongs that are normalized as morally good. Kutz, moreover, is not concerned with complicity that is a product of and that supports systemic ignorance. Kutz's theory is also guided by the sense of responsibility some people report they "feel." Yet it is specifically a lack of such a feeling of responsibility (such complicity is denied) that is characteristic of white complicity. Denials of white complicity, furthermore, are camouflaged by seemingly morally honorable virtues, for instance, assertions of "colorblindness." It is the connection to seemingly moral behavior that contributes to the resistance and that makes explaining white complicity so difficult.

Finally, and related to this latter point, the type of cases that Kutz attempts to explain, such as the Dresden pilots or drivers that collectively pollute the air, do not involve structural injustice that underpins white complicity. Structural injustice is also collective harm but such harms are reproduced through cultural, economic and political institutions that people participate in without any participatory intentions that can be pointed to.

Larry May's[22] *Sharing Responsibility* offers a conception of responsibility that might seem more promising in its ability to capture white complicity. May theorizes individual complicity in collective harms and seems to take seriously how individuals qua group members are implicated in systemic injustice. May's work is situated within a broader debate in recent philosophical scholarship around collective moral responsibility. Most of the debates have revolved around the question of whether or how moral agency, intention and responsibility can be ascribed to a group when these notions have been traditionally understood in individualistic terms.[23] May's distinctive contribution is that he also draws attention to the question of how responsibility can be *distributed* to individual group members for wrongs that the group they are members of commit.

May distinguishes between collective responsibility and shared responsibility. Collective responsibility is nondistributed and involves the case where the group as a whole is responsible for a wrong. Collective responsibility does not entail that *every* member of the group is individually responsible for the wrong. A corporation, for instance, can be collectively responsible for its employees' behaviors if it does not have a policy on sexual harassment, especially if this lack of a policy might convey the message that such behavior will be tolerated. Shared responsibility, in contrast, is *distributed responsibility.* As May underscores, it is "the aggregated responsibility of individuals, all of whom contribute to a result and for that reason are personally responsible, albeit to different degrees, for a given harmful result."[24]

May's work is a bold effort to extend responsibility in less individualist terms by capturing the way that an individual qua group member can be implicated in the harms that his/her group or fellow group members commit. Like Kutz, he understands that "in advanced technological societies, much greater evil is done by groups of persons than by discrete individual persons."[25] May's project is based on the conviction that "seeing one's own moral status as interrelated with that of one's fellow group members will negate the tendency to ignore the most serious moral evils, those which can only be thwarted by the collective efforts of communities."[26]

Drawing on Karl Jaspers' notion of metaphysical guilt (briefly mentioned in Chapter 1), May explains that metaphysical guilt arises from being a member of a group and the wrongful actions that are committed by the group or members of the group. According to Jaspers, metaphysical guilt involves a failure to manifest solidarity with a fellow human being. As a social existentialist, May views the individual as a member of various social groups and insists that such group membership can implicate the individual in what the group or various members of the group do.

May draws out this metaphysical guilt in three ways. First, May insists that responsibility is connected not only to one's causal relation to actions but also connected to who one chooses to be. He focuses on personal attitudes and connects responsibility for the attitudes one *chooses* to hold. Notice that May continues to tie ascriptions of moral responsibility to control and voluntariness. As May puts it,

> . . . one is responsible for all of those things over which one has control, and responsibility for one's states of mind is added to the normal range of things for which responsibility is assigned.[27]

For example, if one lives in a racist society and one *chooses* to hold racist attitudes, one shares responsibility for the racist violence some members of one's society perpetrate even if one does not directly contribute to the violent acts oneself. According to May, holding such negative attitudes is moral reckless-ness and entails responsibility for contributing to the *climate of attitudes* that supports the act and increases the likelihood that the harm will be enacted. May explains,

> In advanced technological societies, much greater evil is done by groups of persons than by discrete individual persons. And evil is made much more likely when people do not understand how failure to change their attitudes or be-haviors facilitates the production of harm within the groups of which they are members.[28]

Although only certain members of a group might have directly perpetrated violence, May insists that *seemingly innocent* group members are also partially responsible if they choose to hold on to racist attitudes.

Second, group members can also be responsible for negligent omission. If one does not register disapproval when confronted with racist wrongs perpetrated by other group members, one also shares responsibility for such wrongs. Borrowing from Sartre, May claims that group members have a duty of authenticity. May explains,

> Authenticity involves, among other things, being conscious of who one is and taking responsibility for the harms of one's class, one's position, and one's situation in the world. To be "unauthentic" is to "deny" or "attempt to escape from" one's condition, to fail to assume responsibility for choosing to be who one is.[29]

Elaborating on what such inauthenticity means, Cassie Striblen[30] argues that inauthenticity is manifested when one does not publicly show disapproval because one allows those members who do harm to define one's group. If one responds with disapproval, one *chooses* not to contribute to the association of doing harm with the definition of the group and, thus, one escapes respon-sibility. Individuals who fail to distance themselves from the group members that are causing harm whether by condemning these people or by ending af-filiation with the group where possible give their implicit endorsement to the harm and become morally tainted.

The third way in which group members can be ascribed shared responsibil-ity is by benefiting from a climate in which such harms exist. A concrete illus-tration of shared responsibility and its relationship to benefit is highlighted in an influential article that May co-authored with Robert Strikwerda[31] discuss-ing the shared responsibility of ordinary men for the prevalence of rape in western culture.

Responsibility for rape is usually attributed to individual males or groups of males who commit the crime. May and Strikwerda contend that responsibility for rape should not be understood merely in individualistic terms. Rape is not an isolated, individual wrong but rather has a group-like orientation and a systemic dimension. As May explains

> . . . individual men are more likely to engage in rape when they are in groups, and men receive strong encouragement to rape from the way they are socialized as men, that is, in the way they come to see themselves as instantiations of what it means to be a man. Both the "climate" that encourages rape and the "socialization" patterns which instill negative attitudes about women are difficult to understand or assess when one focuses on the isolated individual perpetrator of a rape. There are significant social dimensions to rape that are best understood as group-oriented.[32]

All men share responsibility in the prevalence of rape in their culture, according to May and Strikwerda,

> (1) Insofar as most perpetrators of rape are men, then these men are responsible, in most cases, for the rapes they committed. (2) Insofar as some men, by the way they interact with other (especially younger) men, contribute to a climate in our society where rape is made more prevalent, then they are collaborators in the rape culture and for this reason share in responsibility for rapes committed in that culture. (3) Also, insofar as some men are not unlike the rapist, since they would be rapists if they had the opportunity to be placed into a situation where their inhibitions against rape were removed, then these men share responsibility with actual rapists for the harms of rape. (4) In addition, insofar as many other men could have prevented fellow men from raping, but did not act to prevent these actual rapes, then these men also share responsibility along with the rapists. (5) Finally, insofar as some men benefit from the existence of rape in our society, these men also share responsibility along with the rapists.[33]

According to May and Strikwerda, all men share responsibility for rape not only when they contribute to a climate in our society where rape is made more prevalent but also if they benefit from the existence of rape in society.

May and Strikwerda make explicit one of the least discussed benefits of rape that all men gain from, i.e., that "women are made to feel dependent on men for protection against potential rapists."[34] This puts men in a dominant position as "saviors" of women who need to be rescued. This connection between benefits and responsibility is one that is crucially important for understanding white complicity.

May, however, also contends that while shared responsibility involves *moral taint*, it does not entail *moral guilt* and so he believes that the term "metaphysical *guilt*" is unfortunate. Shared responsibility is partial responsibility.[35] For May responsibility is a scalar concept—one can be more or less responsible, although he does not explicate the criteria by which degrees of responsibility should be attributed. He does explicitly claim that one can relieve oneself of responsibility for the crimes that other people commit if one opposes the wrong or if one dissents. Striblen offers an illustration of who would be absolved of shared responsibility when she asks us to

> . . . imagine a hate crime case where a "black" boy is killed by two "white" men in a Mississippi town, after whistling at a "white" woman. May would say that the men are directly responsible, of course, but he would also say that many "white" people, at least those who live in the area of the crime, are indirectly responsible. Those "white" people who hold racist attitudes recklessly contribute to the climate of harm and in that way share responsibility. What is more, those "white" people who do and say nothing share responsibility because of their negligence. On May's account, only those "white" people who respond with disapproval do not share responsibility.[36]

In addition, May also removes responsibility for the individual if there is no control but implies there is never an issue of lack of choice for the future. In his discussion of habits of sensitivity, May contends that

> A white person who has formed the habit of insensitivity to Blacks due to long association with people who are racists may never have consciously chosen to become a racist; for this reason *he may not now be responsible for his racism.* But he may be responsible for his racism in the future if he does not initiate steps now to change the habits of insensitivity.[37]

At first glance, May's approach seems to offer many insights for understanding white complicity because the type of group that May considers in his discussion of shared responsibility is not a nation or a corporation but a social group in which one's group membership is not necessarily under one's control. Moreover, he is interested in distributed responsibility or the responsibility that individuals carry qua group members. Moreover, May explains how well-intentioned men can be responsible for harms against women or how well-intentioned white people can be responsible for racially motivated harms, even when the individual has no direct causal connection to the harm. His discussion about the benefits of some of the harms that follow from group membership is also extremely apt. In addition, he highlights how harms are not isolated acts but instead connected to beliefs and attitudes that are shared in a society.

Although May wants to move away from individualistic notions of responsibility, the problem is that he continues to connect responsibility to some type of individual choice, the choice to choose one's attitudes and, therefore, the behavior that stems from them. As he argues in *Sharing Responsibility,*

> In arguing for the view that the attitudes and beliefs we choose, and not just our overt behaviors, are relevant to judgments of responsibility, I remain committed

to the view that people should only be judged morally responsible for those things that are under our control; but control here does not necessarily mean that one could make the world a different place.[38]

Immediately it becomes clear that his focus on control and choice make it difficult to use May's notion to expose white complicity since the connection between choice and white ways of being/white privilege is more complex.

Moreover, May's approach is exclusively concerned with *negative attitudes* and how such attitudes implicate well-intentioned white people in a type of *partial* responsibility for *overt* harms that *other* white people perpetrate. As Iris Marion Young points out, May concentrates on past wrongs or acts that have reached a terminus and focuses on the enabling conditions that allowed such harms to occur. He assumes that one can relieve oneself of responsibility if only one can purge oneself from negative attitudes or make an attempt to show others one's discontent. Yet structural injustice, as Young insists, is maintained in much more complicated ways where the *harms are ongoing* and they are not just what *someone else* is doing.

There are at least four problems that arise when we attempt to use May's notion of shared responsibility to explain white complicity that I would like to address in detail.

First, May's shared responsibility fails to consider complicity for unintentional ways in which racist systems are perpetuated by white practices or white phenomenology. As Shannon Sullivan[39] makes clear, white practices are so familiar, white people are often unaware of the underlying attitude that motivates them. White practices are unconscious habits that contribute to and reinforce racist systems.

Second, shared responsibility ignores the ways in which white people can perpetuate systemic oppression not through negative attitudes but by actually intending to be good. Peg O'Connor discusses how good intentions can function to protect racial injustice from challenge.

> Those who argued for the *gradual* ending of slavery on the basis of the belief that Black people were like children and unable to care and provide for themselves did not intend to harm Black people. To the contrary, they saw themselves as doing something good because they were trying to end slavery.[40]

O'Connor emphasizes that such unintentional actions become difficult to name because they are accompanied by good intentions.

Third, although he mentions the benefit that dominant group members reap from systemic oppression, May does not acknowledge how systemic privilege might be difficult to denounce and he overlooks the ways in which privilege sticks to white people even when they want to give privilege up.[41] Most significantly, May does not acknowledge the ways in which power circulates through all white bodies in ways that make them *directly* complicit for contributing to the perpetuation of a system they did not, as individuals, create.

Finally, May also reverts to the fault/blame model of responsibility when he explains how well-intentioned group members are *partially* responsible for what other members do. Implicit in this point is that when dominant group members do take action against the violence of their fellow group members, when they resist and actively oppose these practices, they are cleared of all responsibility. The white complicity claim, however, maintains that even when white people act against racism they must still be vigilant about how they may be supporting it and that white privilege sticks to one even as white people attempt to challenge it. May does not consider how, as Sara Ahmed[42] explains, projects of white critique can be complicit with the object of their critique. Thus, May's shared responsibility does not adequately capture such complicity.

Alison Bailey[43] offers additional support for the claim that May reverts to the fault/blame model of responsibility when she observes that May is more concerned with the person who is complicit and the relationship s/he has to the harm than he is about the relationship between the person who is complicit and the one harmed. The victim, Bailey insists, is written completely out of the story. This is especially problematic because it implies that the agency of the one responsible is more important than the agency of the victim. Control over the interpretation of harm remains in the hands of the one responsible and thus dominance is reasserted. Without attempting to understand how the victim feels, Bailey argues, the one responsible cannot understand the harm done. This is especially egregious in cases of white complicity where the racism in a situation might be invisible to those who are not its victims. When the victim is written out of the story, according to Bailey, the motivation for preventing future harms "may be driven more by shame than by genuine concern."[44] In other words, May's approach ends up being more focused on the interests of the perpetrator than with a concern for the victim.

Bailey also finds it problematic that May believes that those who share responsibility are otherwise innocent except that they contribute to an oppressive climate. Like Young, Bailey understands that structural injustice is maintained not just via attitudes but also through subtle practices that the complicit enact often unwittingly and often with the best of intentions. Structural injustice, as has been noted throughout this book, is kept in place by everyday practices and habits of well-intentioned people.

Unlike May, whose notion of responsibility is primarily interested in complicity for *blatant* harms (rape, racial violence) that other people do, white complicity involves the subtle racism that the systemically privileged enact on a day-to-day basis and that can masquerade as moral behavior. It is subtle microaggressions (subtle, that is, for the perpetrator) whose wrongfulness is exactly what is being contested that the white complicity claim attempts to expose. Solorzano et al[45] use the term "microaggression" to highlight the "subtle insults (verbal, nonverbal, and/or visual) directed toward people of color, often automatically or unconsciously."[46] These are brief but commonplace white practices that convey a negative message about non-white people.

The interesting point about microaggressions is that when one focuses one's attention on the microaggression in isolation from the system within which it has meaning, the act indeed may seem harmless. It is the cumulative effects of a lifetime of experiencing microaggressions that can have a dramatic impact on the lives of the racially marginalized. As Pierce explains, " . . . one must not look for the gross and obvious. The subtle, cumulative miniassault is the substance of today's racism."[47] In her discussion of feminist consciousness, Sandra Bartky makes a similar point about the microaggressions that women endure, referring to them as those "pervasive *intimations* of inferiority."[48] As Bailey reminds us, this is one reason why it is so important not to write the experience of the marginalized out of the story of the interpretation of harm.

It is the unintentional actions and inactions that sustain systemic racism that the scholarship on white complicity attempts to name. As a concrete illustration of such unintended habits of whiteness or microaggressions that white people are often ignorant of, recall the uproar in the media when in the early part of 2007 Joseph Biden, the white Senator who Obama eventually appoints as his vice-president, publicly described his then fellow Democratic presidential contender Senator Barack Obama as "the first mainstream African-American who is articulate and bright and clean and a nice-looking guy."[49] Biden insisted that he meant it as an innocent compliment. Indeed, white people, drawing on their own experience, do not normally object when they are described as "articulate" and "clean" and the adjectives are most often intended as a form of praise. Yet some African-Americans were outraged and offended that someone could think that the former president of the *Harvard Law Review* should be complimented by being described as "articulate." As a subtle form of insidious racism, the descriptor has the subtext of amazement (even bewilderment) that implied this person is articulate "for a Black person."

While Senator Obama declared he was personally unharmed by this microaggression, such practices have collective effects that can remain invisible if not noted. On the first day that I taught a graduate course on race and racism, a student of color came into the class clearly incensed. When I inquired what was upsetting him, he explained that as a new student in our department one of the white students approached him to welcome him and asked if he was a new Masters student in our program. Amazed, I asked him why that upset him so and he explained that he is a Ph.D. student and he could not help but wonder if this white student presumed that other new white students were working on their *Masters* degree. Since this was a course on race and racism, I asked him if I could open the class with his experience and he agreed. Most of the white students responded with comments like, "You have to learn how to not be so sensitive" or "The student didn't mean anything bad. He was trying to welcome you." Such microaggressions, as the student explained, are something that he continually encounters and contribute to the general feeling that people that look like him do not belong in academia.

These microaggressions are the result of systemic ignorance. May moves closer to addressing such ignorance when he discusses the issue of racial insensitivity as a form of culpable ignorance.[50] He reverts back to an individualistic notion of ignorance, however, when he follows Holly Smith in contending that one is culpably ignorant if one *chooses* not to do something whose consequence is ignorance that results in harm. As argued in Chapter 2, white ignorance which is systemic does not fit into this paradigm of ignorance. The white students described above were ignorant of the ways in which a seemingly innocent comment can be a microagrresion connected to a larger system of norms, beliefs and values. Let us turn to the philosophical discussion around culpable ignorance to ascertain if and how these discussions might offer some insight into how white people can be responsible for their ignorance.

IGNORANT COMPLICITY

How can one be responsible for perpetrating a wrong that one does not know is wrong? In his discussion of virtue, Aristotle[51] addresses the connection between ignorance and responsibility. For Aristotle, moral responsibility depends on one's actions being voluntary in the sense that "the moving principle (of the action) is in the agent himself."[52] One is an appropriate candidate for moral praise or blame only if the action under consideration was done voluntarily, i.e., the agent must be the primary cause of the action. Choice, according to Aristotle, is ultimately a requisite condition of responsibility.

Voluntary action requires a control condition in the sense that the action or trait must have its origin in the agent and the agent must be free to choose whether or not to perform the action or have the trait. If the individual is externally compelled, one cannot hold the individual responsible. A second and related condition of responsibility, according to Aristotle, is knowledge that one is doing wrong. Unless ignorance can be shown to be a reflection of the agent's choice, individuals are not responsible for something they did not know was wrong. Ignorance, therefore, can be culpable but only when the agent *chooses to be ignorant* and, therefore, it can be said that the agent should have known better.

In her seminal essay, "Culpable Ignorance," Holly Smith[53] fleshes out what it means that someone should have known better. According to Smith, culpable ignorance involves two factors. The first is what she refers to as a "benighting act" or an initial act *that the agent chooses* and that results in ignorance. Second, the "unwittingly wrongful act" is a consequence of the benighting act. Moreover, the connection between the benighting act (or the decision to choose to do x or omit to do x) and the unwittingly wrongful act must involve *the agent having reason to believe that by choosing to do x (or omitting to do x) s/he was risking the wrongful consequence at a later time.* In Smith's illustration of culpable ignorance, a doctor treats a premature infant with harmful levels of oxygen and as a result the infant suffers severe eye damage. Although the doctor caused the damage to the infant's eyesight, s/he did not intend to hurt the infant. Yet the doctor *should have known* that such levels of oxygen were unnecessarily high and s/he would have known if s/he had not *made the choice* not to read the medical journals that s/he had in the office.

In such a case, there is a benighting act in which the one makes a choice that affects one's later actions. It is the benighting act that one is culpable for because it makes knowledge that would be necessary for avoiding the wrongful act epistemically unavailable. Culpable ignorance, according to Smith, is a variant of a broader category of actions in which an agent is morally responsible for an earlier act that affects one's moral state in the perpetration of a later act. Although there is no immediate reprehensible intention to do the wrongful act (hence, it is done unwittingly), the agent is still blameworthy because the benighting act involves an *awareness of the risk of possible wrongful consequences.*

White ignorance, however, does not fit comfortably into this profile of the culpably ignorant. First of all, the benighting act to which blameworthiness can be linked is absent. Charles Mills is clear that the Racial Contract is merely a rhetorical trope that allows us to better understand how racial injustice is kept in place. There is no single act that could be pointed to in regards to the signing of such a contract.

> Although no single act literally corresponds to the drawing up and signing of a contract, there is a series of acts . . . which collectively can be seen . . . as its conceptual, juridical, and moral equivalent.[54]

If there is no intentional decision that individual white people make to agree to the Racial Contract, then if we follow Smith, white ignorance is not culpable.

Culpable ignorance presumes that one is not culpable if one can find absolutely no accountable intention, no benighting choice. Even when white people oppose the system and they have morally good intentions, however, they still benefit from the system in ways that makes them responsible, as I believe is intimated in Mills' claim that "All whites are beneficiaries of the Contract, though some whites are not signatories to it."[55] In her discussion of Mills' work, Peg O'Connor explains that

> The racial system benefits all white people, no matter how hard some of us try to reject our privileges and subvert them. . . . given the way racism constantly reinvents itself, the lines between beneficiaries and signatories blur. Despite my best intentions to the contrary, I may be enacting and embodying my racial privilege. Today's traitorousness is tomorrow's complicity.[56]

Thus, white ignorance can involve white people trying to do what they believe is the morally responsible thing to do, something that has made considering white complicity from within the framework of most philosophical scholarship on moral responsibility exceedingly difficult.

Second, and related to the above, the ignorance that is the focus of the scholarship on culpable ignorance is an individualistic ignorance and not group-based systemically induced ignorance. The harm caused by the doctor to the child's vision is an isolated wrong that the individual perpetrates qua individual. White ignorance, in contrast, is systemic and involves individuals not qua individuals but qua white.

Finally, the philosophical scholarship on culpable ignorance, like the discussions of complicity in the previous section, is focused exclusively on acts of *blatant* wrongfulness. White complicity, in contrast, involves those practices that white people enact but are not perceived as morally wrong because they conform to societal norms and values.

Which leads to another philosophical debate involving ignorance and moral responsibility and that is specifically focused on the relationship between culture and ignorance about the moral dimension of certain practices. The central question in this debate is whether one's culture can be a mitigating factor that diminishes ascriptions of moral responsibility. Can one be held responsible for wrongs that are part of a system of culturally accepted practices? Some philosophers, such as Michael Slote[57] and Bernard Williams,[58] have contended that cultural factors may contribute to a person's *inability* to judge the wrongness of certain actions.

In her often cited, controversial defense of "the inability thesis," Susan Wolf[59] explains, "the ability to act in accordance with the True and the Good"[60] may be thwarted by our cultural upbringing. She equates such an inability with insanity. Just as the insane cannot be held morally responsible for wrongdoing so too those who are mistaken about their values because of the cultural belief system they were brought up in cannot be held accountable. As Wolf puts it, even the slaveowners of the American South, the Nazis of the 1930's and male chauvinists of earlier generations should not be held morally responsible since "given the social circumstance in which they developed," it "may have been inevitable" that they held the false beliefs and false values that they held.[61] In other words, by internalizing one's cultural beliefs and values, one may lose the requisite ability to critically reflect upon such values and beliefs, and if a person is unable to distinguish between right and wrong in regards to a particular range of moral issues, the person should not be held responsible for behavior that follows from such values and beliefs. According to Wolf, if agents could not help but be mistaken about their values and beliefs, they should not be blamed.

The question arises, however, whether culture makes it *impossible* to know right from wrong. In her forceful rejection of "the inability thesis," Michelle Moody-Adams[62] argues that it is ultimately individuals who interpret the rules and values of their culture. Since benefiting from the system may give people a reason *not to probe* the injustice of the practice, when people are ignorant about wrong practices from which they benefit, it is likely that they are *choosing to remain ignorant.* Such "affected ignorance," according to Moody-Adams, is culpable because "it involves a choice not to know something that is morally important and that would *be easy to know but for that choice.*"[63] Affected ignorance involves a *choice to remain ignorant* because of the benefit that ignorance protects.

According to Moody-Adams, affected ignorance is culpable. Although she acknowledges that such wrongdoing is a product of "widespread moral ignorance,"[64] she insists that such ignorance is culpable because members of society are *not unable to know* but rather *choose not to know or are unwilling to know* the moral significance of their actions and this choice is connected to the benefits of being ignorant. Culture does not make one unable to know, Moody-Adams insists, because there is always a way to dissent (although she acknowledges that dissenters risk marginalization). For Moody-Adams, culture influences individuals but individuals can also influence culture. The affected ignorance thesis preserves the agency of the agent that the inability thesis does away with.

There is a sense of inability with regard to critical reflection on one's cultural norms that Moody-Adams, nevertheless, seems to underestimate. Nigel Pleasants[65] also examines the "inability thesis" but distinguishing between two types of wrongdoing. The first involves individual wrongdoing and the second is focused on institutional wrongdoing. In regard to the former type of wrongdoing, individuals are acting *in violation* of the laws, rules, norms and values of their society while in the latter case individuals are acting *in accordance* with their society's rules. In this latter case, individuals, thus, participate, collude or support the harms that are a consequence of following those rules. Pleasants argues,

> Individual wrongdoing results from the aberrational acts of deviant individuals, whereas institutional wrongdoing is chronically embodied in lawful, socially accepted, collectively sustained practices.[66]

Institutional wrongdoing that arises as a result of institutionally supported ignorance is not a "disability" (note the problematic ablest assumptions in this scholarship) and here Pleasants concurs with Moody-Adams.

Pleasants diverges from Moody-Adams' position, however, in that it is *not* easy to obtain moral knowledge to critique one's own society. Inability can mean not being able to do something but it can also mean that something is very difficult to do. In regards to institutional ignorance, Pleasants emphasizes that *it is very difficult* to challenge one's cultural norms even if it is not impossible.

Why this is so difficult to do, Pleasants insists, is because what is required to correct such ignorance is a change in what is understood to be *morally relevant*. Culture may normalize the way we comprehend issues so that certain issues that should be morally relevant do not seem to be so. Affected ignorance in the realm of institutional wrongdoing is not about

> individuals affecting ignorance over their personal involvement in something that they know to be morally wrong, but of affecting ignorance over whether something is morally wrong.[67]

Affective ignorance, according to Pleasants, is about an unwillingness to be open to a perceptual change. It may be difficult to make this perceptual change, yet not unachievable. Pleasants cautions us not to conflate individual with institutional wrongdoing so that we can more clearly assess when ignorance is affected and so that we can acknowledge what exactly must be done to counter ignorance.

Like Pleasants, Cheshire Calhoun[68] also focuses on normalized wrongdoing connected to socially sanctioned ignorance. She opens her essay with a provocative quote from Sandra Lee Bartky who points to an "inability to know" that feminists are often troubled with.

> Feminist consciousness is often afflicted with category confusion—an inability to know how to classify things.[69]

Part of the reason for such confusion, for such inability to know, according to Calhoun, stems from "the atypical character of the wrongdoing that feminists critique."[70] The confusion is a product of the double vision that characterizes feminist consciousness, a vision of victimization and, simultaneously, of offense. Calhoun notes that

> Unlike ordinary cases of individual wrongdoing, oppressive wrongdoing often occurs as the level of *social practice*, where social acceptance of a practice

impedes the individual's awareness of wrongdoing. Thus questions about moral responsibility become very difficult questions about how to weigh the social determinants producing moral ignorance against the individual's competence to engage in moral reasoning. . . .[71]

It is because the wrongdoing is socially sanctioned, the wrongdoing "stands a much greater chance of being perpetuated by its very normalcy,"[72] thus, the ensuing confusion.

For instance, according to Calhoun, most of the perpetrators and supporters of patriarchy are not vicious monsters but ordinary men.

Without the ordinary man's participation in routine social practices—in marriage, in the workplace, in daily conversation—oppression would not take the universal form it does.[73]

But then Calhoun wants to understand, "How do we locate individual responsibility when oppression occurs at the level of social practice?"[74]

Calhoun, like Pleasants and Moody-Adams, rejects Wolf's "inability thesis" but she puts emphasis on *abnormal* social contexts. Although ignorant, ordinary men have full moral capacities. Their ignorance, Calhoun argues, is related to their living in "abnormal" social contexts. Calhoun argues that ignorance in abnormal contexts differs from ignorance in normal contexts because the ignorance is social and systemic. Such ignorance is not only attributable to the feature of particular individuals but is systemic. Moreover, such ignorance occurs in individuals that generally possess good moral reasoning.

Under normal contexts, Calhoun argues, right or wrong is "transparent" to the individual. By that she does not mean that the morality of an action is self-evident but instead that participants in such a context "share a common moral language, agree for the most part on moral rules, and use similar methods of moral reasoning."[75] Under abnormal conditions, in contrast, moral ignorance is widespread because it has become the norm. In abnormal moral contexts, it is possible to be ignorant and still be considered or conceive of oneself as a moral person. Similar to what has been noted about white complicity, systemic benefit is related to such ignorance.

One of the points stressed by feminists is that men's benefiting from oppressive social practices provides them with a *motive* for resisting critical reflection and for exercising self-deception about their own motives and about the consequences for women of their actions.[76]

According to Calhoun, however, it is not that those who benefit from patriarchy are motivated not to examine their moral grammar. Rather, they lack a motive to consider certain practices *as morally relevant to begin with*. Since this is not self-deception, Calhoun does not hold men to be morally responsible for their behavior. It is for this reason, I am arguing, that what is required is a new conception of moral responsibility that captures the moral relevance of such practices.

That Calhoun lacks such a notion of responsibility becomes evident when, in an extremely striking move, she insists that these men *should still be reproached and not excused.* Calhoun offers three reasons for this conclusion. First, if we do not reproach such behavior it may seem that such action is sanctioned. In abnormal contexts, excusing someone by saying that one is not responsible can have the consequence of conveying the message that the behavior is not really wrong. Second, when such wrongs are excused, those who actually do right are presumed to be supererogatory and going above and beyond what is actually expected of them when in fact they are only doing what everyone should be doing. Finally, Calhoun is concerned that without reproach, we set up a view of the individual as lacking agency to change. In other words, in abnormal contexts even when individuals are not blameworthy, it is reasonable to reproach institutionally sanctioned moral failings.

By using the word *reproach*, it is clear that Calhoun is attempting to extricate herself from the problem of blaming individuals for something she believes they are somehow not blameworthy for. Even if there is no justification for such reproach (because the person is not blameworthy), there is a point for such reproach and that being the educational aim of raising awareness of the moral issues that are not recognized. Without reproach, Calhoun intimates, one would not be motivated to act otherwise.

Building upon Calhoun's argument that diminished responsibility is a consequence *not of the agent doing what was wrong thinking it was right* but rather the *agent not knowing that the issue is morally relevant,* Tracy Isaacs[77] argues that when men do not even know that some practice has moral import, they should not be held accountable. When some members of a group, however, *refuse to consider* what the sub group is telling them, their ignorance may certainly be affected ignorance. As an illustration, she explains that when writers who use sexist language are ignorant of the moral dimension of sexist language they should not be held accountable. When they know (and few writers can claim today not to know) but then ignore what everyone else knows is a morally relevant issue, then they should be held responsible.

Few people who write for a living can actually claim to be ignorant of the issue of nonsexist language; by this point they likely have a view about the matter, and whatever their view they must recognize it as a morally charged issue. It is no longer possible seriously to claim, "Well, I was always taught that 'he' is gender neutral, and no one has ever suggested otherwise."[78]

When such writers profess ignorance, after many have claimed that the issue is morally relevant, this is affected ignorance and they are responsible. There is no way they cannot have known that sexist language has moral consequences.

While there is much in this debate that can help us to understand white ignorance and white complicity, the conception of responsibility is still too wedded to notions of blame and fault. Thus it should not be surprising that determinations of responsibility are reduced to willfulness or choice. While white ignorance may be the result of a deliberate and conscious decision to ignore, this is not always the case. If we apply what Tracy Isaacs contends about writers, white ignorance can be a form of affective ignorance. Clearly, Issacs recognizes the systemic nature of such ignorance. Yet, as I have argued in Chapter 2, white ignorance is not always an issue of affecting ignorance about the moral relevance of a practice about which there is social consensus. Traditional tools to determine responsibility, therefore, may be ineffective in exposing responsibility for white complicity.

The problem is not with making traditional notions of responsibility apply to white complicity but rather the problem is that we need another notion of responsibility. Although white ignorance is not necessarily affected ignorance, white ignorance prevents white complicity from being acknowledged. White ignorance does not absolve one from moral responsibility because it is a characteristic of systemic privilege that benefits white people whether or not they are cognizant of their privilege. Even when white people are cognizant of such privilege and want to denounce it, privilege continues to stick, as Sara Ahmed[79] insists, often in very subtle way. If all white people benefit from systemic white privilege and whiteness sticks to them, then *all* white people are implicated in the maintenance and perpetuation of systemic racial injustice. Before examining attempts to rearticulate moral responsibility, there is one last debate in the responsibility literature that might be useful to examine.

THE "ALL ARE COMPLICIT" PROBLEM

The white complicity claim maintains that all whites are complicit in systemic racial injustice and this claim sometimes takes the form of "all whites are racist." When white complicity takes the latter configuration what is implied is *not* that all whites are racially prejudiced but rather that all whites participate in and, often unwittingly, maintain the racist system of which they are part and from which they benefit. Philosophers have debated the general question whether responsibility can be shared across *all* members of a particular group and, in particular, have been skeptical about the claim that all whites are racist. There are two main albeit related objections to the "all are complicit/responsible" claim. The first can be referred to as "the disappearing problem," while the second can be described as "the equalizing problem." Although in both cases responsibility disappears, each objection highlights different sides of the same coin.

After World War II, a haunting question was debated (and is still debated[80]) among scholars as to whether *all* Germans were "guilty" for the atrocities committed by the Nazi regime. On the one hand, many of the younger Germans maintained that they *felt* guilty for the horrors perpetrated by Nazi regime. At the Nuremberg trials in 1946, Hans Frank confessed his role in Nazi crimes and declared, "A thousand years will pass and this guilt of Germany will not be erased."[81] On the other hand, while some Germans clearly had a direct link to the atrocities, many Germans were ordinary people who tried to go about their daily lives and just obeyed the laws of their country. The "disappearing problem" is illustrated in some of the arguments put forth as to why all Germans should not be held responsible for the atrocities that were perpetrated in the name of Nazi Germany.

Some scholars contended that all Germans were guilty. In his seminal work, *The Question of German Guilt*, that has become a paradigm for studying collective guilt, Karl Jaspers, the eminent German psychiatrist and philosopher, maintained that although all Germans are not collectively *criminally* guilty of crimes committed by the Nazis, they share *political* guilt because the members of a nation "must answer for its polity."[82] Because the German people contributed to and/or tolerated the creation of an "atmosphere of submission"[83] that maintains a repressive regime they bear responsibility collectively for the act of violence perpetrated by Hitler's Third Reich.

Jaspers distinguishes between political and criminal guilt that are public and involve the judgment of others, and moral and metaphysical guilt that are private and involve one's own conscience. Criminal guilt involves those acts for which one may be held liable for punishment in a court of law. Political guilt involves the collective responsibility one bears for a political community by virtue of membership in that community. While the Germans as a people share political guilt, they do not bear criminal guilt. According to Jaspers, one can only punish an individual for a crime. All Germans, therefore, should not be brought to trial for war crimes. That all Germans are collectively responsible in the sense of political guilt was not, however, Jaspers' main concern. Rather he was interested in the degree that all Germans should personally *feel* co-responsible. According to Jaspers, to various degrees, each German incurs moral and metaphysical guilt.

Moral guilt is a consequence of violating moral principle whether by conforming to, supporting or failing to resist an immoral regime because of self-interest or perhaps a lack of sensitivity to the suffering of others. Metaphysical guilt, on the other hand, as already noted in the first chapter, involves a failure to show "absolute solidarity"[84] with one's fellow human beings. As human beings, we are co-responsible in the sense of metaphysical complicity if we stand by inactively and let fellow human beings be violated. According to Jaspers, all Germans incur political guilt, as a collective, and, individually, moral and metaphysical guilt to varying degrees although they are not all criminally guilty. Without recognition of political, moral and metaphysical guilt, without feeling this sentiment of guilt, Jaspers thought cultural and political renewal would not be possible.

Hannah Arendt, Jaspers' former student, however, insisted that all Germans were not guilty. Agreeing with Jaspers that Germans are not criminally culpable for crimes done in their name, Arendt rejects Jaspers emphasis on guilt as a means of purification. Arendt makes a sharp distinction between collective responsibility and personal guilt. Guilt and blame, Arendt argues, cannot be applied to entire groups. Guilt can only be ascribed to individual actions. The "disappearing argument" crops up in Arendt's reasons for why all Germans cannot be guilty.

In the beginning of her essay, "Collective Responsibility,"[85] Arendt maintained that "there is no such thing as being or feeling guilty for things that happened without oneself actively participating in them."[86] Yet Arendt was also clearly disturbed by the postwar German cry, "We are all guilty." She believed this claim was both self-indulgent and obscurant. The logic of such confessions of guilt, she explains,

> . . . at first hearing sounded so very noble . . . (but) has actually only served to exculpate to a considerable degree those who actually were guilty. Where all are guilty, nobody is. Guilt, unlike responsibility, always singles out; it is strictly personal. It refers to an act, not to intentions or potentialities.[87]

When Germans who did not directly contribute to Nazi crimes say they feel guilty, Arendt explains, they are being self-indulgent and this can lead to "a phony sentimentality in which all real issues are obscured."[88] Arendt notes that while many Germans were indulging in confessions of guilt, those who were guilty but felt no remorse continued to hold government positions. In even more powerful terms, Arendt claims that the cry "We are all guilty" is "actually a declaration of solidarity with the wrongdoers."[89] In a profound argument that has resonance for white complicity, Arendt argued that what Germans need to do is to invest energies in political change rather than to think that confessions of guilt would purify them.

Moreover, in a clear reference to "the disappearing objection," Arendt noticed how the discourse of "we are all guilty" could function to excuse those who *are* personally guilty. If all are equally guilty, Arendt insists, no one can be considered guiltier than anyone else. Eichmann, for instance, could then have argued that if all are guilty then he cannot be held to be guilty more than anyone else. He was just obeying orders and responsibly doing his job. His misfortune was to have had the horrible job that he had. Why should he be held individually accountable? When people are fungible and anyone could have done what the perpetrator has done under the same conditions it makes no sense to blame a particular individual. Responsibility that is shared by so many people, the reasoning goes, loses its potency and effectiveness. In both cases, responsibility disappears.

Arendt, however, rejects this logic because she wants to hold on to the claim that the Germans are in some sense responsible. While Jaspers maintained that guilt was necessary for acknowledging complicity, Arendt maintained that such self-regarding sentiments drew attention away from real political change. Both Jaspers and Arendt agreed that Germans were in some sense responsible and they each struggled to articulate that responsibility. They also both maintained that everyone is not equally responsible. To brand those who resist in the face of wrong along with those who do not does not seem to make much sense.

Which leads to the "equalizing objection." If all are responsible, does it entail that everyone is *equally* responsible? Here the concern is less with the disappearance of responsibility and more with the loss of *criteria* to distinguish the good from the bad, the innocent from the guilty. How can the same concept of responsibility be applied to the perpetrators of the crime and to those who did not directly cause the harm? H.D. Lewis,[90] who insists that individuals are the center of ascriptions of responsibility, has referred to this move as the "equalizing objection." If we "equalize" moral judgments by distributing it equally over all in a group without consideration of what the individual contributed to outcome, we forfeit any way to distinguish between good and bad, innocent and guilty individuals. If principals and accessories are equally responsible, accessories will be judged too harshly while principals will get off too easily.

Furthermore, what about those who dissent, who publicly oppose evil? Doesn't dissent remove one from responsibility? Howard McGary[91] coined the term the "disassociation condition" for the claim that when one disassociates oneself from evil practices, one is free of shared responsibility. Dissent is always possible, as McGary explains,

A crucial aspect of the disassociation condition is the avenues of action available for disassociation. The avenues of action will be political as well as legal. For example, when chattel slavery was legal in this country, there were laws that closed most of the legal avenues open to those who opposed slavery, but there were still political avenues available, e.g., abolitionist movements. Some people took those avenues available to them and thus they succeeded in disassociating themselves from the horrible practice of slavery.[92]

As discussed in the previous section, Larry May also insists that when one registers opposition one is freed from blame. In addition, May argues for a scalar measure of responsibility. In other words, responsibility should never be ascribed equally but rather in different degrees.

Lawrence Blum[93] offers an interesting perspective that is relevant to white complicity when he argues *against* the claim that all white people are racist. It is clear that Blum recognizes that white people are complicit in systemic racial injustice. Yet he insists that racism should not be equated with having white privilege and that racism should not be defined in a manner that would imply that all whites are racist. The tendency towards "conceptual conflation" or the overuse and overextension of the term racist to cover all sorts of racial behavior, Blum argues, imperils the moral opprobrium of the term. If the only choice available to us is whether a practice is racist or not, Blum is concerned that certain racially wrong practices will be dismissed. Instead he suggests that we distinguish between a variety of racial wrongs and racism proper. For Blum, it is important to distinguish both between different types of racism (intentional and unintentional) and also different degrees of blame.

Although not explicitly a response to the "equalizing objection," Blum clearly wants to ensure that the term "racist" is reserved for the most morally abhorrent forms of racial behavior, beliefs and actions but also does not want unintentional actions to escape accountability. This is a courageous balancing act, for sure. His proposal is to distinguish between racist and racial incidents.

> Not every instance of racial conflict, insensitivity, discomfort, miscommunication, exclusion, injustice, or ignorance should be called "racist." Not all *racial* incidents are *racist* incidents. We need a more varied and nuanced moral vocabulary for talking about the domain of race.[94]

Through the distinction between racist and racial, Blum is able to delineate different degrees of racial culpability.

It is primarily for this reason that Blum finds definitions that equate white privilege with racism problematic. If every act that contributes to or sustains white privilege is racist, the ability to distinguish intentional, race-based exclusions from unintentional stereotyping or cultural ignorance disappears. And this distinction is crucial for Blum. His aim is to keep unintentional acts accountable but not to the same degree that the term "racist" would imply. Blum worries that if racism is understood as an all-or-nothing matter, unintentional stereotyping and cultural ignorance may be dismissed as not being racist and the ability to describe these acts as racial wrongs may be lost.

Blum, therefore, restricts the term "racist" to those actions, beliefs, institutions and policies that involve inferiorization and/or antipathy toward a racial group. Thus, if one holds no antipathy towards Blacks and/or if one is not inferiorizing Blacks, then one should not be considered racist. Blum rejects definitions of racism that put so much emphasis on the *system* of racism that they draw attention away from the *individual*. Concerned to develop ways to describe racially related wrongs that are "less morally evil"[95] than the term racism itself implies and alarmed at the consequences of making racism an all-or-nothing matter, Blum provides a compelling argument as to why different degrees of racism must be delineated.

Blum's proposal is of particular interest because it is also motivated by pedagogical concerns. Blum is troubled about the pedagogical consequences of teaching that all white people are racist. Since the term "racist" is morally charged (and he insists that it should continue to function as a severe condemnation) and since most whites want very much to avoid being accused of racism, Blum envisions (correctly, I believe) that white students who are accused of being racist will tend more towards defensively trying to exonerate themselves from the charge of racism than towards engaging in intercultural communication.

As a philosopher of education and someone who has taught courses about race and racism, I resonate with Blum's pedagogical concerns. Nevertheless, I find his suggestion of substituting "racial" for "racist" to describe race-related practices problematic. Blum's distinction between "racial" and "racist" assumes that certain types of violence are more harmful than others, i.e., racist harms are worse than racial ones. There are a number of dangers in this move that I would like to address. The first involves the recognition that constructing a contrast between "bad" whites and "less bad" whites can contribute to white distancing strategies that whites use to demonstrate their innocence. Many of the scholars who study white denials of complicity observe how white students explicitly make reference in their white talk to family members or friends who are "really" racist in order to protect their own racial standing. The implication is "*I* am not like *them*."

Second, by defining racism exclusively in terms of intentional antipathy or inferiorization, Blum implies that unintentional racism is somehow less harmful, since less violent. The risk, however, is in minimizing the violence perpetuated by social norms that Judith Butler struggles to make visible and that have been discussed in Chapter 3. Blum's scalar approach to responsibility similarly may also lead to a trivialization of the harms of microaggressions. From the viewpoint of the systemically privileged who do not have to endure these harms, such harms traditionally appear as having less weight. As Charles Lawrence III explains,

> The institutionalization of white supremacy within our culture has created conduct on the societal level that is greater than the sum of individual racist acts.

The racist acts of millions are mutually reinforcing and cumulative because the status quo of institutionalized white supremacy remains long after deliberate racist actions subside.[96]

Moreover, one could argue that the racism that well-meaning whites perpetuate is even more destructive than the overt violence inspired by hate because the racism perpetuated by good whites is so often invisible to them and hidden by their helpful and well-intended practices. Such racism becomes immune to disruption.

While I believe Blum recognizes this, the point gets thrust into the background by his focus on the fault of the perpetrator and his concern to minimize white guilt. What makes Blum's work perplexing is that he clearly acknowledges personal, institutional and structural racism and how they are intertwined but, as Anna Stubblefield contends,

> . . . he does not follow this understanding to its conclusion. "Lesser" and/or "unintentional" acts of racism contribute as much to the maintenance of a racist society as intentional and/or overt acts. When we take the latter as paradigmatic or definitional, we lose the big picture.[97]

The validity of scalar conceptions of responsibility, as Kurt Baier[98] argues, depends on what is meant by responsibility. When responsibility is primarily conceived as fault, accountability or culpability, it makes sense to talk of degrees of responsibility. There may, however, be different conceptions of responsibility that need to be considered especially given the pedagogical aims that Blum wants to achieve.

In addition, if we recall Alison Bailey's caution about writing the victims' interpretation of the harms out of the story, skepticism is raised about the efficacy of labeling a practice "racial" instead of "racist." Although this move might help to prevent white people from becoming defensive, this may *not* result in improved cross-racial dialogue or better listening on the part of white students, as Blum assumes. Students of color may perceive the distinction between "racial" and "racist" as a distancing strategy to protect white innocence with the consequence that cross-racial dialogue would be impeded rather than improved. This possibility becomes more pronounced if white denials of complicity are as pervasive as has been argued in previous chapters and if white people often use anything to avoid engaging with their role in the perpetuation of racially unjust systems.

Blum's approach remains focused on the perpetuator's perspective and assumes a particular notion of responsibility that is focused on fault. Those who are harmed must not be written out of the picture. My experience in the classroom has been that white students who protect their moral status frustrate and justifiably anger students of color. Yes, white students have a problem listening to students of color because they feel threatened. Being called "racist" exacerbates white attempts to exonerate themselves. Yet even before the R word is even raised, white students are busy proving their moral innocence and the reason they feel so able to do this may be attributed to the problematic concept of moral responsibility they have available to them.

This chapter has offered some support to the claim that attempts to protect white moral innocence are validated by a particular notion of moral responsibility. Thus, I argue that it is conceptions of moral responsibility that must first change before discussions of the definitions of racism can be addressed.

Iris Marion Young contends that the various attempts in the philosophical scholarship to incorporate individual liability within collective or shared responsibility result in a weaker sense of responsibility. Young is specifically concerned with responsibility for structural injustice and insists that what is required is not a *weaker* sense of responsibility but a *different* kind of responsibility that encourages individuals to take responsibility for what is wrong and collectively work to change it. I want to close this chapter with a brief discussion about why this matters. In brief, this matters because the interpretation of moral responsibility that frames one's understanding of morality will strongly influence how one understands white complicity and how to respond to it.

COMPLICITY IN PHILOSOPHY AND THE COMPLICITY OF PHILOSOPHY

The philosophical scholarship on complicity has provided some interesting insights but has not been very helpful in bringing white complicity to the forefront of our attention. First of all, philosophers have generally been interested in complicity as a concern with how someone can be responsible for something that *other* people have done. When causal attempts to connect the individual to harm they did not perpetrate fail, some philosophers have shifted their attention to intentional participation in collective harm. Even when complicity is raised as a question of culpable ignorance, still most philosophers search for some volitional tidbit upon which to hang ascriptions of responsibility. None of these approaches are helpful in illuminating the responsibility of white complicity that often involves unintentional and non-volitional participation in a system which one perpetuates by one's white practices and habits but also through systemic benefits that are normalized so that they are not perceived as privileges.

Second, in their discussions of complicity most philosophers have focused on blatant wrongs that have reached a terminus. Yet, as Iris Marion Young emphasizes, the harms of structural injustice are ongoing and are often considered the normal state of affairs. Some philosophers have discussed the background conditions that make wrongs possible especially around the topic of affected ignorance. Yet even here, the emphasis has been on finding a volitional moment that links the wrong to responsibility. When complicity is recognized in this scholarship as the product of social practices, blameworthiness is often denied, even if reproach is considered appropriate. Systemic benefit is sometimes acknowledged but never adequately elaborated as connected to systemic ignorance. How systemic ignorance works hand in hand to keep the status quo in place and whether it is possible to voluntarily denounce one's privilege are either ignored or under-theorized. Nor do philosophers who focus on volition take into consideration how systemic privilege is reflected in the very choices one makes and the very things one chooses to give attention to. If we employed the understanding of complicity that most philosophers assume either white complicity would remain invisible or if it became visible, it would not be connected to moral responsibility.

Finally, from the three areas of philosophical discussion associated with complicity addressed in this chapter, it seems clear that the understanding of responsibility that many philosophers work with is focused excessively on some type of causality or control and functions to determine blame and fault. Such a conception of responsibility does not help to name white complicity and may even hide it.

The aforementioned discussions about complicity in the philosophical scholarship are admittedly far from exhaustive. The brief account sketched, however, provides some evidence that philosophical theories of both individual and group-based complicity and culpable ignorance would not bring white complicity to our attention and may even obscure the relationship between white complicity and responsibility. That white people are implicated in an unjust racial system from which they gain systemic benefit and that they reinscribe (most often unwittingly) existing power relations even despite their best intentions cannot be accounted for in the interesting yet inadequate group-based notions of responsibility that are offered by May and Kutz. Nor can most philosophical scholarship on culpable ignorance explain why white people are responsible for their role in maintaining white ignorance. Most importantly, these approaches cannot expose for interrogation how denials of complicity can be supported by white moral sensibilities or how whiteness can be reinscribed even when good intentions to challenge racism are present.

Recall that Kutz writes about traditional conceptions of responsibility that ". . . where individualistic principles (of accountability) *exculpate*, the principle of complicity *implicates*."[99] In addition, he notes,

So long as individuals are only responsible for the effects they produce, then the result of this disparity between collective harm and individual effect is the *disappearance of individual accountability*.[100]

It matters how concepts are defined. A concept can be defined in such a way as to preclude the ability to perceive the social reality of white complicity or even raise awareness of its possibility. As Charles Mills reminds us, "concepts orient us to the world."[101] We understand social reality through the concepts that are available to us. Kutz emphasizes then that it is not just that individualistic principles of accountability do not capture the type of complicity he insists is rampant; it is also that such principles *exonerate* such complicity. Thus, it is important to consider how the concepts we are using might not only be encouraging distortion of social reality but also erasing accountability.

In her discussion of backgrounds that become normalized so that they are just taken for granted and never interrogated, Peg O'Connor maintains that "(p)hilosophy has done its share in contributing to the inability to see backgrounds."[102] She specifically targets philosophy's tendency to presume a particular subject.

The history of Western philosophy is a history of the isolated, autonomous, and atomistic self—the epistemological subject and moral agent—who confronts/ knows/acts in the world *out there* by using his rationality/knowledge/attitudes *in here*. . . . This picture, I argue, has contributed to a host of social harms.[103]

White complicity can be hidden when the notion of the subject underlying principles of accountability are overly individualistic and when conceptions of moral responsibility are similarly individualistic. And as O'Connor highlights, "What is hidden, why it is hidden, and how it remains hidden are all philosophically, politically, and morally compelling questions."[104]

Ultimately much of the philosophical scholarship on complicity depends on a particular conception of moral responsibility that emphasizes fault and blameworthiness or remains haunted by it. In the next chapter, a conception of moral responsibility will be developed that can help to expose rather than conceal white complicity.

NOTES

1. John Gardner, "Complicity and Causality," *Criminal Law and Philosophy* 1, no. 2 (2007): 127–141.
2. Alexander Solzhenitsyn, *One Word of Truth* (London: Bodley Head, 1971) as cited by Gardner, "Complicity and Causality," 127.
3. John Gardner, "Complicity and Causality," 136.
4. Lindsay Farmer, "Complicity Beyond Causality: A Comment," *Criminal Law and Philosophy* 1, no. 2 (2007): 151–156.
5. Ibid., 154.
6. Ibid.
7. Ibid., 155.

8. Ibid.
9. Christopher Kutz, *Complicity: Ethics and Law for a Collective Age* (Cambridge: Cambridge University Press, 2000).
10. Ibid., 1.
11. Ibid., 116–117.
12. Ibid., 50.
13. Ibid., 113, emphasis added.
14. Ibid., 123.
15. Christopher Kutz, *Complicity*, 557.
16. Ibid., 122.
17. Ibid.
18. Ibid.
19. Ibid., 7.
20. Ibid., emphasis in original.
21. Ibid., 9.
22. Larry May, *Sharing Responsibility* (Chicago: University of Chicago Press, 1992).
23. See Peter French (ed.) *Individual and Collective Responsibility* (Rochester VT: Schenkman, 1998); Larry May and Stacey Hoffman (eds.) *Collective Responsibility: Five Decades of Debate in Theoretical and Applied Ethics* (Savage MD: Rowman and Littlefield, 1991).
24. Larry May, *Sharing Responsibility*, 106.
25. Ibid., 53.
26. Ibid., 253.
27. Ibid., 19.
28. Ibid., 53.
29. Ibid., 149.
30. Cassie Striblen, "Guilt, Shame, and Shared Responsibility," *Journal of Social Philosophy* 38, no. 3 (2007): 469–485.
31. Larry May and Robert Strikwerda, "Men in Groups: Collective Responsibility for Rape," *Hypatia* 9, no. 2 (1994): 134–151.
32. Ibid., 127.
33. Ibid., 126.
34. Ibid., 148.
35. Larry May, *Sharing Responsibility*, 120.
36. Cassie Striblen, "Guilt, Shame, and Shared Responsibility," 477–478.
37. Larry May, *Sharing Responsibility*, 68, emphasis added.
38. Ibid., 44.
39. Shannon Sullivan, *Revealing Whiteness: The Unconscious Habits of Racial Privilege* (Bloomington, IN: Indiana University Press, 2006).
40. Peg O'Connor, "If Everyone's Responsible, Then Nobody Is," in her *Oppression and Responsibility: A Wittgensteinian Approach to Social Practices and Moral Theory* (University Park, PA: Pennsylvania State University Press, 2002), 121.
41. Sara Ahmed, "Declarations of Whiteness: The Non-Performativity of Anti-Racism," *borderlands* e-journal 3, no. 2 (2004) http://www.borderlands.net.au/vol3no2_2004/ahmed_declarations.htm (accessed July 19, 2009).

42. Sara Ahmed, "The Phenomenology of Whiteness," *Feminist Theory* 8, no. 2 (2007): 149–168.

43. Alison Bailey, "Taking Responsibility for Community Violence," in *Feminists Doing Ethics,* ed. Peggy DesAutels and Joanne Waugh (Totowa, New Jersey: Rowman and Littlefield, 2001), 219–234.

44. Ibid., 226.

45. Daniel Solorzano, Miguel Ceja and Tara Yosso, "Critical Race Theory, Racial Microaggressions, and Campus Racial Climate: the Experience of African American College Students," *Journal of Negro Education* 69, no. 1–2 (2000): 60–73.

46. Ibid., 60.

47. Chester Pierce, "Psychiatric Problems of the Black Community," in *American Handbook of Psychiatry,* ed. Silvano Arieti (New York: Basic Books, 1974), 516.

48. Sandra Lee Bartky, "Phenomenology of Feminist Consciousness," in her *Femininity and Domination: Studies in the Phenomenology of Oppression* (New York: Routledge, 1990), 18, emphasis mine.

49. "Biden's Description of Obama Draws Scrutiny," http://edition.cnn.com/2007/POLITICS/01/31/biden.obama/ (accessed November 25, 2009).

50. Larry May, *Sharing Responsibility,* 62–64.

51. Aristotle, *Nichomachean Ethics,* translated by Terence Irwin, 2nd edition (Indianapolis, Indiana: Hackett, 350 BCE/1999), Book III.

52. Ibid., 1111a.

53. Holly Smith, "Culpable Ignorance," *The Philosophical Review* 92, no. 4 (1983): 543–571.

54. Charles Mills, *The Racial Contract,* 20–21.

55. Ibid., 11.

56. Peg O'Connor, "If Everybody's Responsible, Then Nobody Is," 128.

57. Michael Slote, "Is Virtue Possible?" *Analysis* 42, no. 2 (1982): 72.

58. Bernard Williams, *Shame and Necessity,* (Berkeley CA: University of California Press, 1993), 124.

59. Susan Wolf, *Freedom within Reason* (New York: Oxford University Press, 1990).

60. Susan Wolf, *Freedom within Reason,* 118.

61. Susan Wolf, "Sanity and the Metaphysics of Responsibility," in *The Inner Citadel: Essays on Autonomy,* ed. John Christman (Oxford: Oxford University Press, 1989), 146.

62. Michelle Moody-Adams, "Culture, Responsibility, and Affected Ignorance," *Ethics* 104, no. 2 (1994): 291–309.

63. Michelle Moody-Adams, *Fieldwork in Familiar Places: Morality, Culture and Philosophy* (Cambridge, MA: Harvard University Press, 1997), 102, emphasis added.

64. Ibid., 292.

65. Nigel Pleasants, "Institutional Wrongdoing and Moral Perception," *Journal of Social Philosophy* 39, no. 1 (Spring 2008): 96–115.

66. Ibid., 96.

67. Ibid., 112.

68. Cheshire Calhoun, "Responsibility and Reproach," *Ethics* 99, no. 2 (1989): 389–406.

69. Sandra Lee Bartky, *Femininity and Domination: Studies in the Phenomenology of Oppression*, 18.
70. Cheshire Calhoun, "Responsibility and Reproach," 389.
71. Ibid., 389, emphasis in original.
72. Ibid., 389.
73. Ibid., 390.
74. Ibid.
75. Ibid., 394.
76. Ibid., 399.
77. Tracy Isaacs, "Cultural Context and Moral Responsibility," *Ethics* 107, no. 4 (1997): 670–684.
78. Ibid., 682.
79. Sara Ahmed, *The Cultural Politics of Emotions* (New York: Routledge, 2004). Also see her "Declarations of Whiteness: The Non-Performativity of Anti-racism."
80. Daniel Jonah Goldhagen, *Hitler's Willing Executioners: Ordinary Germans and the Holocaust* (New York: Knopf, 1996).
81. Klaus P. Fischer, *Nazi Germany: A New History* (New York: Continuum, 1997) as cited at http://mars.wnec.edu/~grempel/courses/hitler/lectures/german_guilt.html (accessed November 25, 2009).
82. Karl Jaspers, *The Question of German Guilt* (Westport, Connecticut: Greenwood, 1948/1978), 61.
83. Ibid., 78.
84. Ibid., 32.
85. Hannah Arendt, "Collective Responsibility."
86. Ibid., 147.
87. Ibid.
88. Ibid., 148.
89. Ibid.
90. H. D. Lewis, "Collective Responsibility," in *Collective Responsibility: Five Decades of Debate in Theoretical and Applied Ethics*, ed. Larry May and Stacey Hoffman (Savage, MD: Rowman and Littlefield, 1991), 21–22.
91. Howard McGary, "Morality and Collective Liability," *Journal of Value Inquiry* 20, no. 2 (1986): 157–165.
92. Ibid., 163.
93. Lawrence Blum, "What Is 'Racism' in Antiracist Education?" *Teachers College Record* 100, no. 4 (Summer 1999): 860–880; also see his *"I'm Not A Racist, But . . . ": The Moral Quandary of Race* (Ithaca: Cornell University Press, 2002).
94. Lawrence Blum, *"I'm Not A Racist, But . . . ,"* 2.
95. Lawrence Blum, *"I'm Not A Racist, But . . . ,"* 13.
96. Charles R. Lawrence III, "If He Hollers Let Him Go: Regulating Racist Speech on Campus," in *Words That Wound: Critical Race Theory, Assaultive Speech, and The First Amendment*, ed. Marie Matsuda (Boulder, CO: Westview Press, 1993), 61.
97. Anna Stubblefield, "Review of Lawrence Blum, *'I'm Not a Racist, But . . . ,'*" *Socialism and Democracy Online* 17, no. 2 (2003): 239–244, http://www.sdonline.org/34/anna_stubblefield.htm (accessed July 24, 2009).

98. Kurt Baier, "Guilt and Responsibility" in *Collective Responsibility: Five Decades of Debate in Theoretical and Applied Ethics*, 211–213.
99. Christopher Kutz, *Complicity*, 122, emphasis added.
100. Ibid., 113, emphasis added.
101. Charles W. Mills, "White Ignorance," 27.
102. Peg O'Connor, *Oppression and Responsibility*, 7.
103. Ibid., 7–8.
104. Ibid., 20.

CHAPTER 6

Rearticulating White Moral Responsibility

Understanding how racism works, he (a white man) can see the way in which whiteness acts to terrorize without seeing himself as bad, or all white people as bad, and all black people as good.[1]

This is not about making you feel guilty. This is about understanding how being White has shaped us, as well as provided us with unearned privileges, and armed with this understanding, to do something about racism.[2]

IN THE FIRST CHAPTER OF HIS INSIGHTFUL BOOK, BLACK BODIES, WHITE GAZES: THE *Continuing Significance of Race,* George Yancy[3] explains how his body has been confiscated and blackened by a white woman's gaze in an elevator.

Well-dressed, I enter an elevator where a white woman waits to reach her floor. She "sees" my black body, though not the same one I have seen reflected back to me from the mirror on any number of occasions. Buying into the myth that one's dress says something about the person, one might think that the markers of my dress (suit and tie) should ease her tension. What is it that makes the markers of my dress inoperative? . . . Over and above how my body is clothed, she "sees" a criminal, she sees me as a threat . . .[4]

Yancy describes the white woman's behavior and bodily comportment on the basis of the history of the experiences of many black men in elevators with white women. The white woman appears uncomfortable and she displays signs of apprehension. She clutches her purse as if to protect it, her eyes not daring to meet his. It appears as if these brief moments in the elevator, for her, are experienced as an eternity.

Challenged to justify his observations, Yancy maintains that white "seeing" is mediated through historically structured forms of "knowledge" or "lack of knowledge considered as knowledge" that mark black men's bodies as criminal even when enveloped in upper-class apparel. Tacit racist scripts frame whitely-being-in-the world so that how whites "see" others is not transparent but a "reading." As Yancy puts it, "She performs her white body, ergo, I 'become' the predatory Black."[5] Co-constitutively, such mediated "seeing" shapes and sustains white innocence. Yancy explains that

> . . . not only does the white woman in the elevator ontologically freeze my 'dark' embodied identity *but she also becomes ontologically frozen in her own embodied (white) identity.* . . . She "sees," but does not necessarily reflect upon, herself as normative, innocent, pure. Her performances reiterate the myth of the *proverbial white victim* at the hands of the Black predator.[6]

The white woman is co-constructed as "not threatening" and morally innocent all the while as she is, as the epigram from bell hooks that opens this chapter intimates, "terrorizing."

Yancy insists her behavior is racist even if she is like the "walking dead" and is "unaware of how the feeling of her white bodily upsurge and expansiveness is purchased at the expense of my Black body independently of any threatening action on my part."[7] Her racist comportment involves "habits of the body and not simply cognitively false beliefs."[8] In other words,

> The white woman is not simply influenced by racist practices, but she is the *vehicle* through which such practices get performed and sustained.[9]

Her gaze is a reiteration of power relations and perpetuates the "larger social racist imaginary" which simultaneously "sanction(s) her performance of the gaze in the first place, guaranteeing its performance with impunity and ensuring material effects on the gazed-upon Black body."[10] Thus, her complicity in racism is not a matter of her intentions nor any consciously held prejudices about the criminality of Black men.

More accurately, her practices are deeply ingrained somatic habits which she reiterates and which are socially sanctioned. Yancy insists that

> to reduce whiteness to a set of false beliefs overlooks the fact that many whites, those who have very honorable intentions, those who might be described as "goodwill" whites, who deny holding racist beliefs, benefit from acting whitely-in-the-world in ways that they themselves may not consciously intend. On this score, benefiting from acting whitely-in-the-world can have negative implications for nonwhites, even if whites are unaware of the consequences of their actions.[11]

One benefits from being whitely. In the elevator, white innocence is purchased on the back of Black criminality even when conscious racist beliefs are obstinately denied.

Such an understanding of what is taking place in the elevator coincides with the provocative insights that Michel Foucault offers about power. Nancy Fraser articulates this well when she writes about the insights (and limitations) of Foucault's work,

> . . . power is in our bodies, not in our heads. When it comes to understanding the hold power has on us, we must look more at our practices than to beliefs in our heads.[12]

From the perspective of common assumptions of responsibility that focus primarily *on what goes on in our heads*, it might be absurd to claim that this woman, whose actions seem unintended and not based on explicitly conscious racist beliefs, is in any way accountable for her responses.

Traditional conceptions of moral responsibility will find it difficult to explain why this woman bears any responsibility for what Yancy claims is happening in the elevator. More significantly, traditional conceptions may provide reasons (more accurately excuses) for believing she is *in no way* responsible and thus promote incredulity in regards to the racial dimension of Yancy's claims. (Yancy, in fact, describes how he has encountered such incredulity and that he analyzes in detail.) If the white woman does not intend to discriminate or if there is no racist belief that can be pointed to, why is she to blame? To understand what Yancy is describing, I submit, we need a conception of responsibility that is different from the standard notion that focuses on blame or liability.

THE SOCIAL CONNECTION MODEL OF RESPONSIBILITY

Iris Marion Young attempts to flesh out responsibility in the context of structural social injustice and offers some optimism for finding a conception of moral responsibility under the condition of complicity. Young is specifically concerned with articulating a conception of responsibility that can account for responsibility for global injustice.[13] The Social Connection Model of Responsibility (SCM) that she develops has links with complicity because the model claims, "all agents who contribute by their actions to the structural processes that produce injustice have responsibilities to work to remedy these injustices."[14]

Young recognizes that the standard model of responsibility that she refers to as "the liability model" cannot explain why individuals who contribute to the perpetuation of global injustice but do not have a direct causal relationship to harm are responsible. She uses the anti-sweatshop movement to demonstrate the logic of the SCM. Anti-sweatshop activists call on consumers to take responsibility for the apparel they purchase that are produced under structurally unjust conditions. Under the liability model of responsibility, it would seem odd to maintain that consumers are responsible for unjust working conditions on the other side of the globe. It would not seem surprising for consumers to disassociate themselves from responsibility by claiming, "We didn't create those unjust conditions. We are not liable; we are not to blame."

Young, however, contends that consumers *are* responsible for their contributions to the perpetuation of structural injustice. She provides a detailed definition of "structural injustice" that can be summed up in these few sentences.

> Structural injustice occurs as a consequence of many individuals and institutions acting in pursuit of their particular goals and interests, within given institutional rules and accepted norms. All the persons who participate by their actions in the ongoing schemes of cooperation that constitute these structures are responsible for them, in the sense that they are part of the process that causes them. They are not responsible, however, in the sense of having directed the process or intended its outcomes.[15]

In other words, social injustice that has structural causes presumes social connections so that all those who participate in producing and reproducing the structures are implicated in the outcomes of those structures. What is required is a conception of responsibility that is derived from our social connections in the sense of "belonging together with others in a system of interdependent processes of cooperation and competition through which we seek benefits and aim to realize projects."[16]

The liability model of responsibility not only cannot explain why those who indirectly contribute to structurally caused harm are responsible, such a model may even provide excuses for why contributors are not to blame. Liability models of responsibility require that a *clear* connection be made between an identifiable individual or group of individuals and the harm be drawn. If structural injustice is the product of the actions of a multitude of persons along with policies that normalize and rationalize such actions, however, in most cases it will be impossible to clearly trace such a causal connection.

According to Young, the liability model of responsibility is fundamentally concerned with finding guilt or fault in the sense of accountability for some wrong. The primary question is "who is to blame for this?" That is why finding a causal connection between the perpetrator(s) and the harm is crucial. Moreover, the actions that caused the wrong must be voluntary and performed with adequate knowledge. Thus, as we have seen in the previous chapter, if an agent's action was not voluntary or if the agent was excusably ignorant, responsibility is diminished or completely dissolved. While strict liability seems to depart from this model in the sense that one is liable even without intention or even when one is unable to control the outcome, Young insists that strict liability nevertheless "shares the conceptual and functional features of the liability model."[17] These conceptual and functional features come into sharper focus when Young defines SCM.

Young defines SCM by contrasting the characteristics of this model with the characteristics of the liability model of responsibility. Before doing so, however, she reminds us that she is not rejecting the liability model but rather contending that the model inadequately confronts responsibility under conditions of structural injustice. She insists, however, that we need both models of responsibility.

Young details the five features of SCM. First of all, SCM does not isolate perpetrators as the liability model demands. The liability model, with its predominant focus on sanctions and compensation, must be able to point to those who are to blame and distinguish them from who are not so that guilt and fault are justifiably applied. Yet under structural injustice harms are the result of "the participation of thousands or millions of people in institutions and practices."[18] Thus, pointing to an isolated perpetrator in order to attribute causal blame is not only difficult but also unfeasible. In addition, where there is structural injustice, even when a guilty perpetrator can be pointed to, this does *not* absolve others who contribute to the reproduction of the conditions of injustice. Isolating and punishing any particular sweatshop owner under the liability model, for instance, does not absolve those who continue to purchase the apparel produced in sweatshops from responsibility in upholding unjust systems. Structural injustice involves systems that are upheld by more than isolated guilty individuals.

The second feature of SCM involves the background conditions of actions. The liability model assumes that what counts as a wrong consists in a deviation from some baseline that is considered normal and acceptable. Consonant with the "abnormal conditions" that Cheshire Calhoun describes and that support widespread moral ignorance (as discussed in the previous chapter), Young understands that under structural injustice it is precisely the "normal background" conditions that are problematic. Unlike the liability model, SCM does not judge harm that deviates from the normal and acceptable but rather "brings into question precisely the background conditions that ascriptions of blame or fault assume as normal."[19] Young elucidates that well-intentioned people going about their daily practices and often habitually following the "accepted and expected rules and conventions"[20] hold structural injustice in place.

SCM is also more forward looking than backward looking. This third feature contrasts sharply with the liability model that is primarily backward looking and concerned with how to hold one accountable for a wrong that has reached a terminus. Structural injustice, however, involves an "ongoing set of processes that we understand is likely to continue producing harms unless there are interventions in it. . . . The injustices produced through structures have not reached a terminus, but rather are ongoing."[21] SCM allows for a notion of responsibility that is not primarily about blame or punishment and thus may be able to motivate those who contribute to sustaining the system to join in the collective process of trying to change it.

This leads to the fourth feature of SCM that focuses on the shared nature of such responsibility. All who contribute by their actions to the production and reproduction of the structural process that lead to the harm are responsible. This entails the final, and extremely significant, characteristic of SCM that emphasizes how such responsibility can only be discharged through collective action. Again, the emphasis is NOT on blame or guilt but instead on "changing the institutions and processes so that their outcomes will be less unjust."[22] As Young powerfully underscores, "No one of us can do this on our own."[23]

As a final and related note, Young highlights the practical advantages of SCM. Since SCM does not focus on fault or blame, it is a concept of responsibility that can help to motivate people to take responsibility for making social change. The liability model, Young argues, too often encourages persons to deny their participation in social injustice.

> The actors addressed hear themselves being blamed for harms. More often than not, agents who believe themselves being blamed react defensively: they look for other agents to blame instead of themselves, or find excuses that mitigate their liability in cases where they admit that their actions do causally contribute to the harm.[24]

The liability model of responsibility, therefore, encourages rather than inhibits denials of complicity. Given that in the context of structural injustice it is not easy to find isolated individuals to blame, employing a liability model of responsibility exclusively promotes the discourse of blame shifting or exoneration. If others are also responsible and if there are socially sanctioned discourses that normalize complicity then complicity becomes what is considered everyday practice. As such, it becomes difficult to discern. Because it does not focus on blame and guilt, SCM has the potential to minimize denials of complicity and instead direct energy towards the possibility of mobilizing collective action for the sake of social change.

Young's SCM of responsibility seems especially suited to explain responsibility for white complicity because white complicity is a form of structural injustice. SCM has the potential to expose rather than conceal white complicity because this model acknowledges that well-intentioned agents, through their everyday practices, play a role in the perpetuation of systemic injustice. SCM also recognizes that structural injustice, of which whiteness is a part, is ongoing and involves the contributions of many people. Such a conception of responsibility shifts attention away from a primary focus on guilt, fault and blame and so can help motivate people to take responsibility instead of deny responsibility. Thus, those who perpetuate systemic injustice may be responsible without being liable.

It could be argued, however, that Young's emphasis on shifting the focus away from blame or fault and her concern with alleviating the perpetrator's discomfort and resentment recenters systemically privileged affect.[25] While I acknowledge this potentially problematic aspect of SCM, it is also important to underscore that Young insists that background conditions must always be critiqued even when such critique is uncomfortable. SCM acknowledges that the norms, such as whiteness, that form the background conditions of our everyday practices require critical analysis and this clearly is not something that will be comfortable for white people to do.

Finally, SCM draws our attention away from focusing solely on the individual and towards understanding how we can work collectively to change norms. Young emphasizes the need for continued vigilance in working against unjust practices that are ongoing. Her focus on such vigilance has the potential to minimize the tendency for "heroism" and "exceptionalism" that is a common white response to anti-racism.

Nevertheless, SCM falls short of adequately accounting for white complicity. First, the agent that her model of responsibility hangs on to is astonishingly abstract given her emphasis on social connections and the relationship between persons and structures. In her earlier work on oppression and on the category of woman,[26] Young has forcefully demonstrated the importance of understanding agents qua members of social groups or serialities. One might specifically recall how, in reference to Heidegger, Young argues that one senses a kind of "thrownness" that characterizes how one's identity is related to being a member of a social group "whose existence and relations one experiences as always already having been."[27]

While in her recent work, Young repeatedly acknowledges that persons occupy different social locations and that social structures put "large groups of people under the systemic threat of domination or deprivation of the means to develop and exercise their capacities, at the same time as these processes enable others to dominate or have a wide range of opportunities for developing and exercising their capacities," missing in her recent work on responsibility is a recognition of this "thrownness." When she claims, "all agents who contribute by their actions to the structural processes that produce injustice have responsibilities to work to remedy these injustices,"[28] one wonders who these agents are? Thus, in her more recent work, Young does not sufficiently critically analyze who is the "I" who is responsible, a point that Judith Butler's work on responsibility can help to remedy.

Second, and related to the above, under SCM, responsibility ends up being exclusively focused on actions and practices that are somewhat separate from how one is constituted. Young ignores how doing is related to subject formation. Although she contends that agents are responsible not for the harms they directly cause but "in the sense that they are part of the process that causes them,"[29] Young focuses on actions that individuals do. Persons are responsible for their active contribution *to the process* that produces outcomes that unjustly harm others. As Jacob Schiff[30] notes,

> She doesn't say that individuals who purchase sweatshop clothing contribute to injustice. She says that such individuals "contribute by their actions to the *processes* that produce unjust outcomes."[31]

While Young's model of responsibility and its emphasis on the connection between individual practices and social structures is appealing, it nevertheless overlooks the deep and entrenched ways in which "doing" is connected to "being," a point that Judith Butler's work underscores so well.

Moreover, Young's model ends up not giving adequate attention to the ways in which those who are responsible *benefit* from their contribution to the processes. The benefits involved in white complicity are different then the material benefits of purchasing apparel. In the aforementioned elevator incident, it is not only that the white women clutching her purse blackens Yancy but also that this somatic habit constitutes her as innocent. SCM seems unable to capture this important detail.

This, however, is not Schiff's point. Schiff maintains that Young underestimates how difficult it is to change our practices. Change is difficult, according to Schiff, because structural injustice is normalized and so pervasive. In an important remark, Schiff notes that in the case of structural injustice, "the immediate facts that we need to notice (our purchasing practices, for instance) are *so* quotidian, and *so* frequent, that they easily escape our attention."[32] This point resonates with the discussion in Chapter 2 of systemic ignorance and socially sanctioned denials of complicity. Schiff points to three dispositions that make it difficult to acknowledge complicity in structural injustice: thoughtlessness, bad faith and misrecognition. These are related to excuses, but as Schiff highlights, "they seem more resilient."[33] Turning to Butler's conception of normative violence and subject formation, I suggest, can better help to explain this unrelenting resilience.

Finally, Young recognizes the importance of critiquing the norms that constitute the background conditions that make it difficult to acknowledge how we are complicit in structural injustice. Yet she assumes that norms are somehow *outside* of us. Instead, Butler draws attention to the materiality of bodies and how material bodies get to mean what they mean as material via regulatory norms. She maintains that subject formation is "*indissociable* from the regulatory norms that govern their materialization and signification of those material effects."[34] How bodies are socially positioned is an effect of discourse and involves regulatory norms.

Whiteness as a regulatory norm compels reiteration of white practices such that even in attempts to act against white norms, as noted in previous chapters, whiteness can be reproduced. For Butler, there is no racial purity or innocence and this does not preclude responsibility but, instead, is a resource for responsibility, as will be subsequently made clear. Butler can complement Young's attempt to rearticulate responsibility because she underscores that to critique norms is to risk one's own subjectivity in that one is constituted by the very norms that one needs to critique.

Bringing Butler into dialogue with Young might seem, as Amy Allen puts it about her own work integrating Foucault, Butler and Arendt, "the height of theoretical poaching."[35] However, I contend that there are some philosophical and ethical commonalities between Young and Butler. Both critique traditional conceptions of responsibility for focusing on fault and blame. Both do not reject the traditional model but merely its exclusiveness in our thinking. Both are concerned with one's responsibility for complicity in systemic injustice and both draw our attention to the need to critique norms, although here is one place that their paths diverge. Young targets norms that are involved in background conditions while Butler draws our attention to normative violence as an inherent aspect of subject formation.

Certainly, Butler's conception of responsibility deviates from Young's in a number of crucial ways. I submit, however, that important insights can be gleaned about responsibility under conditions of white complicity from considering these scholars' rearticulations of responsibility in conjunction. Moreover, although I will not address this in too much detail here, Young's emphasis on the collective action is something sorely lacking in Butler's work, as already noted in Chapter 3.

JUDITH BUTLER AND RESPONSIBILITY

. . . ethics undermines its own credibility when it does not become critique.[36]

In her most recent work, Judith Butler "turns to ethics" and more specifically (like Young) attempts to postulate a new conception of responsibility (but unlike Young) that does not rely on the sovereign subject. Allusions to such a project are already evident in *Excitable Speech* when Butler struggles with a seeming dilemma: Can one be responsible for hate speech if speech cannot be said to originate with the sovereign subject? Butler maintains that an ethics that presumes a sovereign subject is unethical in that it ignores how the subject of ethics is formed. In *Giving an Account of Oneself*, Butler gives a full account of how it is possible to attribute moral responsibility to a subject that is not self-grounding by developing an ethics that is established in the characteristic features of such an understanding of the subject, i.e., its opacity to itself and a vulnerability entailed by the subject's existence being dependent on others. Butler exposes the following question as fundamental for ethics: "How are we formed within social life, *and at what costs?*"[37]

On the one hand, Butler's *Giving an Account of Oneself* is a response to the charge that poststructuralism necessarily results in moral relativism or even moral nihilism. She asks, "does the postulation of a subject who is not self-grounding . . . whose conditions of emergence can never fully be accounted for, undermine the possibility of responsibility and, in particular, of giving an account of oneself?"[38] In other words, does the critique of the humanist subject necessarily forfeit responsibility? Postmodernism and ethics, Butler responds, are *not* mutually exclusive. The unknowability of oneself, the unknowability of others and our vulnerability to others do not dissolve responsibility but rather are the springs from which ethics can be derived.

On the other hand, like Young, Butler's recent work is also a scathing critique of moral philosophy that has traditionally relied on the ability of the moral subject to give an account of oneself and one's actions: Why did x do y? One is responsible primarily for things one has consciously done and that are within one's control. Such a notion of responsibility requires an "I" who can give an account of oneself in the sense of providing reasons for why one did what one did. Responsibility as accountability, as Young so articulately explains, presumes a self that can be linked to the wrong done in order to justify attributions of praise and blame. While Young is concerned that this link cannot be made under conditions of structural injustice because there are scores of people who indirectly support the structures and processes that cause the injustice, Butler is concerned that the link cannot be made because the subject as obscure to oneself is always an effect of discourse. What moral philosophy does not adequately interrogate, Butler insists, is "who is the 'I' that is accountable?" And this is not inconsequential. Butler wants to make the subject not the grounds *of* ethics but a problem that is a source *for* ethics.[39]

Butler builds upon some of her earlier arguments about subject formation already discussed in Chapter 3 to develop her understanding of responsibility. More specifically, she focuses on the opacity of the subject to oneself and also the subject's vulnerability to others. One cannot give an account of oneself, according to Butler's understanding of subject formation, because the subject is an effect of the normative conditions of intelligibility at work in systems of power. As Butler puts it, "the very terms by which we give an account, by which we make ourselves intelligible to ourselves and to others, are not of our making."[40] The subject emerges as intelligible only through regulatory, discursive norms that limit what the subject can be.

Norms, according to Butler, work at two levels. First, norms function to direct conduct but, second, at a more fundamental level, norms are the necessary condition for the possibility of an "I" who acts as an agent. Norms not only guide how we act but also constitute subjects as ones who can lead "livable lives" or "lives worth living." To become intelligible, subjects require language. Language or discourse is not something subjects construct and then use but rather is something that uses subjects as subjects simultaneously make use of it.

Norms are violent, Butler argues, both because they limit whom we can be by regulating what will or will not appear in the sphere of the social but also because they constitute whose lives are livable. Norms operate by demanding a "constitutive outside." Butler's concern with the injustice of political exclusion has always been clear. In *Precarious Life* she implores us to ask, "Who counts as human? Whose lives count as lives? . . . What makes for a grievable life?"[41] In the volume of *Gender Trouble* published to celebrate the tenth anniversary of the original publication, Butler notes her real-life experiences with normative violence.

> I grew up understanding something of the violence of gender norms: an uncle incarcerated for his anatomically anomalous body . . . gay cousins forced to leave their homes . . . my own tempestuous coming out at the age of 16.[42]

Butler's concern with keeping open possibilities to reiterate norms differently is an ethical one as she intimates when she claims

> . . . one might wonder what use "opening up possibilities" finally is, but no one who has understood what it is to live in the social world as what is "impossible," illegible, unrealizable, unreal and illegitimate is likely to pose that question.[43]

Butler worries about "unlivable lives" and how they can become livable. She acknowledges that livable lives require being received by others as intelligible.

Samuel Chambers and Terrell Carver offer a valuable insight when they highlight how normative violence functions to make other types of violence invisible. Normative violence

> can be thought of as a primary form of violence, because it both *enables* physical violence that we routinely recognize and simultaneously *erases* such violence from our ordinary view.[44]

Norms are violent because intelligible subjects require the "simultaneous production of a domain of abjected beings, those who are not yet 'subjects' but who form the constitutive outside to the domain of the subject."[45] Through this process, other types of violence become normalized and the harms that ensue are erased and selectively ignored.

Norms are thus violent both because they limit who we can be but also because they are exclusionary. A subject's intelligibility (or in the case of the woman in the elevator, a subject's moral innocence) is dependent on abject others who preserve the borders that protect one's ability to be perceived as intelligible. Regulatory norms operate through the subject who repeats and perpetuates the norms that sustain the subject's intelligibility. It is the repetition of norms that, as Catherine Mills explains, "establishes one's 'being' in complicity with power and operates to define and delimit the possibilities of existence."[46] Normative violence is, thus, inherent to subject formation; an interpretation of subject formation that traditional ethics completely ignores. Such an interpretation of the subject is never even raised as an issue for debate within traditional philosophical scholarship around ethics.

If the subject is understood as an effect of discourse and power, it is dependent on discourse that is not of one's making. It follows that the subject can never be transparent to oneself. Butler explains,

> And since one never chooses the language in which one is addressed, nor can one ever possess the origin of this address, one will always be unknown to oneself.[47]

The question, "Who are you?" cannot be answered once and for all. Responsibility involves a constant vigilance whose elaboration we will come back to subsequently.

In addition, Butler also highlights how the subject is primarily vulnerable to others for its social existence. There is a fundamental sociality at the core of subject formation.[48] Borrowing from Emmanuel Levinas and Jean Laplanche (among others), Butler describes the subject as the product of social relations emphasizing the constitutive character of "address." The very demand that one give an account of oneself requires a "you" that calls me to be "me." Recognition is always mediated through names and labels that assume norms that call the subject into being. This, however, entails that the subject is also vulnerable to the risk of misrecognition. Because of this dependency and vulnerability to misrecognition, the subject is always constitutively incomplete. More specifically, Butler argues that this dependency on the social involves a subject that becomes possible only as a dispossession from oneself in relation to the other. "It is only in dispossession that I can and do give any account of myself."[49] And this dispossession, according to Butler, implies an acknowledgement that such an account cannot be a story that is my story alone, that is only about "me."

One is dispossessed by the language that one uses and that at the same time uses the subject. Consequently, one can never totally explain one's origins or the origins of one's actions. Annika Thiem, whose book is a complimentary commentary on Judith Butler's critical responsibility, explains this point well when she writes,

This dispossession by social norms is precisely that which I cannot render transparent to myself as I speak, because I can make myself understood—paradoxically—only insofar as I undergo this dispossession, which cannot be made into a narrative account of the "I."[50]

Not only are we not transparent to ourselves but also the linguistic frameworks that are not of our making always mediate our recognition of others.

Thus, not only our sense of self but also our sense of others is always already mediated by social norms and linguistic frameworks, frameworks that although we did not make, we can repeat differently. Butler describes this process within the framework of complicity,

my very formation implicates the other in me . . . my own foreignness to myself is, paradoxically, the source of my ethical connection with others.[51]

We are constituted by others through regulatory norms. But we also understand others through the same normative frameworks. We cannot escape these mediating frameworks. It is because of our dependency on norms and on others for our intelligibility, for our existence, that we are never totally transparent to ourselves and can thus never give a full account of ourselves or of others. This being given over from the start to another implies that the subject is always vulnerable to others while also opaque to oneself.

The subject's vulnerability to violence because it is a product of sociality highlights the possible pain and injury that is entailed by such relationality. Violence, Butler maintains, is a condition of our being. It is "a situation we do not choose. It forms the horizon of choice, and it grounds our responsibility. In this sense, we are not responsible for it, but it creates the conditions under which we assume responsibility."[52] As subjects, we are vulnerable to the pain and injury of misrecognition and abjection because we are dependent on others and the norms that constitute our very being.

What follows from this opacity and vulnerability, according to Butler, is humility about our self-understanding. Humility is an expression of an acknowledgement of the opacity of the subject. Because one can never give a complete account of oneself, a new understanding of ethics emerges based on the "willingness to acknowledge the limits of acknowledgment itself."[53] To understand opacity and vulnerability at the basis of ethics means to eschew certainty and to always be vigilant about disrupting the closure of possibilities. Thus, willingness to constantly critique norms becomes an essential aspect of ethics. Thiem describes this type of critique as a willingness to interrogate "power in relations to (social) justice."[54] Jodi Dean aptly articulates this understanding of critique at the heart of ethics when she writes,

> Although we don't choose the norms through which we emerge, insofar as we speak within them, or recognize an other in a way that they frame, we transmit these norms and thus bear a responsibility for their consequences. *To this extent, an ethics that does not involve critique, that does not call into question these norms and their consequences, is itself unethical, culpable, unresponsive as it disavows the relations of power on which it depends.*[55]

Butler pushes Young's call for critique of norms both further and in a different direction. This is especially important because for those who fit comfortably within norms, norms do not appear to be norms but just "what is." One is responsible in as much as one is complicit in the repetition of norms. Yet this is not the end of responsibility but rather the beginning of it. Such responsibility calls for a very special type of responsiveness whose characteristics are vigilance, critique, humility and uncertainty.

Butler locates critique at the core of ethics. Ethics requires us to risk ourselves exactly when we think we understand the other. This involves *constant* critique. Butler writes,

> Ethics requires that we must risk ourselves precisely there, at the moment of our unknowingness, when what conditions us and what lies before us diverge from one another, when our willingness to become undone constitutes our chance of becoming human, a becoming whose necessity knows no end."[56]

Butler makes this more concrete when she asks, "What would it mean, in the face of violence, to refuse to return it?"[57] To repeat norms differently requires an undoing of the self that is

> a primary necessity, an anguish, to be sure, but also a chance—to be addressed, claimed, bound to what is not me, but also to be moved, to be prompted to act, to address myself elsewhere, and so to vacate the self-sufficient "I" as a kind of possession.[58]

For Butler, we are responsible in as much as our being is dependent on the repetition of norms. Being compelled to reiterate norms does not relieve us of responsibility but instead is the start from which our responsibility springs, a responsibility that begins with uncertainty and is rooted in our vulnerability. Butler thus puts social and political critique at the core of ethical practice.

BUTLER'S "ETHICS OF NON-VIOLENCE"

Young's Social Connection Model facilitates our understanding of why the liability model of responsibility is ineffective in capturing complicity in structural injustice and why an exclusive focus on liability can normalize and prevent such complicity from being acknowledged and interrogated. The type of reproduction of race that occurs in the elevator described in the opening of this chapter cannot be captured by the liability model of responsibility. The woman's complicitity in reproducing racism and her responsibility is very likely to be dismissed as long as we are exclusively focused on liability. While Young also draws attention to the role of norms in normalizing and erasing such complicity, it is Butler who recognizes how power works through the constitution of subjects in often unconscious and unintentional ways.

Butler, however, goes further by calling for an "ethics of non-violence" as a response to the normative violence that conditions subject formation. Such an ethics of non-violence requires exposure and constant critique of the norms that produce and hide harm from appearing as harm. Butler draws our attention to a different type of violence that traditional ethics does not take into account. It is a violence that is not as much focused on physical violence done to a preformed subject (although she does not dismiss this type of violence) but rather involves a violence that is discursive and is prior to subjectivity. Normative violence is alluded to in George Yancy's description of what is going on in the elevator. Recall Chambers and Terrell's insistence that normative violence is the primary violence that *enables* the more traditionally understood type of violence.

Butler draws our attention to the need to expose the violence that is a product of normative violence. An ethics of non-violence, then calls for first and foremost

> unmasking the operations of normative violence so as to (1) to interrupt its capacity to enable other violences and (2) to render them visible when they do occur.[59]

But Butler takes an additional step when she focuses on our vulnerability to injury and grief. To better appreciate what she means by a non-violent ethics that centers vulnerability to injury and grief, it is important to place her recent work in the context of the violence that occurred in the events of September 11th, 2001 (commonly referred to as 9/11).

Although she does not dismiss the violent atrocity of the events of 9/11 in which approximately three thousand people lost their lives, Butler urges us not to understand these terrorist acts *only* within the frame of the physical violence that took place. She recognizes that "those who commit acts of violence are surely responsible for them"[60] but she insists that this conception of responsibility does not exhaust our understanding of responsibility. Butler also wants to expose the normative violence that many in the United States refused to be attentive to involving the unintelligibility of those who perpetrated the violence of 9/11. Chambers and Carver put Butler's point like this,

> Butler reads the violence of 9/11 and its aftermath through and with the lens of normative violence. Thus rendered, the terrorist acts of that day cannot be *merely* acts of physical violence (although they most certainly are that as well); they must be situated in the context of prior human dependency. . . . the extent that Al-Qaeda saw itself reacting to suffering caused by America . . . [61]

Similarly, Moya Lloyd[62] explains that Butler is concerned to bring to the forefront the political opportunity that was lost when the United States "heightened national discourse, extended surveillance mechanisms, suspended constitutional rights and developed forms of explicit and implicit censorship"[63] instead of acknowledging our vulnerability and that our lives depend on people we do not know and may never know.

Butler asks us to consider "what, politically, might be made of grief besides a cry for war"[64] and how could we have begun "to imagine a world in which violence might be minimized, in which an inevitable interdependency becomes acknowledged as the basis for a global political community."[65] In *Giving an Account*, Butler insists that

> It may be that the question of ethics emerges precisely at the limits of the schemes of intelligibility, the site where we ask ourselves what it might mean to continue in a dialogue where no common ground can be assumed, where one is, as it were, at the limits of what one knows and still under the demand to offer and receive recognition.[66]

Moreover, when we acknowledge the limits of our epistemological horizon, we are more willing to acknowledge that "the question is not simply whether I can or will know you, but whether 'you' qualify in the scheme of the human within which I operate."[67] What many people in the United States refused to ask, were *unwilling to consider*, was who were these people who wanted to destroy us and why? What did we not know and not want to know? There was resistance to interrogating or even considering our complicity in how we are understood by others. Butler concludes that

> Ethics requires that we must risk ourselves precisely there, at the moment of our unknowingness, when what conditions us and what lies before us diverge from one another, when our willingness to become undone constitutes our chance of becoming human, a becoming whose necessity knows no ends.[68]

Like Young, the type of responsibility that Butler is concerned to develop is deeply global.

Grief plays an important role in Butler's non-violent ethics. Butler insists that grief is not only something exclusively private. She maintains that mourning can open up the possibility to develop a sense of political community. By acknowledging our vulnerability and dependency we might begin to "reimagin(e) the possibility of community."[69]

> That we can be injured, that others can be injured, that we are subject to death at the whim of another, are all reasons for both fear and grief. . . . One insight that injury affords is that there are others out there on whom my life depends, people I do not know and may never know. This fundamental dependency on anonymous others is not a condition that I can will away. No security measure will foreclose this dependency; no violent act of sovereignty will rid the world of this fact.[70]

Moreover, when Butler refers to grief, she compels us to pay attention to the ethical problem that we do not consider all deaths worth of grieving.

Ethics requires that we consider whose life is understood as worthy of grief and whose deaths are selectively ignored. This becomes particularly salient in *Precarious Life* where Butler argues that the violence of the United States foreign policy depends on the dehumanization that is the product of normative violence. She rhetorically asks: Whose deaths are considered worthy of concern, whose deaths become invisible?

> I am referring not *only* to humans not regarded as humans, and thus to a restrictive conception of the human that is based on their exclusion. It is not a matter of simple entry of the excluded into an established ontology, but an insurrection at the level of ontology, a critical opening up of the questions, What is real? Whose lives are real?[71]

When normative violence renders a life less worthy of living, then the violence done to such a life is erased. Butler wants to highlight grief as a source for ethical questions about normative violence that might be invisible to us and she is vigilantly concerned with keeping open possibilities for resignification. Butler, however, also acknowledges how difficult it is to be critical of the norms that constitute us. She recognizes that " . . . *when one calls a set of norms into question one always runs the risk of calling the self into question.*"[72]

"ETHICS OF NON-VIOLENCE": LIMITATIONS, CLARIFICATIONS
Catharine Mills[73] and Jodi Dean[74] are sympathetic to Butler's rearticulation of responsibility as grounded in the normative violence of subject formation.

They both raise concerns, however, about her move to an ethics of non-violence. Briefly addressing these concerns helps to clarify what Butler means when she puts "non-violence" at the center of her ethics of responsibility. Mills argues that if Butler maintains that norms are inherently violent and norms are necessary for subject formation, it seems inconsistent for her to reject all forms of violence. Jodi Dean contends that Butler's strong emphasis on openness and constant critique sacrifices the possibility of the condemnation and conviction that are required for politics.

Butler's primary concern, however, is less with whether or not violence is always unjustified and more with exposing the invisibility of *normative* violence. In her response to Mills, she draws a sharp distinction between different types of violence that parallels the distinction made by Chambers and Terrell's above. She argues for the need to distinguish between the

> violence by which we are formed and the violence by which we conduct ourselves once formed. Indeed, it may be that precisely because—or rather, when—someone is formed in violence, the responsibility not to repeat the violence of one's formation is all the more pressing and important.[75]

Butler consistently wants to draw attention to "the more subtle ruses of coercive power."[76] Because she maintains that norms do not do their violence once and for all and that one can reiterate norms differently, her call for an ethics of non-violence involves a type of responsibility that disrupts the closure of the possibility to repeat norms differently.

Butler's understanding of responsibility is one "that makes good use of the iterability of those norms and, hence, their fragility and transformability."[77] Non-violence, for Butler, involves a struggle, as she explains

> ... (t)he mired and conflicted position of a subject who is injured, rageful, who has access to violent retribution and nevertheless struggles against that action. The struggle *against* violence is one that accepts that violence is one's own possibility. If that acceptance were not there, if one postured rather as a beautiful soul, as someone who is definitionally without violent aggression, there could be no ethical quandary, no struggle, no problem.[78]

Thus, Butler's call for an ethics of non-violence does not imply a "cleansing or expiating violence from the domain of normativity"[79] but instead it is a call that conceives of non-violence as a type of struggle. This point can be clarified through a question raised by Jodi Dean in regards to Butler's call for non-violence.

Dean is concerned that an ethics of non-violence entails a rejection of condemnation and conviction. Without condemnation we are left with no way to condemn racists or homophobes, Dean argues, and a politics of avoidance is encouraged. Butler, however, clearly does not avoid condemnation. She does not recoil from condemning the Bush administration and U.S. foreign policy. She does not refuse to condemn the violence done against Americans during the events of 9/11 and, specifically, rejects the justification of this violence as "'just punishment' for prior sins."[80]

Dean is skeptical of Butler's discourse of condemnation, especially when she criticizes the perpetrators of 9/11 prior to her critique of the response by the United States government to this attack. Does Butler use this statement of condemnation to give her arguments credence, as if this condemnation "gives her permission to argue"?[81] Dean also surmises that when Butler displays such discourse of condemnation, it is as if "she finds herself in that moment trapped within a discourse she rejects."[82]

Butler, however, seems less worried about whether or not we should reject condemnation altogether and more concerned to expose the dangers of *the rush to condemnation*. Butler writes,

Condemnation, denunciation, and excoriation work as *quick ways* to posit an ontological difference between judge and judged, even to purge oneself of another. Condemnation becomes the way in which we establish the other as nonrecognizable or jettison some aspect of ourselves that we lodge in the other, whom we then condemn. In this sense, *condemnation can work against self-knowledge, inasmuch as it moralizes a self by disavowing commonality with the judged.* Although self-knowledge is surely limited, that is not a reason to turn against it as a project. Condemnation tends to do precisely this, to purge and externalize one's own opacity. In this sense, *judgment can be a way to fail to own one's limitations and thus provides no felicitous basis for a reciprocal recognition of humans as opaque to themselves, partially blind, constitutively limited.*[83]

Instead of rejecting condemnation and conviction, Butler wants to highlight how in our making judgments, we can forget or ignore our own limitations. In other words, she cautions that condemnation and conviction can hide normative violence.

Dean makes a compelling point when she insists that failure to condemn can be a way of refusing to challenge systems of power and one's complicity in them. She argues,

My condemnation . . . may be a way of grappling with, of confronting, additional elements of the contexts of address, elements that involve power, hierarchy, and responsibility for other futures, other contexts, other beings. Failure to condemn, then, risks disavowing relations of power and confronting one's complicity in them.[84]

Again, Butler's ethics does not preclude condemnation. Instead, Butler takes pains to underscore that even when we undertake political action, we are not outside of the system and may still be reproducing it.

Butler's theory does not undermine political action and conviction, but rather cautions us that even when we take political action, we must be vigilant that we are not reproducing what we claim to be challenging. This is always a struggle. Dean subsequently clarifies that what Butler rejects is *condemnation that involves closure, finality and disconnection.*[85] Butler does not reject condemnation that involves a call for continued analysis and interrogation.

Butler's call for an ethics of non-violence is a call for vigilance based on unknowability and a troubling of what is considered certain, even our moral convictions. When Butler interrogates the "I" and compels us to consider the conditions of its possibility, her concern is to expand the possibility of livable lives. Her early work focused not only on challenging the presumptions of heteronormativity but also compelled presumably progressive feminists to ask: What normative violence does particular versions of feminist theory preserve? Like her early work that troubled the ethical and political moves of second wave feminism, Butler's call for an ethics of non-violence cautions that even when we express convictions and fight for social justice, we must be willing to interrogate how we might be reinscribing rather than challenging norms that transmit power. The educational implications of these new articulations of responsibility will be taken up in the next and final chapter.

NOTES

1. bell hooks, "Representations of Whiteness in the Black Imagination," in her *Black Looks: Race and Representation* (Boston, MA: South End Press, 1992), 177.
2. Nado Aveling, "'Hacking at Our Very Roots': Rearticulating White Race Identity within the Context of Teacher Education," *Race, Ethnicity & Education* 9, no. 3 (2006): 269.
3. George Yancy, *Black Bodies, White Gazes: The Continuing Significance of Race* (Lanham, Maryland: Rowman & Littlefield, 2008).
4. Ibid., 4.
5. Ibid., 23.
6. Ibid., 19, emphases added.
7. Ibid., 4.
8. Ibid., 22.
9. Ibid.
10. Ibid., 23.
11. Ibid., 24.
12. Nancy Fraser, "Foucault on Modern Power: Empirical Insights and Normative Confusions," in her *Unruly Practices, Power, Discourse and Gender in Contemporary Social Theory* (Minneapolis: University of Minnesota Press, 1989), 25.

13. Iris Marion Young, "Responsibility, Social Connection, and Global Labor Justice," in her *Global Challenges: War, Self-Determination and Responsibility for Justice* (Malden, MA: Polity Press, 2008), 159–186.
14. Ibid., 159–160.
15. Ibid., 170–171.
16. Ibid., 175.
17. Ibid., 173.
18. Ibid., 176.
19. Ibid., 177.
20. Ibid.
21. Ibid., 178.
22. Ibid., 179.
23. Ibid.
24. Ibid., 180.
25. Alice McIntyre, *Making Meaning of Whiteness: Exploring Racial Identity with White Teachers* (Albany, State University of New York Press, 1997), 69.
26. Iris Marion Young, "Gender as Seriality: Thinking about Women as a Social Collective," *Signs* 19, no. 3 (1994): 713–738.
27. Iris Marion Young, *Justice and the Politics of Difference* (Princeton, New Jersey: Princeton University Press, 1990), 46.
28. Iris Marion Young, "Responsibility, Social Connection, and Global Labor Justice," 159–160.
29. Ibid., 170.
30. Jacob Schiff, "Confronting Political Responsibility: The Problem of Acknowledgment," *Hypatia* 23, no. 3 (2008): 99–117.
31. Ibid., 107, emphasis added by Schiff.
32. Ibid., 105.
33. Ibid., 102.
34. Judith Butler, *Bodies That Matter: On the Discursive Limits of "Sex"* (New York: Routledge, 1993), 2, emphasis added.
35. Amy Allen, *The Power of Feminist Theory: Domination, Resistance, Solidarity* (Boulder, Colorado: Westview Press, 1999), 4.
36. Judith Butler, *Giving an Account of Oneself* (New York: Fordham University Press, 2005), 77.
37. Ibid., 136, emphasis added.
38. Ibid., 19.
39. Ibid., 110.
40. Ibid., 21.
41. Judith Butler, *Precarious Life: The Powers of Mourning and Violence* (New York: Verso, 2004), 20.
42. Judith Butler, *Gender Trouble: Feminism and the Subversion of Identity* (New York: Routledge, 1999), xix.
43. Ibid., viii.

44. Samuel A. Chambers and Terrell Carver, *Judith Butler and Political Theory: Troubling Politics* (New York: Routledge, 2008), 76.
45. Judith Butler, *Bodies That Matter*, 3.
46. Catherine Mills, "Normative Violence, Vulnerability, and Responsibility," *differences: A Journal of Feminist Cultural Studies* 18, no. 1 (2007): 136.
47. Judith Butler, *Giving An Account of Oneself*, 78.
48. Ibid., 33.
49. Ibid., 37.
50. Annika Thiem, *Unbecoming Subjects: Judith Butler, Moral Philosophy, and Critical Responsibility* (New York: Fordham University Press, 2008), 110.
51. Judith Butler, *Giving an Account of Oneself*, 84.
52. Ibid., 101.
53. Ibid., 42.
54. Annika Thiem, *Unbecoming Subjects*, 13.
55. Jodi Dean, "Change of Address: Butler's Ethics at Sovereignty's Deadlock," in *Judith Butler's Precarious Politics: Critical Encounters*, ed. Terrell Carver and Samuel A. Chambers (New York: Routledge, 2008), 121–122, emphasis added.
56. Judith Butler, *Giving an Account of Oneself*, 80.
57. Ibid., 100.
58. Ibid., 136.
59. Samuel A. Chambers and Terrell Carver, *Judith Butler and Political Theory*, 80.
60. Judith Butler, *Precarious Life*, 15.
61. Samuel Chambers and Terrell Carver, *Judith Butler and Political Theory*, 87.
62. Moya Lloyd, "Toward a Cultural Politics of Vulnerability: Precarious Lives and Ungrievable Deaths," in *Judith Butler's Precarious Politics*, 93.
63. Judith Butler, *Precarious Life*, xi.
64. Ibid., xii.
65. Ibid., xii–xiii.
66. Judith Butler, *Giving an Account of Oneself*, 18.
67. Ibid., 80.
68. Ibid.
69. Ibid., 20.
70. Ibid., viii.
71. Ibid., 33.
72. Ibid., 100.
73. Catherine Mills, "Normative Violence."
74. Jodi Dean, "Change of Address."
75. Judith Butler, "Reply from Judith Butler to Mills and Jenkins," *differences: A Journal of Feminist Cultural Studies* 18, no. 2 (2007): 181.
76. Ibid.
77. Ibid., 185.
78. Ibid., 186.
79. Ibid., 185.
80. Judith Butler, *Precarious Life*, 40.

81. Jodi Dean, "Change of Address," 123.
82. Ibid.
83. Judith Butler, *Giving an Account of Oneself,* 46, emphasis added.
84. Ibid.
85. Ibid.

CHAPTER 7

White Complicity Pedagogy

It is students' very desires to preserve these positive self-identities which I investigate for pedagogical possibilities and for a consideration of the question "What does 'good' look like now?"[1]

We suggest that instructors openly address conflicts about the meaning of responsibility in discourses of social action and engage students in give-and-take talk about how Whites and people of color might join together to ameliorate racism in educational settings and other contexts.[2]

THE WHITE COMPLICITY CLAIM MAINTAINS THAT ALL WHITES, BY VIRTUE OF SYSTEMIC white privilege that is inseparable from white ways of being, are implicated in the production and reproduction of systemic racial injustice. Uncovering systemic white ignorance and white denials of complicity that are so prevalent in everyday white discourse and practices and that protect white moral innocence facilitates our understanding of the connection between systemic benefit and the maintenance of the racial system. I have argued in this book, however, that such attempts to causally connect benefit and perpetuation of unjust systems do not adequately acknowledge the type of responsibility involved in white complicity. It is important to rearticulate notions of white responsibility in order for white people to be able to acknowledging their white complicity and to form alliances with others to challenge systemic racial injustice. The required notion of responsibility must be able to aim a critical gaze on white desires for moral goodness and innocence.

Acknowledging white complicity does not rule out responsibility but instead demands a rearticulated notion of responsibility. While traditional conceptions of responsibility have been found ineffective in exposing, and may even conceal, white complicity thereby contributing to its normalization, rearticulated models of responsibility can help white people to acknowledge their complicity in systemic racial injustice. Iris Marion Young's Social Connection Model of Responsibility offers a notion of responsibility that takes the individual's role in perpetuating structural injustice seriously. Young calls for a shift from a focus from blame and liability to a type of response-ability that can facilitate white students' acknowledgement of their complicity in structural injustice.

While going a long way, Young's model does not adequately epitomize the type of white moral responsibility that whites can aspire to. For that, we moved to an exposition of Judith Butler's recent work on ethical responsibility that clarifies in sharper details the contours of responsibility under complicity by focusing on vigilance that is based on uncertainty, humility and critique.

Fiona Probyn's provocative and penetrating assertion that "Complicity . . . is the starting point and the condition of ethics itself"[3] should by now be clear. Complicity does not preclude but, in fact, is the condition of white moral responsibility. Probyn argues that awareness of complicity is required for white engagement with racial injustice. If the acknowledgement of complicity is the starting point for white engagement with others, what are the implications for teaching white students about systemic racial injustice? This chapter introduces what I refer to as "white complicity pedagogy" but, at the same time, will also address the question, given white complicity, "What does 'good' look like now?"

THE MEANING AND AIMS OF WHITE COMPLICITY PEDAGOGY

In contrast to the problems with white privilege pedagogy addressed in the first chapter, white complicity pedagogy begins with the principle that the recognition of complicity, not just privilege, is the starting point for white engagement with systemic racial injustice. Acknowledging white complicity entails more than just a facile confession. It involves understanding how whiteness works through white bodies and the discursive practices of well-intentioned, caring and even progressive white people. The questions framing white complicity pedagogy are: How do white people reproduce and maintain racist practices even when, and especially when, they believe themselves to be morally good? How do these practices function to protect their white moral innocence? What allows whites to see themselves as part of the solution and to deny that they are part of the problem? The focus is on racism perpetuated by "good," well-meaning whites that, as Sherry Marx and Julie Pennington[4] argue,

> is even more destructive than the violence inspired hate of the Klan because to the good whites the racism they perpetuate is invisible to them, hidden by their helpful, knowledgeable and well-intentioned practices.[5]

Contemporary forms of racism are extremely lethal because they are perpetrated by good white folk whose moral agency, as has been argued throughout this book, is implicated in their complicity. White complicity pedagogy aims to help white students understand how their most benevolent practices may be contributing to systemic racism.

Unlike white privilege pedagogy, however, the emphasis is not on personal revelation. Although awareness is necessary, confessions and public assertions of awareness do not redeem one from complicity that is ongoing. Thus, a distinctive feature of white complicity pedagogy is the development of constant vigilance and openness to the ways that whiteness transforms its invisibility so as to protect the status quo. George Yancy[6] argues that whiteness is insidious and he refers to the *ambush* of whiteness as a powerful metaphor to express how whiteness snares and traps white people unexpectedly. Yancy maintains,

> The moment a white person claims to have arrived, he/she often undergoes a surprise attack, a form of attack that points to how whiteness ensnares even as one strives to fight against racism.[7]

In white complicity pedagogy, however, white ambush can be harnessed for its productive possibilities, a point that will be subsequently taken up in more detail.

This book has examined the conceptual shifts in understanding the subject, language and moral responsibility required to understand and critically reflect upon how whites are complicit in perpetuating systemic racial injustice. Specific attention has been given to the ways in which traditional conceptions of moral responsibility that rely to a considerable extent on intention, knowledge and/or choice and control obscure rather than promote the contemplation of white complicity.

It has been argued that such conceptions of responsibility encourage and support white denials of complicity that protect white moral innocence as well as shield the status quo from critique. In her examination of common white reasoning about responsibility for racism, Robin DiAngelo[8] notes,

> . . . as long as we didn't intend to perpetuate racism, then our actions don't count as racism. We focus on our intentions and discount the impact, thereby invalidating people of color's experiences and communicating that the effects of our behavior on them are unimportant. We then spend great energy explaining to people of color why our behavior is not racism at all. *This invalidates their perspectives while enabling us to deny responsibility for making the effort to understand enough about racism to see our behavior's impact in both the immediate interaction and the broader, historical context.*[9]

As long as individual intention, knowledge and/or choice and control are the cornerstones for the only conception of moral responsibility one can appeal to, white complicity will be obstinately denied.

Traditional conceptions of responsibility, focused as they are on liability and blame, encourage white students to be defensive. Researchers and theorists in the area of social justice education who have studied the resistance of white students to learning about systemic racial injustice observe how when white students are exposed to even the intimation that they might be racist, they interpret this as an attack and they are motivated towards avoidance and defensiveness rather than engagement. Using Janet Helm's model of white identity development, Beverly Daniel Tatum[10] explains how white students can learn about racism without guilt by presenting to them a positive white identity that they can aspire to.

Along with others[11] who have been critical of white identity development theory, the arguments made in this book suggest that striving for a positive white identity is dangerous. Although recognizing the desire to move in this direction, positive white identity is at least partially defined as a non-racist identity and this assumes that whites can move themselves outside of racist systems just by a willingness to do so. In addition, putting the spotlight on the desire to be a "good white" encourages white exceptionalism and white heroism that are forms of white denials of complicity. Audrey Thompson,[12] for instance, argues that whites have to resist the "Lone Hero" stance. As an illustration of the "Lone Hero" stance, she notes how white students who take only a few classes about whiteness and privilege think that they are

> well positioned to make pronouncements about race and racism. Some of us are quick to practice surveillance over others; others want to take charge and lead the way. Many of us demand that our antiracist activism be acknowledged and celebrated. Above all, we expect our own anxieties, feelings, opinions, and questions about race to organize discussions around race and racism.[13]

Thompson also points out how white exceptionalism ("I am not like those 'bad' whites.") impedes white listening and makes cross-racial dialogue fractious.

Iris Marion Young's Social Connection Model of Responsibility offers a conception of responsibility that does not forefront blame. This model is not concerned with isolating perpetrators, focuses on critically analyzing the background conditions or accepted rules and conventions that support ascriptions of blame and fault as "normal," is more forward looking than backward looking, involves shared responsibility and, finally, is a responsibility that can only be discharged by collective action. One might argue after the arguments put forth in this book that responsibility without blame is exactly what social justice education should avoid. White students need to be pushed out of their comfort zones. Does the move to a notion of responsibility that is not focused on blame re-center white affect?

White complicity pedagogy, with its emphasis on not being able to exit the system through individual will and its insistence on the collective action needed to change the system, does not aim to make white students feel comfortable. Instead, "the capacity of complicity to disorient and unsettle also constitutes its political agency."[14] White complicity pedagogy encourages white students to learn to be constantly vigilant as there is no innocence to hide behind.

Moreover, white complicity is not exclusively centered on white affect because it takes seriously the feelings of students of color who are often frustrated with white students' dismissive arrogance. White complicity pedagogy is not about blaming whites but instead about helping white students to understand how even their best moral intentions must be scrutinized for their potential to reproduce racist systems, for their potential to reproduce the "culture of power" in the classroom. White complicity pedagogy invites white students to consider what discourse does and how their everyday practices require critique. Such an approach to social justice education can also help white students recognize that when they are making a "case for our racial innocence" it is not so much a case of trying to persuade others, but rather about persuading ourselves of our own goodness.[15]

White complicity pedagogy, like other forms of social justice education, begins by eliciting students' presumed beliefs but goes farther. It does not stop at exposing hidden stereotypes or uncovering privileges that students take for granted, but, also, addresses ideologies and the ontological, epistemological and ethical frameworks that support and maintain racial injustice. White complicity pedagogy troubles "normal" moral discourse and practices because, as Carol Schick reminds us, "it is the appearance of normality in the conversations of would-be teachers who intend to 'make a difference', for example, which gives racism its license."[16]

Finally, white complicity pedagogy shifts the focus from white identity to how the system of racism is perpetuated and maintained by and through individuals. The focus is not on rearticulating a positive white identity but instead on how whites can be "part of an alliance against racism."[17] Although I only have anecdotal evidence, when white students recognize that their discourse and practices function to deny complicity, they become more careful listeners. Because white complicity pedagogy is not about "finger-pointing" it can promote whites' willingness to be vulnerable.

Early on in my course white students are often eager to ask, "What can we do?" We discuss how prematurely asking this question is a distancing strategy. White complicity, however, does not preclude responsibility. Complicity, as Probyn insists, is a starting point for understanding white moral agency. The type of responsibility that emerges when one recognizes that one is always part of the system of power and privilege ("my mobs are always with me"), that power works through subject formation in often unconscious and unintentional ways, and that we are not transparant to ourselves can lead to a type of humble uncertainty about our self-understanding. Indeed, it can open possibilities for critique about the limits of our knowledge.

Responsibility, thus conceived, involves exposure and constant critique of norms that produce and hide harm from appearing as harm. In her critique of normative violence, Judith Butler[18] advocates a willingness to disrupt the closure that norms bring about. These harms are different from the type of wrongful harms traditional ethics considers. Less focused on physical violence (although she is not discounting this type of violence), Butler exposes the types of injury that is discursively produced and that has its source prior to subjectivity. Normative violence not only helps to give a name to what George Yancy is alluding to in his description of the "elevator effect" but, also, explains the discursive violence involved in white denials of complicity and white distancing strategies. Acknowledging the complicity involved in normative violence calls for a special type of responsibility based on vigilance that involves uncertainty, humility and critique. In what follows, I briefly discuss the type of vigilance that is endorsed by white complicity pedagogy by examining uncertainty, humility and critique.

WHITE VIGILANCE

Uncertainty

Recounting an experience he had when he gave an invited presentation about racism to a group of students taking a course about multiculturalism, George Yancy notes that immediately after telling the story of the "elevator effect" that introduced Chapter 6, a white student got up with a resounding cry, "Bullshit!" expressed with the all the certainty of the one who knows. This positioned her, as Yancy explains, as the "discerner of bullshit, and so as the one who ought to be believed."[19] The white student's "Bullshit!" not only erased *his* credibility but also

> functioned as a form of erasure of the experiences of Black men who have indeed encountered the white gaze within contexts of elevators and other social spaces.[20]

The response discounted the knowledge that marginalized people have accrued from their lived experiences and reflects a white arrogant certainty about one's ability to know. Moreover, as Yancy notes,

> She did not *listen* to me and did not take any steps toward conceding my understanding of the social world as legitimate.[21]

Yancy maintains that this was not just a disagreement about and defense of a position like when one defends an ontological theory of numbers. This issue was about race and racism.

In other words, the student's response was not merely disagreement but, also, a defensive strategy in which she was "protecting her sense of 'goodness,' which functioned to mask how she is implicated in the subtle workings of white racism."[22] Not knowing but thinking that one knows, as has been argued, is characteristic of systemic white ignorance and, on the one hand, protects the presumption of white innocence and shields the status quo from challenge, on the other.

Cris Mayo calls for the centering of "not knowing" rather than "knowing" as a way to work against whiteness because, as she explains, the "certainty" of whiteness is expressed in the

> confidence in knowing the contours of a situation precisely because whites do not actually have to know very much about any situation. Whites can make assumptions about their welcome, their dominant knowledge, the acceptability of their practices, and rarely need to worry about challenge because they define the norm.[23]

The type of "not knowing" and "uncertainty" that Mayo advocates aims to "push them to see the limits of their understanding precisely because they are white in a white dominant society."[24] Mayo is not proposing that whites simulate "not knowing" but, rather, she is pointing to the ways in which privilege

> gives whites a way to not know that does not even fully recognize the extent to which they do not know that race matters or that their agency is closely connected with their status.[25]

White complicity pedagogy involves helping white students to acknowledge systemic white ignorance that is couched in a sense of white certainty. It centers uncertainty and attempts to disrupt white certainty.

Humility

Although related to uncertainty, humility involves an *ethical* stance that steers clear of arrogance and involves being open to always interrogating white moral sensibilities. White complicity pedagogy not only centers uncertainty and an acknowledgment of the limits of what we can know, it also encourages vigilance about one's own moral and antiracist projects. In my courses, I insist that white students explore how even discourses that are presumed to be "progressive" must "be monitored for their repressive strains."[26]

Towards the end of the course, my white students often write in their journals how much they have learned. We read the part of John Warren's article in which he claims that he "cannot rest under the banner of the transformed."[27] We discuss and critically examine any feelings they might have that they have now "arrived" and interrogate how this might be reproducing whiteness. Because whiteness is sedimented in ways of being white, especially white ways of being moral, because whiteness is something that is working through us, even when we think we are progressive and anti-racist, we must be open to examining how our progressiveness might be oppressive in ways we are not aware of. Echoes of Young's Social Connection Model can be heard in Yancy's claim that, "Dismantling whiteness is a continuous project."[28] It is a project that always needs another step. There are always unexplored layers of whiteness to examine because whiteness finds ways to hide "even as one attempts honest efforts to resist it."[29]

Thus, an essential element of white vigilance involves the attitude that Dreama Moon and Lisa Flores point to when they contend that

> while we cannot avoid taking an action step, neither can we become so committed to our particular vision for change that we fail to see the possibility that every strategy for change can also become oppressive."[30]

Rather than resting assured that one is fighting racism, white students must continually be open to "questioning the effects of her activism on both the self and the world."[31]

In one of my classes, we discussed the distancing strategy of keeping silent and one of my white students insisted that she remains silent in class because she doesn't want to offend anyone. While expressing a good intention, I pushed her to probe further what she just said by reminding her of the article by Case and Hemmings that we had recently discussed. Was her silence a way to avoid confrontation? Was her silence the product of a fear of disapproval and critique? What is the responsibility of white people to work through their fears rather than respond to the anger and frustration of students of color with silence or resentment? This led to an intense discussion of how whites can be stuck in defensive emotions (in feeling guilty, in feeling attacked, in feeling anger) that is unproductive and can be a way that whites further disengage from the difficult and critical self-reflection necessary for genuine learning to occur.

Constant critique does not mean that, as one of my white students once offered, "whites are doomed" and the only position is silence or inaction. On the contrary, this should lead whites to be less defensive about their mistakes and rather to attempt to learn from them. Screwups with regard to race and racism, Shannon Sullivan[32] explains, are inevitable. Accepting this inevitability means

> that white people can stop focusing more or less solely on themselves—what is the impact on me and my moral standing if I do or do not do X in this situ-

ation?—and spend more energy figuring out the situation and what might be done to improve it.[33]

White complicity pedagogy does not reject the possibility of whites challenging systemic racism but insists on a willingness to hear how what one thinks is the right thing to do might have effects that one does not intend. Resonating with Butler's emphasis on the opacity of self, Yancy contends that

> being a white antiracist is never completely in one's control because such an identity is deferred by the sheer complexity of the fact that one is never self-transparent, that one is ensconced within structural and material power racial hierarchies, that the white body is constituted by racist habits that create a form of racist inertia even as the white body attempts to undermine its somatic normativity, and that the white self undergoes processes of interpellation even as the white self engages in agential acts of racist disruption. . . . This does not mean . . . that all is hopeless . . . One ought to exercise vigilance . . . [34]

Critique

Criticality is considered a highly valued aim in contemporary theories of education in the West but, as Nicholas Burbules and Rupert Berk[35] have argued, there are many kinds of criticality. Burbules and Berk compare and contrast the types of criticality promoted by advocates of Critical Thinking and advocates of Critical Pedagogy, two prominent movements in foundations of education. While both movements aim to help students develop skepticism to commonly held beliefs, their understandings of what it means to be critical differ in significant respects.

Critical thinking advocates are primarily concerned with ideals of autonomy and presume that reasons and rationality are the routes to the "examined life." Therefore, they are focused on teaching formal and informal logic and reason assessment. Students are taught to be

> more discerning in recognizing faulty arguments, hasty generalizations, assertions lacking evidence, truth claims based on unreliable authority, ambiguous or obscure concepts, and so forth.[36]

The individual who is able to weigh reasons and choose what to believe is one who is not deceived and is self-sufficient. For some, critical thinking is *the* aim of education.

Critical Pedagogy, in contrast, begins from a very different premise. Critical Pedagogy starts out with the understanding that systems of power and knowledge are linked in ways that support social injustice. Criticality is primarily understood as the practice of interrogating those systems of power, its truth regimes and the discourse through which such power circulates. The question, "who benefits?" is prior to questions of truth because "a crucial dimension of this approach is that certain claims, even if they might be 'true' or substantiated without particular confines and assumptions, might nevertheless be partisan in their effects."[37] Although Critical Pedagogy has itself been the target of critique,[38] this approach has brought to the forefront questions about the relationship between knowledge and power that go unaddressed when dominant interpretations become so normalized and naturalized that such questions are not deemed warranted to ask.

The pros and cons of both approaches are beyond the scope of this chapter. (For an excellent review of the debates, I strongly recommend Burbules and Berk's essay.) It is significant, however, that Burbules and Berk end their essay with a brief description of an *alternate* approach to criticality that arises from postmodernism and poststructuralism because this is similar to the type of criticality that white complicity pedagogy seeks to promote.

Critique, according to Michel Foucault,[39] is the practice of interrogating the norms that constitute subjects and exposing the ways in which systems of power are maintained. Foucault insists, however, that this is a practice that transpires *from within* rather than *external to* existing discursive structures. The point of such criticality is to expose the limits of knowing and to disrupt epistemological and ontological certainty. Regimes of truth and the discursive practices they allow, Foucault argues, determine what can be said, what must remain unsaid but most important, what it is possible to think. Thus this type of criticality involves an openness to challenge the impossible and even our own beliefs and practices, *the ones without which we literally do not know how to think and act.*[40]

Gert Biesta[41] explains that interrogating what is impossible involves "what cannot be foreseen, predicted and calculated as a possibility"[42] because of the foreclosure entailed by regimes of truth. Criticality, in this sense, involves being open to interrogating what our worldview does not even raise as a possibility for consideration. Foucault implores,

There are times in life when the question of knowing if one can think differently than one thinks, and perceive differently than one sees, is absolutely necessary if one is to go on looking and reflecting at all. In what does (philosophical activity) consist, if not in the endeavor to know how and to what extent it might be possible to think differently, instead of legitimating what is already known?[43]

Such critique promotes a willingness to entertain certain questions about how and why knowledge gets constructed, and, most significantly, a willingness to question why certain constructions of reality are validated by the dominant culture and why others are marginalized and dismissed. The objective is to bring to critical awareness what we view as natural, common sense, and, thus, *unchangeable.* Biesta remarks that in his discussion of genealogy, Foucault refers to this type of awareness as "to question . . . what is postulated as self-evident . . . to dissipate what is familiar and acceptable."[44]

For Foucault, critique is not about judgments and he, in fact, argued that the task of exposing how power works is impeded by making judgments. This deserves mention because it highlights an important element of criticality. In her erudite exposition of Foucault's conceptualization of critique, Judith Butler[45] explains Foucault's avoidance of judgments. Judgments presume that one stands outside of the social world and, thus, ignores the framework within which judgments are made. When critique involves judgment, the frameworks upon which judgments are made escape interrogation. As Butler explicates,

Judgments operate . . . as ways to subsume a particular under an already constituted category, whereas critique asks after the occlusive constitution of the field
of categories themselves.[46]

Butler explains that the primary task of critique for Foucault

will not be to evaluate whether its objects—social conditions, practices, forms of
knowledge, power, and discourse—are good or bad, valued highly or demeaned,
but to bring into relief the very framework of evaluation itself. What is the relation of knowledge to power such that our epistemological certainties turn out
to support a way of structuring the world that forecloses alternative possibilities
of ordering?[47]

This bracketing of judgment and normative certainty has exposed Foucault's theory to much criticism (in the fault finding sense).

In her defense of Foucault, Butler asks who benefits from such judgments and such certainty.

To what extent . . . is that certainty orchestrated by forms of knowledge precisely
in order to foreclose the possibility of thinking otherwise?[48]

To critics who question the value of thinking otherwise when there are no normative criteria to determine when thinking otherwise is valuable, Butler responds,

Indeed, the only rejoinder . . . is to return to a more fundamental meaning of
"critique" in order to see what may well be wrong with the question as it is posed
and, to pose the question anew, so that a more productive approach to the place
of ethics within politics might be mapped.[49]

Foucault is making an important point that is occluded by the way his critics frame the issue. Foucault's point is that critique does not take us outside of power but is itself implicated in power systems. Our very ways of knowing, our very ways of being are constituted by power. What he offers is a reframing of critique as a practice in which we interrogate the limits of our most certain ways of thinking and most taken for granted practices, even those about critique.

I never understood this extreme reticence to assume normative foundations until I read Butler's essay about the censorship of dissent that was rampant in the United States after the attacks of 9/11. Butler[50] offers a compelling and concrete illustration of how judgments may obstruct "what we can hear." She examines the claim heard in the media against the Left's question, "Why do they hate us so much?" The claim was that asking this question implied an exoneration of the acts of terror committed on 9/11. Butler contends that the assertion that "there is no excuse for 9/11" has been used as a way to silence dissent and to preclude certain questions from even being considered. In addition, the focus on who is to blame for 9/11 and exclusively focusing on isolating the individuals involved "absolves us of the necessity of coming up with a broader explanation for events."[51]

This is not to imply, Butler insists, that those who committed the violence perpetrated on 9/11 are innocent, nor is it to say that what happened on that day was the "fault" of the United States but rather to open up for consideration questions that are at the limits of our knowledge. As Butler puts it,

> If we believe that to think radically about the formation of the current situation is to exculpate those who committed acts of violence, we will freeze our thinking in the name of a questionable morality. But if we paralyze our thinking in this way, we will fail morality in a different way. We will fail to take collective responsibility for a thorough understanding of the history that brings us to this juncture. We will, as a result, deprive ourselves of the very critical and historical resources we need to imagine and practice another future, one that will move beyond the current cycle of revenge.[52]

Significantly, we must ask what is protected when we are not allowed to interrogate how *our own actions* can be considered terrorist.

Butler distinguishes between conditions and causes and implores us to consider how we might contribute to the conditions of terrorism, even if we are not the cause. This is crucial because

> to understand how U.S. imperialism figures here, we have to understand not only how it is experienced by those who understand themselves as its victims, but how it enters into their own formation as acting and deliberating subjects.[53]

In a provocative and insightful assertion, Butler asks us to rethink responsibility that is not so focused on causes that it occludes our ability to interrogate the conditions that contribute to violent acts. Such a notion of responsibility can encourage us to hear beyond the limits of what we can hear and "to take stock of how the world has become formed in this way precisely in order to form it anew, and in the direction of nonviolence."[54]

Similarly, the notion of responsibility that I am advocating is a requirement of social justice pedagogy that must be understood as, borrowing from the title of Butler's essay, about *explanation* and not *exculpation or exoneration*. Only with this notion of responsibility, I submit, can we educate white students to hear beyond what they can hear. This is not to imply that judgments are always to be eschewed. Butler is not endorsing rampant relativism and Butler does not eschew making judgments. She makes judgments when she is critical of the war in Iraq, when she insists that she is not exonerating the perpetrators of 9/11 and even when she advocates for "hearing beyond the limits of what we can hear." Her point rather is to endorse a willingness to consider a critique of our judgments even when they seem so certainly right to us. Her concern is with what judgments make impossible to think or consider.

In addition, it is important to emphasize that critiquing something does not mean one is necessarily rejecting it entirely. In her examination of the discourse of tolerance in "liberal" societies, Wendy Brown[55] provides illustrations that support how such discourse works to constitute "the West" as superior. Although she demonstrates how power works through the discourse of tolerance, Brown insists she is not rejecting or condemning tolerance. She insists that

> To remove the scales from our eyes about the innocence of tolerance in relation to power is not thereby to reject tolerance as useless or worse. Rather, it changes the status of tolerance from a transcendental virtue to a historically protean element of liberal governance, a resituating that casts tolerance as a vehicle for producing and organizing subjects, a framework for state action and state speech, and an aspect of liberalism's legitimation.[56]

Similarly, Butler does not abstain from making judgments even as she critiques its use.

The critique she advocates, however, has a particular ethical dimension. Writing and extending Butler's recent work, Annika Thiem describes critique as a willingness to interrogate "power in relation to (social) justice."[57] Such critique, as Linda Martin Alcoff puts it, "helps to free us from locked-in ways of thinking in which we have lost the ability to reflect critically on our *dominant* concepts."[58] This is especially relevant about the ethical concepts that frame our moral sensibilities.

Butler explains that critique involves two undertakings. First, critique works to expose how power works to order our social world but, second, to find those places of fissure where new possibilities can emerge.

So not only is it necessary to isolate and identify the peculiar nexus of power and knowledge that gives rise to the field of intelligible things, but also to track the way in which that field meets its breaking point, the moments of discontinuities, the sites where it fails to constitute the intelligibility for which it stands. What this means is that one looks for both the conditions by which the object field is constituted, but also for the limits of those conditions, the moments where they point up their contingency and their transformability.[59]

Because whites have investments in the system, this type of critique is not a project that whites should undertake alone. Yancy reminds us why this is so important when he writes

that the dynamics of white racism (should) not solely be left in the hands of whites to theorize. Whites' insights must be challenged and corrected by those bodies of color that stand to suffer from the subtle blinkers that inhibit efforts of anti-racist whites. People of color must keep whites cognizant of the limits of their visions, their "certainty" regarding how to tackle whiteness.[60]

This does not necessitate face-to-face dialogue with those who can help them to expose these fissures but it does require the development of new ways of listening, new ways of reading and new ways of engaging with what people of color can teach them.

WHITE COMPLICITY PEDAGOGY AND LISTENING

How might we learn to listen if we gave up the need to feel like and be seen as good Whites?[61]

In her interviews with students after they took her course on systemic social injustice, Jessica Ringrose[62] reports on a comment made to her by a student of color.

I can't say the course is meeting up to my expectations . . . The sense that I get is some white women want validation that they're not racists. Rather than coming into the course deciding that they want to do active work towards being critical of their racism, they're, like, (high-pitched voice) "I'm not going to listen to anyone trying to tell me that I am a racist. There are other white people out there who are racist but I'm not."[63]

The student recounts her frustration when many white students interpreted an essay read in class by Lee Maracle, a Canadian First Nations poet and author, as "too angry." The student recalls her feelings.

The moment women of colour resist white dominant discourse . . . it's always, "Well, you're angry, therefore I'm exempted from needing to listen to what you're saying" . . . Power and privilege affect how white women read black women's scholarship. . . . I don't want to have to come to class and have to deal with "this author is too angry and is making generalizations about all white women." I get that it's hard to critique your privilege but that doesn't exempt you from needing to do it. A lot of women in the class are like (high voice) "Oh well, we're all people, and we're women and we should all just be the same and get along" . . . It's incredibly frustrating. It's like going to that class every week and *feeling like you're talking to a brick wall.*[64]

White defensiveness obstructs whites' ability to listen to what people of color are trying to tell them and contributes to students' of color desire to retreat from dialogue with them.

Lisa Delpit coined the term "the silenced dialogue" to explain why students of color often withdraw from having discussions with white students. Some of the comments of students of color that Delpit[65] reports are:

I'm tired of arguing with those White people, because they won't listen. *Well, I don't know if they really don't listen or if they just don't believe you.* . . .
When you're talking to White people they still want it to be their way. You can try to talk to them and give them examples, but they're so headstrong, they think they know what's best for everybody . . . They won't listen, . . . No, they listen, but they don't hear . . . So I just try to shut them out so I can hold my temper.[66]

Delpit explains that what is even more distressing is that the white people that these students of color are speaking about were seldom even aware that the dialogue has been silenced. They tended, instead, to interpret the silence as agreement. "After all, they stopped disagreeing, didn't they?"[67] Those who have power to control such discussions can pretend to listen (which is a form of not listening) but also they have the privilege to blatantly not listen if they don't want to. Audrey Thompson[68] offers important insights about listening and privilege.

They have the prerogative of not being persuaded. They have the prerogative of being offended. If the conversation gets too disruptive, too annoying, too agitating, or too frustrating, they can stop the conversation. Not only do those in power have the freedom to declare when enough listening has been done . . . , but their power usually ensures that certain things never get said in the first place.[69]

In her analysis of her white students' "desire for the other," Alison Jones[70] critically examines her white students' responses to a situation where her students of color preferred separated rather than integrated classes. Jones begins her analysis by noting that the call for cross-racial dialogue in education is for the benefit of the dominant group. As she explains, "members of marginalized or colonized groups do not need to encounter the voice of the powerful—they are immersed in it and hear it daily."[71] While such calls for dialogue presumably focus on empowering the voice of the marginalized, Jones emphasizes that the problem is "not the *telling*, but the *hearing* of stories. . . . Most important in educational dialogue is not the *speaking voice*, but the *voice heard*."[72]

As she continues to probe her white students' comments of disappointment and anger in regard to the students' of color preference for separation, Jones realizes that the real exclusion was not the exclusion of the subordinate but rather the dominant group's exclusion from the voice of the marginalized. The white students were so upset that the students of color desired separation because the white students were looking for redemption through the access they had to the cultures and lives of students of color in integrated courses. *They needed the students of color to teach them but not so much to learn from the marginalized but rather as a way to redeem themselves from any implication in racism.* The very act of white students wanting to know the "Other" functioned as a demonstration of white, anti-racist goodness. When the students of color preferred separation this was a threat to the white students' ability to be seen as "good whites." They lost their opportunity for absolution.

Jones makes explicit some of the distancing strategies behind the white students' confessions of ignorance. The white students complained about how ignorant they are and how they need students of color to help them to learn. While outwardly appearing to indicate "an openness, a lack of prejudice, a pure 'desire to know',"[73] Jones contends that such confessions are themselves requests for redemption. Audrey Thompson draws our attention not only to white students but also to white "progressive" academics, like myself, whose practices of white denials and problematic listening may take different forms. Thompson cautions white academics to not "come to say no" and she recommends reading and listening from "(a racially) engaged position."[74] What Thompson means by this is, first of all, that white projects and interests must not be at the forefront of our concern. Whites must address our investments and interests as they steer "our research and teaching, our personal and professional relationships, our politics, and our way of life."[75] Thompson points to Audre Lorde's admonition to Mary Daly, "Did you ever read my words, or did you merely finger through them for quotations which you thought might valuably support an already conceived idea?"[76] The type of listening that Thompson advocates is radical for whites.

It is a demand not just to register or include the voices of women of color but to change how we as white women act and think. It is a call to rethink our theories.[77]

Whites, according to Thompson, must be willing to work together with others to change the center.

Second, this radical call for listening requires that whites be able to hear anger and criticism without becoming defensive. As Maria Lugones and Elizabeth Spelman urge,

> you need to learn to become unintrusive, unimportant, patient to the point of tears, while at the same time open to learning any possible lessons. You will also have to come to terms with the sense of alienation, of not belonging, of having your world thoroughly disrupted, having it criticized and scrutinized from the point of view of those who have been harmed by it, having important concepts central to it dismissed, being viewed with mistrust, being seen as of no consequence except as an object of mistrust.[78]

Does this mean that whites can never disagree with people of color? Such a position would entail another form of disengagement and would not promote social justice. Again, Thompson is so insightful here.

> To fail to engage the work of feminists of color thoughtfully is only to exercise relativistic tolerance. . . . Studying the work of women of color means becoming the kind of scholar who *can* exercise judgment, who knows how to listen to, how to read different scholars.[79]

Disagreement, however, should only be expressed *after* one knows how to listen "passionately, responsively, lovingly . . . desperately."[80]

In her discussion of how to listen to others whose views are different from our own, Naomi Scheman[81] makes a similar point. She is particularly interested in listening on the part of those whose views conform to dominant norms. Scheman argues,

> Not to leave ourselves open and vulnerable to alternative understandings when our own come in part from locations of discursive privilege is to close ourselves to the possibility of learning from others whose social locations on the borders of intelligibility equip them precisely for dismantling the structures we may deplore but cannot ourselves see beyond—since they are, for those of us who are intelligible in their terms, the 'limits of our language.'[82]

Scheman recognizes that some might argue that such openness is the height of "epistemic promiscuity" by which she means "opening ourselves up to every passing argument" and never being able to defend any position. Scheman makes a profound point in her rejoinder. She writes,

> All of us pick and choose, as we must, which challenges to our own beliefs we will seriously entertain. (We have to . . .) examine how we make these choices: in

what venues, for example, do we try out our ideas: to whom do we make them intelligible; whose critiques do we especially try to understand and respond to; whom do we read; where do we look for ways of thinking that might wake us up?[83]

Whites must not only make choices but *how* those choices are made must be honestly and critically examined.

Finally, Thompson emphasizes that white people must understand how they are complicit. In her discussion of white feminists, Thompson argues that they have to learn how they "are oppressors as well as oppressed persons."[84] White complicity pedagogy has the potential to avert many of the barriers that preclude whites from genuinely listening to what people of color are trying to tell them. It may also minimize the frustration that people of color experience when they are willing to attempt to teach white people about racism. In my classrooms, I have experienced how white complicity pedagogy can help white students listen and read differently. Such differences in listening and reading, I argue, are a result of a decline in denials of complicity and an increased willingness to correct ignorance. This is an empirical claim that I believe is worthy of further study.

CONCLUSION

George Yancy highlights the constructive dimensions of white ambush and he maintains that when whites listen and learn from people of color they open themselves up to "the possibility of being ambushed in new and radical ways."[85] He encourages white people to become more aware of their defensiveness so they can develop "an openness to having one's world transformed and cracked."[86] Yancy insightfully explains that being ambushed is, in actuality, valuable to white growth. Whites should not take being ambushed as "a sign of defeat."[87]

> Indeed, there are transformative possibilities in the valorization of an ambush experience as a mode of surprise, as an experiential opening from which one learns and teaches about the insidious nature of whiteness.[88]

And, so, whites should develop a sense of thankfulness, not fear, when they are ambushed.

> For in that moment, whites come to learn more about themselves, expanding knowledge of the self, revealing how the white self is other to itself. In this way, not only does the humility of thankfulness on the part of whites function as a bridge to others, but it also functions as a bridge to the white self.[89]

In this book, I have introduced an approach to social justice education that I refer to as white complicity pedagogy. The theoretical and conceptual frameworks that it presumes have been examined. The advantages of white complicity pedagogy have been addressed. Some may be disappointed, however, because I have not offered any lesson-plans or concrete pedagogical suggestions. There is, however, no formula for how to do white complicity pedagogy. I encourage others to share their attempts.

Writing this book was prompted by a question posed to me after I presented a paper at a conference. Do I implement what I argue for theoretically? I believe I do, but I realized that at that time I could not give more than a few examples of how my pedagogy is consistent with the theoretical position on social justice education I advocate. I see my project in this book, however, more in the register of providing guidelines. These are the ideas, concepts and frameworks that give direction to my choice of curriculum, my ways of teaching and the exercises that I chose to use in my courses. And they change all the time, even during the course, as I get to know my students better and as I learn how I can more effectively provoke them to do whiteness differently. In addition, they change as I continue to learn more about my own social location and how it influences my theorizing and my pedagogy. Pedagogy, I submit, should never be static or fixed.

Fiona Probyn-Rapsey, whose work has had a profound influence on my thinking, suggests that we rethink complicity *as a methodology and as a practice* that forms the grounds of ethically engaging with others. Complicity, she maintains, is unavoidable but this unavoidability does not preclude responsibility. On the contrary, it is a condition of ethical responsibility because, as she argues employing a quote from Sara Ahmed's discussion of "ethical communication," it brings to our attention "a certain way of holding proximity and distance together: one gets close enough to others to be touched by that which cannot be simply got across."[90]

Calling upon Derrida's notion of "hauntology" in which "the thing that represents the demise of something also signals its continuation in a different form"[91] and Wendy Brown's[92] elaboration of the same concept, Probyn-Rapsey underscores how complicity as a methodology works similarly to remind us of the ongoing presence of injustice and how we might unwittingly be perpetuating it. Brown expands this notion of hauntology in helpful ways when she writes,

> The phenomenon remains alive, refusing to recede into the past, precisely to the extent that it meaning is open and ambiguous . . . To be haunted by something is to feel ourselves disquieted or disoriented by it, even if we cannot name or conquer its challenge.[93]

As previously noted, but it is worth repeating here nonetheless, Probyn-Rapsey underscores that "the capacity of complicity to disorient and unsettle also constitutes its political agency."[94] As a methodology, complicity does not assume a solution which itself would elicit a multitude of problems. I have argued, however, that complicity can serve as a framework for pedagogy that aims at, as John Warren suggests, doing whiteness differently. This assumes that

I cannot escape whiteness, nor can I discount the ways I am reproducing whiteness. . . . I argued that I cannot claim to be nonracist, to rest in the ideal of a positive racial identity. Rather, I contend that the only alternative I have is to do whiteness differently . . . It is the desire to work against whiteness in these more subtle and everyday ways that I think we have hope.[95]

In her essay, "Tiffany, Friend of People of Color: White Investments in Antiracism,"[96] Audrey Thompson relates a story about some friends who left her in charge of their children when they went on vacation but forgot to leave her the keys to their car. For days, the friends argued back and forth on the phone about how they didn't want to send her the keys for fear of this or fear of that. All Thompson wanted was the keys. White complicity pedagogy aims to help white people shift their focus from their needs and their investments to investing their energy in just sending the keys.

NOTES

1. Carol Schick, "'By Virtue of Being White': Resistance in Anti-Racist Pedagogy," *Race, Ethnicity and Education* 3, no. 1 (2000): 86.
2. Kim Case and Annette Hemmings, "Distancing: White Women Preservice Teachers and Antiracist Curriculum," *Urban Education* 40, no. 6 (2005): 625.
3. Fiona Probyn, "Playing Chicken at the Intersection: The White Critic in/of Critical Whiteness Studies," *Borderlands* 13, no. 2 (2004) http://www.borderlandsejournal .adelaide.edu.au/vol3no2_2004/probyn_playing.htm (accessed July 19, 2009).
4. Sherry Marx and Julie Pennington, "Pedagogies of Critical Race Theory: Experimentations with White Preservice Teachers," *Qualitative Studies in Education* 16, no. 1 (2003): 91–110.
5. Ibid., 102.
6. George Yancy, "Whiteness as Ambush and the Transformative Power of Vigilance," in his *Black Bodies, White Gazes: The Continuing Significance of Race* (Lanham, Maryland: Rowman & Littlefield, 2008), 227–250.
7. Ibid., 229.
8. Robin J. DiAngelo, "My Class Didn't Trump My Race: Using Oppression to Face Privilege," *Multicultural Perspectives* 8, no. 1 (2006): 52–56.
9. Ibid., 56, emphasis added.
10. Beverly Daniel Tatum, "Teaching White Students About Racism: The Search for White Allies and the Restoration of Hope," *Teachers College Record* 95, no. 4 (1994): 462–476.

11. Rosa Hernandez Sheets, "Whiteness and White Identity in Multicultural Education," *Multicultural Education* 8, no. 3 (2001): 38–40; Audrey Thompson, "Tiffany, Friend of People of Color: White Investments in Antiracism," *International Journal of Qualitative Studies in Education* 16, no. 1 (2003): 7–29; Cris Mayo, "Certain Privilege: Rethinking White Agency," *Philosophy of Education 2004*, ed. Chris Higgins (Urbana, Ill.: Philosophy of Education Society, 2005): 308–316.

12. Audrey Thompson, "Resisting the 'Lone Hero' Stance," in *Everyday Anti-Racism: Getting Real about Race in School*, ed. Mica Pollack (New York: The New Press, 2008), 328–333.

13. Ibid., 329.

14. Fiona Probyn-Rapsey, "Complicity, Critique, and Methodology," *Ariel* 38, no. 2–3 (2007): 79.

15. Audrey Thompson, "White Alibis in Academe." (Paper presented Colloquium, Teachers College, Columbia University, New York, August 2007).

16. Carol Schick, "'By Virtue of Being White,'" 84.

17. Cris Mayo, "Certain Privilege," 308.

18. Judith Butler, *Giving an Account of Oneself* (New York: Fordham University Press, 2005).

19. George Yancy, "Whiteness as Ambush," 228.

20. Ibid.

21. Ibid.

22. Ibid. 229.

23. Cris Mayo, "Certain Privilege," 310.

24. Ibid.

25. Ibid., 309.

26. Dreama Moon and Lisa A. Flores, "Antiracism and the Abolition of Whiteness: Rhetorical Strategies of Domination among 'Race Traitors'," *Communication Studies* 5, no. 1 (2000): 97.

27. John T. Warren, "Performing Whiteness Differently: Rethinking the Abolitionist Project," *Educational Theory*, 51, no. 4 (2001): 465.

28. George Yancy, "Whiteness as Ambush," 232.

29. Ibid., 240.

30. Dreama Moon and Lisa A. Flores, "Antiracism and the Abolition of Whiteness," 111.

31. Shannon Sullivan, "On Revealing Whiteness: A Reply to Critics," *Journal of Speculative Philosophy* 21, no. 3 (2007): 231–242.

32. Shannon Sullivan, *Revealing Whiteness: The Unconscious Habits of Racial Privilege* (Bloomington, Indiana: Indiana University Press, 2006), 197.

33. Shannon Sullivan, "On Revealing Whiteness," 234.

34. George Yancy, "Whiteness as Ambush," 231.

35. Nicholas Burbules and Rupert Berk, "Critical Thinking and Critical Pedagogy: Relations, Differences, and Limits," in *Critical Theories in Education*, ed. Thomas S. Popkewitz and Lynn Fendler (New York: Routledge, 1999), 45–65.

36. Ibid., 46.

37. Ibid., 47.

38. See Elizabeth Ellsworth, "Why Doesn't This Feel Empowering?: Working Through the Repressive Myths of Critical Pedagogy," *Harvard Educational Review* 59, no. 3 (1989): 297–324; Carmen Luke, *Feminism and Critical Pedagogy* (New York: Routledge, 1992); Ilan Gur-Ze'ev, ed., *Critical Theory and Critical Pedagogy Today: Toward a New Critical Language in Education* (Haifa: University of Haifa Press, 2005).

39. Michel Foucault, "What is Critique?" in *The Political*, ed. David Ingram (Boston: Blackwell, 2002), 191–211.

40. Nicholas Burbules, "Critical Thinking and Critical Pedagogy," 61.

41. Gert Biesta, "What Can Critical Pedagogy Learn from Postmodernism? Further Reflections on the Impossible Future of Critical Pedagogy," *Critical Theory and Critical Pedagogy Today*, 143–159.

42. Ibid., 147.

43. Michel Foucault, *The History of Sexuality Vol. 2* (New York: Vintage Books, 1985), 8–9.

44. Michel Foucault, "The Concern for Truth," in *Politics, Philosophy, Culture: Interviews and Other Writings 1977–1984*, ed. Lawrence D. Kutzman (New York: Routledge, 1998), 265.

45. Judith Butler, "What is Critique? An Essay on Foucault's Virtue," in *The Political*, ed. David Ingram (Boston: Blackwell, 2002), 212–228.

46. Ibid., 213.

47. Ibid., 214.

48. Ibid.

49. Ibid., 215.

50. Judith Butler, "Explanation and Exoneration, or What We Can Hear," *Social Text* 72, 20, no. 3 (2002): 177–188 (also in *Precarious Lives*).

51. Ibid., 180.

52. Ibid., 183.

53. Ibid., 184.

54. Ibid., 188.

55. Wendy Brown, *Regulating Aversion: Tolerance in the Age of Identity and Empire* (Princeton: Princeton University Press, 2006).

56. Ibid., 11.

57. Annika Thiem, *Unbecoming Subjects: Judith Butler, Moral Philosophy, and Critical Responsibility* (New York: Fordham University Press, 2008), 4.

58. Linda Alcoff, "Objectivity and Its Politics," *New Literary History* 31, no. 4 (2001): 838, emphasis added.

59. Judith Butler, "What is Critique?" 222.

60. George Yancy, "Whiteness as Ambush," 240.

61. Audrey Thompson, "Tiffany, Friend of People of Color," 21.

62. Jessica Ringrose, "Rethinking White Resistance: Exploring the Discursive Practices and Psychical Negotiations of 'Whiteness' in Feminist, Anti-racist Education," *Race, Ethnicity and Education* 10, no. 3 (2007): 323–344.

63. Ibid., 333.

64. Ibid., 333, emphasis added.
65. Lisa Delpit, "The Silenced Dialogue: Power and Pedagogy in Educating Other People's Children," *Harvard Educational Review* 58, no. 3 (1988): 280–298.
66. Ibid., 280.
67. Ibid., 281.
68. Audrey Thompson, "Listening and Its Asymmetries," *Curriculum Inquiry* 33, no. 1 (2003): 79–100.
69. Ibid., 79.
70. Alison Jones, "The Limits of Cross-Cultural Dialogue: Pedagogy, Desire, and Absolution in the Classroom," *Educational Theory* 49, no. 3 (1999): 299–316.
71. Ibid., 307.
72. Ibid.
73. Ibid., 312.
74. Audrey Thompson, "Listening and Its Asymmetries," 82.
75. Ibid., 84.
76. Audre Lorde, *Sister Outsider: Essays and Speeches* (Freedom, CA: The Crossing Press, 1984), 68 as cited in Audrey Thompson, "Listening and Its Asymmetries," 83.
77. Audrey Thompson, "Listening and Its Asymmetries," 89.
78. Maria C. Lugones and Elizabeth V. Spelman, "Have We Got a Theory for You! Feminist Theory, Cultural Imperialism and the Demand for the 'Woman's' Voice," in *Hypatia Reborn: Essays in Feminist Philosophy*, ed. A.Y. al-Hibri and M. A. Simmons (Bloomington, IN: Indiana University Press, 1990), 31.
79. Audrey Thompson, "Listening and Its Asymmetries," 90–91.
80. Ibid., 91.
81. Naomi Scheman, "Openness, Vulnerability, and Feminist Engagement," *APA Newsletter* 00, no. 2 (Spring 2001) http://www.apaonline.org/publications/newsletters/v00n2_Feminism_11.aspx (accessed July 26, 2009).
82. Ibid.
83. Ibid.
84. Gloria Joseph, "The Incompatible Menege a Trois: Marxism, Feminism, and Racism," in *Women and Revolution: A Discussion of the Unhappy Marriage of Marxism and Feminism*, ed. Lydia Sargent (Boston: South End Press, 1981), 105 as cited in Audrey Thompson, "Listening and Its Asymmetries," 84.
85. George Yancy, "Whiteness and Ambush," 240.
86. Ibid.
87. Ibid.
88. Ibid., 240–241.
89. Ibid., 241.
90. Fiona Probyn-Rapsey, "Complicity, Critique, and Methodology," 57.
91. Jacques Derrida, *Spectres of Marx: The State of the Debt, the Work of Mourning, and the New International* (New York, Routledge, 1994), 4.
92. Wendy Brown, *Politics Out of History* (Princeton: Princeton University Press, 2001).

93. Ibid., 152–153.
94. Fiona Probyn-Rapsey, "Complicity," 79.
95. John Warren, "Performing Whiteness," 465.
96. Audrey Thompson, "Tiffany, Friend of People of Color."

Bibliography

Ahlquist, Roberta. "Position and Imposition: Power Relations in a Multicultural Foundations Class." *Journal of Negro Education* 60, No. 2 (Spring, 1991): 158–169.

Ahmed, Sara. "The Phenomenology of Whiteness." *Feminist Theory* 8, no. 2 (2007): 164–165.

Ahmed, Sara. "Declarations of Whiteness: The Non-Performativity of Anti-Racism." *borderlands* e-journal 3, no. 2 (2004) http://www.borderlands.net.au/vol3no2_2004/ahmed_declarations.htm (accessed July 19, 2009).

Ahmed, Sara. *The Cultural Politics of Emotions*. New York: Routledge, 2004.

Aristotle. *Nichomachean Ethics*. Translated by Terence Irwin, 2nd edition. Indianapolis, Indiana: Hackett, 350 BCE/1999.

Averling, Nado. "'Hacking at Our Very Roots': Rearticulating White Racial Identity Within the Context of Teacher Education." *Race, Ethnicity and Education* 9, no. 3 (2006): 261–274.

Alcoff, Linda Martin. "Epistemologies of Ignorance: Three Types." In *Race and Epistemologies of Ignorance*, 39–58.

Alcoff, Linda Martin. "Objectivity and Its Politics." *New Literary History* 31, no. 4 (2001): 835–848.

Alcoff, Linda Martin. "What Should White People Do?" *Hypatia* 13, no. 3 (1998): 6–26.

Alcoff, Linda Martin. "The Problem of Speaking for Others." *Cultural Critique* 20 (Winter 1991): 5–32.

Allen, Amy. *The Politics of Our Selves: Power, Autonomy, and Gender in Contemporary Critical Theory*. New York: Columbia University Press, 2007.

Allen, Amy. *The Power of Feminist Theory: Domination, Resistance, Solidarity*. Boulder, Colorado: Westview Press, 1999.

Althusser, Louis. *Lenin and Philosophy and Other Essays*. New York: Monthly Review Press, 1971.

Appiah, Kwame Anthony. *In My Father's House: Africa in the Philosophy of Culture*. New York: Oxford University Press, 1992.

Arendt, Hannah. *Eichmann in Jerusalem*. New York: Viking Press, 1964.

Arendt, Hannah. *Responsibility and Judgment*. New York: Schocken Books, 2003.

Arendt, Hannah. "Organized Guilt and Universal Responsibility (1948/1991)." In *Collective Responsibility: Decades of Debate in Theoretical and Applied Ethics*, ed. Larry May and Stacey Hoffman. Savage, Maryland: Rowman & Littlefield, 273–284.

Armour, Ellen T. and Susan M. St. Ville. "Judith Butler—in Theory." In *Bodily Citations: Religion and Judith Butler*, ed. Ellen T. Armour and Susan M. St. Ville. New York: Columbia University Press, 2006, 1–15.

Austin, J.L. *How to Do Things with Words*. Oxford: Oxford University Press, 1962.

Aveling, Nado. "Student Teachers' Resistance to Exploring Racism: Reflections on 'Doing' Border Pedagogy." *Asia-Pacific Journal of Teacher Education* 30, no. 2 (2002): 119–130.

Aveling, Nado. "'Hacking at Our Very Roots': Rearticulating White Race Identity within the Context of Teacher Education." *Race, Ethnicity & Education* 9, no. 3 (2006): 261–274.

Baier, Kurt. "Guilt and Responsibility." In *Collective Responsibility: Five Decades of Debate in Theoretical and Applied Ethics*, ed. Larry May and Stacey Hoffman. Savage, MD: Rowman & Littlefield, 1991, 197–218.

Bailey, Alison. "Taking Responsibility for Community Violence." In *Feminists Doing Ethics*, ed. Peggy DesAutels and Joanne Waugh. Totowa, New Jersey: Rowman and Littlefield, 2001, 219–234.

Bartky, Sandra Lee. *Femininity and Domination: Studies in the Phenomenology of Oppression*. New York: Routledge, 1990.

Bartky, Sandra Lee. *"Sympathy and Solidarity": And Other Essays*. Lanham: Rowman & Littlefield, 2002.

Bartlett, Thomas. "Guidelines for Discussion, or Thought Control?" *The Chronicle of Higher Education* 45, no. 9 (September 27, 2002): A10–A11.

Barvosa-Carter, Edwina. "Strange Tempest: Agency, Poststructuralism, and the Shape of Feminist Politics to Come." *International Journal of Sexuality and Gender Studies* 6, nos. 1–2 (2001): 123–137.

Bell, Linda. *Rethinking Ethics in the Midst of Violence: A Feminist Approach to Freedom*. Lanham, MD: Rowman & Littlefield, 1993.

Benhabib, Seyla. "Feminism and Postmodernism: An Uneasy Alliance." In *Feminist Contentions*, 17–34.

Benhabib, Seyla. "On Contemporary Feminist Theory." *Dissent* 36 (1989): 366–370.

Benhabib, Seyla, Judith Butler, Drucilla Cornell and Nancy Fraser, *Feminist Contentions: A Philosophical Exchange*. New York: Routledge, 1995.

Berlak, Ann. "Teaching and Testimony: Witnessing and Bearing Witness to Racisms in Culturally Diverse Classrooms." *Curriculum Inquiry* 29, no. 1 (1999): 99–127.

Berlak, Ann. "Confrontation and Pedagogy: Cultural Secrets, Trauma, and Emotion in Antioppressive Pedagogies." In *Democratic Dialogue in Education: Troubling Speech, Disturbing Silence*, ed. Megan Boler. New York: Peter Lang, 2004, 123–144.

Biesta, Gert. "What Can Critical Pedagogy Learn from Postmodernism? Further Reflections on the Impossible Future of Critical Pedagogy." In *Critical Theory and Critical Pedagogy Today: Toward a New Critical Language in Education*, ed. Ilan Gur-Ze'ev. Haifa, Israel: Haifa University Press, 2005, 143–159.

Bingham, Charles W. "A Dangerous Benefit: Dialogue, Discourse, and Michel Foucault's Critique of Representation." *Interchange* 33, no. 4 (2002): 351–369.

Blum, Lawrence. "What Is 'Racism' in Antiracist Education?" *Teachers College Record* 100, no. 4 (Summer 1999): 860–880.

Blum, Lawrence. *"I'm Not a Racist, But...": The Moral Quandary of Race.* Ithaca: Cornell University Press, 2002.

Boler, Megan. "All Speech Is Not Free: The Ethics of `Affirmative Action Pedagogy.'" In *Philosophy of Education 2000*, ed. Lynda Stone. Urbana, IL: Philosophy of Education Society, 2001, 321–329.

Bonilla-Silva, Eduardo. *Racism without Racist: Color-Blind Racism and the Persistence of Racial Inequality in the United States.* New York: Rowman and Littlefield, 2003.

Boyd, Dwight. "The Legacies of Liberalism and Oppressive Relations: Facing a Dilemma for the Subject of Moral Education." *Journal of Moral Education* 33, no. 1 (2004): 3–22.

Boyd, Dwight. "The Place of Locating Onself(Ves)/Myself(Ves) in Doing Philosophy of Education," *Philosophy of Education 1997*, ed. Susan Laird (Urbana, Illinois: Philosophy of Education Society, 1998): 1–19.

Britzman, Deborah. *Lost Subjects, Contested Objects: Toward a Psychoanalytic Inquiry of Learning.* Albany: State University of New York Press, 1998.

Britzman, Deborah. "Decentering Discourses in Teacher Education: Or, The Unleashing of Unpopular Things." *Journal of Education* 173, no. 3 (1991): 60–80.

Brown, Wendy. *Regulating Aversion: Tolerance in the Age of Identity and Empire.* Princeton: Princeton University Press, 2006.

Brown, Wendy. "Gender in Counterpoint." *Feminist Theory* 4, no. 3 (2003): 365–368.

Brown, Wendy. *Politics Out of History.* Princeton: Princeton University Press, 2001.

Brown, Wendy. *States of Injury: Power and Freedom in Late Modernity.* Princeton, New Jersey: Princeton University Press, 1995.

Burbules, Nicholas and Rupert Berk. "Critical Thinking and Critical Pedagogy: Relations, Differences, and Limits." In *Critical Theories in Education*, ed. Thomas S. Popkewitz and Lynn Fendler. New York: Routledge, 1999, 45–65.

Butler, Judith. "Reply from Judith Butler to Mills and Jenkins." *differences: A Journal of Feminist Cultural Studies* 18, no. 2 (2007): 180–195.

Butler, Judith. *Giving an Account of Oneself.* New York: Fordham University Press, 2005.

Butler, Judith. *Precarious Life: The Powers of Mourning and Violence.* New York: Verso, 2004.

Butler, Judith. *Kritik der ethischen Gewalt Adorno Lectures, 2002.* Frankfurt am Main: Institute fur Sozialforschung an der Johann Wolfgang Goethe-Universitat, 2002.

Butler, Judith. "Explanation and Exoneration, or What We Can Hear." *Social Text 72*, 20, no. 3 (2002): 177–188 (also in *Precarious Lives*, 1–18).

Butler, Judith. "What is Critique? An Essay on Foucault's Virtue." In *The Political*, ed. David Ingram. Boston: Blackwell, 2002, 212–228.

Butler, Judith. *Psychic Life of Power: Theories in Subjugation.* Stanford: Stanford University Press, 1997.

Butler, Judith. *Excitable Speech: A Politics of the Performative.* New York: Routledge, 1997.

Butler, Judith. "Contingent Foundations." In *Feminist Contentions: A Philosophical Exchange.* Seyla Benhabib, Judith Butler, Drucilla Cornell and Nancy Fraser. New York: Routledge, 1995, 35–58.

Butler, Judith. "Collected and Fractured: Response to Identities." In *Identities,* ed. K.A. Appiah and H.L. Gates. Chicago IL: University of Chicago Press, 1995, 439–447.

Butler, Judith. *Bodies That Matter: On the Discursive Limits of Sex.* New York: Routledge, 1993.

Butler, Judith. *Gender Trouble: Feminism and the Subversion of Identity.* New York: Routledge, 1990; also *Gender Trouble: Feminism and the Subversion of Identity* (Tenth Anniversary Edition). New York: Routledge, 1999.

Butler, Judith. "Imitation and Gender Subordination." in *Inside/Out: Lesbian Theories, Gay Theories,* ed. Diana Fuss. New York: Routledge, 1991, 13–31.

Butler, Judith. "Conversation with Judith Butler IV." In *Judith Butler in Conversation: Analyzing the Texts and Talk of Everyday Life,* ed. Bronwyn Davies. New York: Routledge, 2008, 187–216.

Calhoun, Cheshire. "Responsibility and Reproach." *Ethics* 99, no. 2 (1989): 389–406.

Carby, Hazel V. "The Multicultural Wars." In *Black Popular Culture,* ed. Gina Dent. Seattle: Bay Press, 1992, 187–199.

Carby, Hazel V. "White Woman Listen! Black Feminism and the Boundaries of Sisterhood." In *Theories of Race and Racism: A Reader,* ed. Les Back and John Solomos. London: Routledge, 2000, 389–403.

Case, Kim and Annette Hemmings, "Distancing: White Women Preservice Teachers and Antiracist Curriculum." *Urban Education* 40, no. 6 (2005): 606–626.

Chambers, Samuel A. and Terrell Carver, *Judith Butler and Political Theory: Troubling Politics.* New York: Routledge, 2008.

Chavez Chavez, Rudolfo and James O'Donnell. *Speaking the Unpleasant: The Politics of (non)Engagement in the Multicultural Education Terrain.* Albany: State University Press, 1998.

Chizhik, Estella Williams. "Reflecting on the Challenge of Preparing Suburban Teachers for Urban Schools." *Education and Urban Society* 35, vol. 4 (2003): 443–461.

Chizhik, Estella Williams and Alexander Williams Chizhik. "Are You Privileged or Oppressed? Students' Conceptions of Themselves and Others." *Urban Education* 40, no. 2 (2005): 116–143.

Dalton, Harlon L. *Racial Healing: Confronting the Fear Between Blacks and Whites.* New York: Doubleday, 1995.

Dean, Jodi. "Change of Address: Butler's Ethics at Sovereignty's Deadlock." In *Judith Butler's Precarious Politics: Critical Encounters,* ed. Terrell Carver and Samuel A. Chambers. New York: Routledge, 2008, 109–126.

de Beauvoir, Simone. *The Second Sex.* Translated by H. M. Parshley. New York: Penguin, 1949/1972.

de Laurentes, Teresa. "Eccentric Subjects: Feminist Theory and Historical Consciousness." *Feminist Studies* 16, no. 1 (1990): 115–150.

de Saussure, Ferdinand. *Course in General Linguistics.* London: Fountana, 1974.

Delpit, Lisa. "The Silenced Dialogue: Power and Pedagogy in Educating Other People's Children." *Harvard Educational Review* 58, no. 3 (1988): 280–298.

Derrida, Jacques. "Signature Even Context." In *Limited, Inc.,* ed. Gerald Graff. Evanston: Northwestern University Press, 1988, 1–24.

Derrida, Jacques. *On Grammatology.* Baltimore: Johns Hopkins University Press, 1976.

Derrida, Jacques. *Spectres of Marx: The State of the Debt, the Work of Mourning, and the New International.* New York, Routledge, 1994.

DiAngelo, Robin J. "My Class Didn't Trump My Race: Using Oppression to Face Privilege." *Multicultural Perspectives* 8, no. 1 (2006): 52–56.

Diller, Ann. "Facing the Torpedo Fish: Becoming a Philosopher of One's Own Education." *Philosophy of Education 1998,* ed. Steven Tozer. (Urbana, IL.: Philosophy of Education Society, 1999): 1–9.

Doane, Woody. "Rethinking Whiteness Studies." In *White Out: The Continuing Significance of Racism,* ed. Ashley W. Doane and Eduardo Bonilla-Silva. New York: Routledge, 2003, 13–14.

Dovidio, John F. and Samuel L. Gaertner. *Prejudice, Discrimination and Racism: Theory and Research.* Orlando, FL: Academic Press, 1986.

Dreyfus, Hubert L. and Paul Rabinow. *Michel Foucault: Beyond Structuralism and Hermeneutics.* Chicago: Chicago University Press, 1982.

Du Bois, W. E. B. *The Souls of Black Folk.* Boston: Bedford Books, 1920.

Duncan, Patti. "Decentering Whiteness: Resisting Racism in the Women's Studies Classroom." In *Race in the College Classroom,* eds. Bonnie TuSmith and Maureen T. Reddy, New Brunswick, New Jersey: Rutgers University Press, 2002, 45–56.

Elias, Karen and Judith C. Jones, "Two Voices from the Front Lines: A Conversation about Race in the Classroom," in *Race in the College Classroom,* 7–18.

Ellsworth, Elizabeth. "Why Doesn't This Feel Empowering?: Working Through the Repressive Myths of Critical Pedagogy." *Harvard Educational Review* 59, no. 3 (1989): 397–324.

Farmer, Lindsay. "Complicity Beyond Causality: A Comment." *Criminal Law and Philosophy* 1, no. 2 (2007) 151–156.

Feagin, Joe and Henan Vera. *White Racism: The Basics.* New York: Routledge, 2001.

Felman, Shoshana. "Psychoanalysis and Education: Teaching Terminable and Interminable." *Yale French Studies* 63 (1982): 21–44.

Felman, Shoshana and Dori Laub, *Testimony: Crisis of Witnessing in Literature, Psychoanalysis, and History.* New York: Routledge, 1992.

Fischer, Klaus P. *Nazi Germany: A New History.* New York: Continuum, 1997.

Flagg, Barbara J. "Foreword: Whiteness as Metaprivilege." *Washington University Journal of Law and Policy,* 16 (2005): 1–11.

Foreman, Tyrone and Amanda Lewis, "Racial Apathy and Hurricane Katrina: The Social Anatomy of Prejudice in the Post-Civil Rights Era." *DuBois Review* 3, no. 1 (2006): 175–202.

Foucault, Michel. *"Society Must Be Defended": Lectures at the College de France, 1975–76,* ed. Mauro Bertani and Alessandro Fontana, New York: Picador, 2003.

Foucault, Michel. "What is Critique?" In *The Political*, ed. David Ingram, Boston: Blackwell, 2002, 191–211.

Foucault, Michel. "The Concern for Truth." In *Politics, Philosophy, Culture: Interviews and Other Writings 1977–1984*, ed. Lawrence D. Kutzman, New York: Routledge, 1998, 255–270.

Foucault, Michel. "The Ethics of Concern for the Self as a Practice of Freedom." In *Ethics, Subjectivity, and Truth Volume 1 of the Essential Works of Michel Foucault*, ed. Paul Rabinow. New York: The New Press, 1997, 281–302.

Foucault, Michel. "On the Genealogy of Ethics." In *Michel Foucault: Beyond Structuralism and Hermeneutics*, ed. Hubert L. Dreyfus and Paul Rabinow, Chicago: The University of Chicago Press, 1983, 231–232. Also in *Ethics, Subjectivity and Truth: Essential Works of Foucault 1954–1984, Volume 1*, ed. Paul Rabinow, New York: The New Press, 1994, 253–280.

Foucault, Michel. *The History of Sexuality Vol. 2*. New York: Vintage Books, 1985.

Foucault, Michel. *Power/Knowledge: Selected Interviews and Other Writings*. New York: Pantheon, 1980.

Foucault, Michel. "Truth and Power." In his *Power/Knowledge: Selected Interviews and Other Writings 1972–1977*, ed. Colin Gordon, New York: Pantheon, 1980, 109–133.

Foucault, Michel. *The History of Sexuality: An Introduction*. New York: Vintage Books, 1978/1990.

Foucault, Michel. *Discipline and Punish: The Birth of the Prison*. New York: Pantheon Books, 1977.

Foucault, Michel. *The Archaeology Knowledge and the Discourse on Language*. New York: Pantheon Books, 1972, 215–237.

Frankenberg, Ruth. *White Women, Race Matters: The Social Construction of Whiteness*. Minneapolis: University of Minnesota Press, 1993.

Fraser, Nancy. *Justice Interruptus: Critical Reflections on the "Postsocialist" Condition*. New York: Routledge, 1997.

Fraser, Nancy. "Foucault on Modern Power: Empirical Insights and Normative Confusions." In her *Unruly Practices, Power, Discourse and Gender in Contemporary Social Theory*. Minneapolis: University of Minnesota Press, 1989, 17–34.

Fraser, Nancy. "Pragmatism, Feminism, and the Linguistic Turn." In *Feminist Contentions*, 157–172.

Freeman, Alan David. "Legitimizing Racial Discrimination through Antidiscrimination Law: A Critical Review of Supreme Court Doctrine." In *Critical Race Theory: The Key Writing that Formed the Movement*, eds. Kimberle Crenshaw, Neil Gotanda, Gary Peller and Kendall Thomas, New York: New Press, 1995, 29–45.

French, Peter. *Individual and Collective Responsibility*. Rochester VT: Schenkman, 1998.

Frye, Marilyn. *Willful Virgin: Essays in Feminism 1976–1992*. Freedom, CA: Crossing Press, 1992.

Frye, Marilyn. *The Politics of Reality: Essays in Feminist Theory*. Trumansburg, New York: The Crossing Press, 1983.

Gardner, John. "Complicity and Causality." *Criminal Law and Philosophy* 1, no. 2 (2007): 127–141.

Giroux, Henry. "Race, Pedagogy, and Whiteness in *Dangerous Minds*," *Cineaste* 22, no. 4 (1997), 46–49.

Goldhagen, Daniel Jonah. *Hitler's Willing Executioners: Ordinary Germans and the Holocaust*. New York: Knopf, 1996.

Gordon, Jenny. "Inadvertent Complicity: Colorblindness in Teacher Education." *Educational Studies: A Journal of the American Educational Studies Association* 38, no. 2 (2005): 135–153.

Green, Thomas. "On the Illusion that We Can Choose to Believe." *Philosophy of Education Society 1994*, ed. Michael Katz (Urbana, Illinois: Philosophy of Education Society, 1995): 69–73.

Griffin, Pat. "Facilitating Social Justice Education Courses." In *Teaching for Diversity and Social Justice: A Sourcebook*, ed. Maurianne Adams, Lee Anne Bell and Pat Griffin, New York: Routledge, 1997, 279–298.

Gur-Ze'ev, Ilan. *Critical Theory and Critical Pedagogy Today: Toward a New Critical Language in Education*. Haifa: University of Haifa Press, 2005.

Hall, Stuart. "Foucault: Power, Knowledge and Discourse." In *Discourse Theory and Practice: A Reader*, eds. Margaret Wetherell, Stephanie Taylor and Simeon Yates, London: Sage, 2001, 72–81.

Hall, Stuart. "The West and the Rest: Discourse and Power." In *Formations of Modernity*, ed. S. Hall and B. Gieben, Cambridge: Polity Press/The Open University, 1992, 275–332.

Hamilton, Kendra. "'Race in the College Classroom': Minority Faculty Often Face Student Resistance When Teaching about Race." *Black Issues in Higher Education* 19, no. 1 (March 14, 2002): 32–37.

Harding, Sandra. *Whose Science? Whose Knowledge? Thinking from Women's Lives*. Ithaca, New York: Cornell University Press, 1991.

Harris, Cheryl. "Whiteness as Property." *Harvard Law Review* 106, no. 8 (1993): 1707–1791.

Haslanger, Sally. "'But Mom, Crop-Tops *Are* Cute!': Social Knowledge, Social Structure and Ideology Critique." *Philosophical Issues* 17, no. 1 (2007): 70–91.

Haslanger, Sally. "Gender and Social Construction: Who? What? When? Where? How?" In *Theorizing Feminisms: A Reader*, ed. Elizabeth Hackett and Sally Haslanger. Oxford: Oxford University Press, 2006, 16–22.

Haslanger, Sally. "What Are We Talking About? The Semantics and Politics of Social Kinds." *Hypatia* 20, no. 4 (2005): 10–26.

Henderson, Mae G. "The Stories of O(Dessa): Stories of Complicity and Resistance." In *Female Subjects in Black and White: Race, Psychoanalysis, Feminism*, ed. Elizabeth Abel, Barbara Christian and Helen Moglen, Berkeley: University of California Press, 1997, 285–306.

Hernández Sheets, Rosa. "Advancing the Field or Taking Center Stage: The White Movement in Multicultural Education." *Educational Researcher* 29, no. 9 (2000): 15–21.

Hernández Sheets, Rosa. "Whiteness and White Identity in Multicultural Education." *Multicultural Education* 8, no. 3 (2001): 38–40.

Higginbotham, Elizabeth. "Getting All Students to Listen." *American Behavioral Scientist* 40, no. 2 (November/December 1996): 203–211.

hooks, bell. *Black Looks: Race and Representation*. Boston: South End Press, 1992.

Hughes, Langston. *The Ways of White Folk*. New York: A.A. Knopf, 1969.

Hytten, Kathy and Amee Adkins. 'Thinking Through a Pedagogy of Whiteness." *Educational Theory* 51, no. 4 (2001): 433–450.

Hytten, Kathy and John Warren. "Engaging Whiteness: How Racial Power Gets Reified in Education." *Qualitative Studies in Education* 16, no. 1 (2003): 65–89.

Isaacs, Tracy. "Cultural Context and Moral Responsibility." *Ethics* 107, no. 4 (1997): 670–684.

James, Susan. "Complicity and Slavery in *The Second Sex.*" In *The Cambridge Companion to Simone de Beauvoir*, ed. Claudia Card, Cambridge: Cambridge University Press, 2003, 149–167.

Jaspers, Karl. *The Question of German Guilt*. Westport, Connecticut: Greenwood, 1948/1978.

Jensen, Robert. *The Heart of Whiteness: Confronting Race, Racism and White Privilege*. San Francisco: City Light Publishers, 2005.

Jones, Alison. "The Limits of Cross-Cultural Dialogue: Pedagogy, Desire, and Absolution in the Classroom." *Educational Theory* 49, no. 3 (1999): 299–316.

Jones, Gayle. *Corregidora*, Random House, 1975.

Karenga, Maulana. "Whiteness Studies: Deceptive or Welcome Discourse?" Interview, *Black Issues in Higher Education* 16, no. 6 (May 13, 1999): 26.

Kaufman, Cynthia. "A User's Guide to White Privilege." *Radical Philosophy Review* 4, no. 1–2 (2002): 30–38.

Kaufman, Cynthia. "Postmodernism and Praxis: Waving Radical Theory from Threads of Desire and Discourse." *Socialist Review* 24, no. 3 (1994): 57–80.

King, Joyce E. "Dysconscious Racism: Ideology, Identity and Miseducation." In *Critical White Studies: Looking Behind the Mirror*, eds. Richard Delgado and Jean Stefancic, Philadelphia: Temple University Press, 1997, 128–132.

Kleinman, Sherryl. *Opposing Ambitions: Gender and Identity in an Alternative Organization*. Chicago: University of Chicago Press, 1996.

Kruks, Sonia. "Simone de Beauvoir and the Politics of Privilege." *Hypatia* 20, no. 1 (2005): 178–205.

Kumashiro, Kevin. "Teaching and Learning through Desire, Crisis, and Difference: Perverted Reflections on Anti-Oppressive Education." *Radical Teacher* 58 (2000): 6–11.

Kutz, Christopher. *Complicity: Ethics and Law for a Collective Age*. Cambridge: Cambridge University Press, 2000.

Ladson-Billings, Gloria. "Silences as Weapons: Challenges of a Black Professor Teaching White Students." *Theory and Practice* 35, no. 2 (Spring, 1996): 80–85.

Lawrence III, Charles. "If He Hollers Let Him Go: Regulating Hate Speech." In *Hate Speech on Campus: Cases, Case Studies and Commentary*, ed. Milton Heumann and Thomas W. Church, Boston: Northeastern University Press, 1997, 270–288. (Also in *Words That Wound: Critical Race Theory, Assaultive Speech, and The First Amendment*, ed. Marie Matsuda, Boulder, CO: Westview Press, 1993, 53–88.)

Lawrence III, Charles. "The Id, the Ego, and Equal Protection: Reckoning with Unconscious Racism." *Stanford Law Review* 39, no. 2 (1987), 317–288.

Leonardo, Zeus. "Reading Whiteness: Antiracist Pedagogy Against White Racial Knowledge." *Handbook of Social Justice in Education,* ed. William C. Ayers, Therese Quinn and David Stovall, New York: Routledge, 2008, 231–248.

Leonardo, Zeus. "The Color of Supremacy: Beyond the Discourse of 'White Privilege.'" *Educational Philosophy and Theory* 36, no. 2 (2004): 137–152.

Levine-Rasky, Cynthia. "Framing Whiteness: Working Through the Tensions in Introducing Whiteness to Educators." *Race Ethnicity and Education* 3, no. 3 (2000): 271–292.

Levine-Rasky, Cynthia. "The Practice of Whiteness Among Teacher Candidates." *International Studies in Sociology of Education* 10, no. 3 (2000): 263–284.

Lewis, Amanda E. "Whiteness Studies: Past Research and Future Directions." *African American Research Perspectives* 8, no. 1 (2002): 1–16.

Lewis, Amanda E. "There is No 'Race' in the Schoolyard: Colorblind Ideology in An (Almost) All White School." *American Educational Research Journal* 38, no. 4 (2001): 781–812.

Lewis, Amanda E., Mark Chesler, and Tyrone A. Forman. "The Impact of 'Colorblind' Ideologies on Students of Color: Intergroup Relations at a Predominantly White University." *The Journal of Negro Education* 69, no. 1–2 (2000): 74–91.

Lewis, H. D. "Collective Responsibility." In *Collective Responsibility: Five Decades of Debate in Theoretical and Applied Ethics,* ed. Larry May and Stacey Hoffman, Savage, MD: Rowman and Littlefield, 1991, 17–34.

Lewontin, Richard C. "The Apportionment of Human Diversity." *Evolutionary Biology* 6 (1972): 381–398.

Lloyd, Moya. "Toward a Cultural Politics of Vulnerability: Precarious Lives and Ungrievable Deaths." in *Judith Butler's Precarious Politics,* 2008, 92–105.

Lloyd, Moya. "Politics and Melancholia." *Women's Philosophical Review* 20 (Winter 1998–1999), 25–43.

Lorde, Audre. *Sister Outsider: Essays and Speeches.* Freedom, CA: The Crossing Press, 1984.

Ludwig, Jack. "Perceptions of Black and White Americans Continue to Diverge Widely on Issues of Race Relations in the U.S." Gallup Poll, February 28, 2000, http://www.gallup.com/poll/3193/Perceptions-Black-White-Americans-Continue-Diverge-Widely.aspx (accessed July 19, 2009).

Lugones, Maria C. and Elizabeth V. Spelman, "Have We Got a Theory for You! Feminist Theory, Cultural Imperialism and the Demand for the 'Woman's' Voice." In *Hypatia Reborn: Essays in Feminist Philosophy,* eds. A.Y. al-Hibri and M. A. Simmons, Bloomington, IN: Indiana University Press, 1990, 18–33.

Luke, Carmen. *Feminism and Critical Pedagogy.* New York: Routledge, 1992.

MacKinnon, Catharine A. *Only Words.* London: HarperCollins, 1994.

Magnus, Kathy Dow. "The Unaccountable Subject: Judith Butler and the Social Conditions of Intersubjective Agency." *Hypatia* 21, no. 2 (2006): 81–103.

Martin, Jane Roland. "Gender in the Classroom: Now You See It, Now You Don't." *Democracy and Education* 9, no. 3 (Winter 1999): 9–13.

Marx, Sherry and Julie Pennington. "Pedagogies of Critical Race Theory: Experimentations with White Preservice Teachers." *Qualitative Studies in Education* 16, no. 1 (2003): 91–110.

Matsuda, Mari J., Charles R. Lawrence III, Richard Delgado and Kimberle Williams Crenshaw. *Words that Wound: Critical Race Theory, Assaultive Speech and the First Amendment.* Boulder, CO: Westview, 1993.

May, Larry. *Sharing Responsibility.* Chicago: University of Chicago Press, 1992.

May, Larry and Robert Strikwerda. "Men in Groups: Collective Responsibility for Rape." *Hypatia* 9, no. 2 (1994): 134–151.

May, Larry and Stacey Hoffman. *Collective Responsibility: Five Decades of Debate in Theoretical and Applied Ethics.* Savage, MD: Rowman and Littlefield, 1991.

May, Vivian M. "Trauma in Paradise: Willful and Strategic Ignorance in *Cereus Blooms at Night.*" *Hypatia* 21, no. 3 (2006): 107–135.

Mayo, Cris. "Certain Privilege: Rethinking White Agency." *Philosophy of Education 2004*, ed. Chris Higgins (Urbana, Ill.: Philosophy of Education Society, 2005): 308–316.

Mayo, Cris. "Civility and Its Discontents: Sexuality, Race, and the Lure of Beautiful Manners." *Philosophy of Education 2001*, ed. Suzanne Rice (Urbana, Ill.: Philosophy of Education Society, 2002): 78–87.

McDonough, Kevin. "Overcoming Ambivalence about Foucault's Relevance for Education." *Philosophy of Education Society 1993*, ed. Clive Beck (Urbana, Illinois: Philosophy of Education Society, 1994): 86–90.

McGary, Howard. "Morality and Collective Liability." *Journal of Value Inquiry* 20, no. 2 (1986): 157–165.

McIntosh, Peggy. "White Privilege and Male Privilege: A Personal Account of Coming to See Correspondences through Work in Women's Studies." In *Critical White Studies: Looking Behind the Mirror*, eds., Richard Delgado and Jean Stefancic, Philadelphia: Temple University Press, 1997, 291–299.

McIntyre, Alice. *Making Meaning of Whiteness: Exploring Racial Identity with White Teachers.* Albany, New York: State University of New York Press, 1997.

McNay, Lois. *Gender and Agency: Reconfiguring the Subject in Feminist and Social Theory.* Polity Press, 2000.

McNay, Lois. "Subject, Psyche, and Agency." *Theory, Culture and Society* 16, no. 2 (1999): 175–193.

McPhail, Mark. "(Re) Constructing the Color Line: Complicity and Black Conservativism." *Communication Theory* 7, no. 2 (1997): 162–175.

McWhorter, Ladelle. "Where Do White People Come From? A Foucaultian Critique of Whiteness Studies." *Philosophy & Social Criticism* 31, no. 5–6 (2005): 533–556.

McWhorter, Ladelle. "Foucault's Analytics of Power." In *Crisis in Continental Philosophy (Selected Studies in Phenomenology and Existential Philosophy, 16)*, eds. Charles E. Scott, Arleen B. Dallery and P. Holly Roberts, Albany: State University of New York Press, 1990, 119–126.

Mills, Catherine. "Normative Violence, Vulnerability, and Responsibility." *differences: A Journal of Feminist Cultural Studies* 18, no. 1 (2007): 133–156.

Mills, Catherine. "Efficacy and Vulnerability: Judith Butler on Reiteration and Resistance." *Australian Feminist Studies* 15, no. 32 (2000): 265–279.

Mills, Charles W. "White Ignorance." In *Race and Epistemologies of Ignorance*, ed. Shannon Sullivan and Nancy Tuana, Albany: State University of New York Press, 2007, 13–38.

Mills, Charles W. *Blackness Visible: Essays on Philosophy and Race*. Ithaca: Cornell University Press, 1998.

Mills, Sara. *Michel Foucault*. New York: Routledge, 2003.

Mills, Sara. *Discourse*. New York: Routledge, 2005.

Minow, Martha. *Making All the Difference: Inclusion, Exclusion, and American Law*. Ithaca: Cornell University Press, 1990.

Moody-Adams, Michelle. *Fieldwork in Familiar Places: Morality, Culture and Philosophy*. Cambridge, MA: Harvard University Press, 1997.

Moody-Adams, Michelle. "Culture, Responsibility, and Affected Ignorance." *Ethics* 104, no. 2 (1994): 291–309.

Moon, Dreama and Lisa A. Flores. "Antiracism and the Abolition of Whiteness: Rhetorical Strategies of Domination among 'Race Traitors.'" *Communication Studies* 51, no. 2 (2000): 97–115.

Morrison, Toni. *Playing in the Dark: Whiteness and the Literary Imagination*. New York: Vintage Books, 1992.

Nelson, Lise. "Bodies (and Spaces) Do Matter: The Limits of Performativity." *Gender, Place and Culture* 6, no. 4 (1999): 331–353.

Nicholson, Linda. "Feminism and the Politics of Postmodernism." *boundary 2*, 19, no. 2 (1992): 53–69.

Nietzsche, Friedrich. *The Basic Writings of Nietzsche*, edited and translated by Walter Kaufmann, New York: Modern Library, 1992.

O'Connor, Peg. *Oppression and Responsibility: A Wittgensteinian Approach to Social Practices and Moral Theory*. University Park, PA: Pennsylvania State University Press, 2002.

Oliver, Kelly. *Witnessing: Beyond Recognition*. Minneapolis: University of Minnesota Press, 2001.

Olson, Gary A. and Lynn Worsham, "Changing the Subject: Judith Butler's Politics of Radical Resignification." *JAC: A Journal of Composition Theory* 20, no. 4 (2000): 759, 727–765.

Omi, Michael and Howard Winant. *Racial Formation in the United States: From the 1960s to the 1980s*, New York: Routledge, 1987.

Phillips, Carol Brunson and Louise Derman-Sparks. *Teaching/Learning Anti-Racism: A Developmental Approach*. New York: Teachers College Press, 1997.

Pierce, Chester. "Psychiatric Problems of the Black Community." In *American Handbook of Psychiatry*, ed. Silvano Arieti, New York: Basic Books, 1974, 515–523.

Pleasants, Nigel. "Institutional Wrongdoing and Moral Perception." *Journal of Social Philosophy* 39, no. 1 (Spring 2008): 96–115.

Probyn-Rapsey, Fiona. "Complicity, Critique, and Methodology." *Ariel* 38, no. 2–3 (2007): 65–82.

Probyn, Fiona. "Playing Chicken at the Intersection: The White Critic in/of Critical Whiteness Studies." *Borderlands* 13, no. 2 (2004) http://www.borderlandsejournal. adelaide.edu.au/vol3no2_2004/probyn_playing.htm (accessed July 19, 2009).

Rich, Adrienne. *On Lies, Secrets, and Silence: Selected Prose 1966-1978.* New York: W. W. Norton, 1979.

Riggs, Damien. "Benevolence and the Management of Stake: On Being 'Good White People.'" *Philament* 4 (2004) http://www.arts.usyd.edu.au/publications/philament/ issue4_Critique_Riggs.htm (accessed July 19, 2009).

Ringrose, Jessica. "Rethinking White Resistance: Exploring the Discursive Practices and Psychical Negotiations of 'Whiteness' in Feminist, Anti-racist Education." *Race, Ethnicity and Education* 10, no. 3 (2007): 323–344.

Rodriguez, Nelson M. "Emptying the Content of Whiteness: Toward an Understanding of the Relation between Whiteness and Pedagogy." In *White Reign: Deploying Whiteness in America,* ed. Joe L. Kincheloe, Shirley R. Steinberg, Nelson M. Rodriguez. and Ronald E. Chennault, New York: MacMillan, 2000, 31–62.

Roediger, David R. *Black Writers on What It Means to Be White.* New York: Schocken Books, 1998.

Roediger, David R. *The Wages of Whiteness: Race and the Making of the American Working Class.* New York: Verso, 1991.

Roman, Leslie G. "White is a Color! White Defensiveness, Postmodernism and Anti-racist Pedagogy." In *Race, Identity and Representation in Education,* eds. Cameron McCarthy and Warren Crinchlow, New York: Routledge, 1993, 71–88.

Ruitenberg, Claudia. "Check Your Language! Political Correctness, Censorship, and Performativity in Education." *Philosophy of Education 2004,* ed. Chris Higgins (Urbana, IL: Philosophy of Education Society, 2005): 37–45.

Salih, Sara. "Judith Butler and the Ethics of 'Difficulty.'" *Critical Quarterly* 45, no. 3 (2003): 42–51.

Sandland, Ralph. "Seeing Double? Or, Why 'To Be or Not to Be' is (Not) the Question for Feminist Legal Studies." *Social and Legal Studies* 7, no. 3 (1998): 307–338.

Schaap, Andrew. "Guilty Subjects and Political Responsibility: Arendt, Jaspers and the Resonance of the 'German Question' in Politics of Reconciliation." *Political Studies* 49, no. 4 (2001): 749–766.

Scheman, Naomi. "Openness, Vulnerability, and Feminist Engagement." *APA Newsletter,* 00, no. 2, (Spring 2001) http://www.apaonline.org/publications/newsletters/ v00n2_Feminism_11.aspx (accessed July 26, 2009).

Schick, Carol. "'By Virtue of Being White': Resistance in Anti-Racist Pedagogy." *Race, Ethnicity and Education* 3, no. 1 (2000): 83–102.

Schiff, Jacob. "Confronting Political Responsibility: The Problem of Acknowledgment." *Hypatia* 23, no. 3 (2008): 99–117.

Sedgwick, Eve Kosofsky. *Epistemology of the Closet.* New York: Oxford University Press, 1980.

Slote, Michael. "Is Virtue Possible?" *Analysis* 42, no. 2 (1982): 70–76.

Smith, Holly. "Culpable Ignorance." *The Philosophical Review* 92, no. 4 (1983): 543–571.

Solorzano, Daniel, Miguel Ceja and Tara Yosso, "Critical Race Theory, Racial Micro-aggressions, and Campus Racial Climate: the Experience of African American College Students." *Journal of Negro Education* 69, no. 1–2 (2000): 60–73.

Solzhenitsyn, Alexander. *One Word of Truth*. London: Bodley Head, 1971.

Spelman, Elizabeth. *Fruits of Sorrow: Framing Our Attention to Suffering*. Boston: Beacon, 1997.

Srivastava, Sarita. "'You're Calling Me a Racist?' The Moral and Emotional Regulation of Antiracism and Feminism." *Signs* 31, no. 1 (2005): 29–62.

Stern, David. "The Return of the Subject? Power, Reflexivity and Agency." *Philosophy and Social Criticism* 26, no. 5 (2000): 109–122.

Striblen, Cassie. "Guilt, Shame, and Shared Responsibility." *Journal of Social Philosophy* 38, no. 3 (2007): 469–485.

Stubblefield, Anna. "Review of Lawrence Blum, *'I'm Not a Racist, But...'*" *Socialism and Democracy Online* 17, no. 2 (2003): 239–244, http://www.sdonline.org/34/anna_stubblefield.htm (accessed July 24, 2009).

Sullivan, Shannon. "On Revealing Whiteness: A Reply to Critics." *Journal of Speculative Philosophy* 21, no. 3 (2007): 231–242.

Sullivan, Shannon. *Revealing Whiteness: The Unconscious Habits of Racial Privilege*. Bloomington, Indiana: Indiana University Press, 2006.

Sullivan, Shannon and Nancy Tuana. *Race and Epistemologies of Ignorance*. Albany, New York: State University of New York Press, 2007.

Tatum, Beverly Daniel. *"Why are All the Black Kids Sitting Together in the Cafeteria?" And Other Conversations About Race*. New York: Basic Books, 1997.

Tatum, Beverly Daniel. "Teaching White Students About Racism: The Search for White Allies and the Restoration of Hope." *Teachers College Record* 95, no. 4 (1994): 462–476.

Thiem, Annika. *Unbecoming Subjects: Judith Butler, Moral Philosophy, and Critical Responsibility*. New York: Fordham University Press, 2008.

Thompson, Audrey. "Resisting the 'Lone Hero' Stance," in *Everyday Anti-Racism: Getting Real about Race in School*, ed. Mica Pollack, New York: The New Press, 2008, 328–333.

Thompson, Audrey. "White Alibis in Academe." Invited address for Teachers College, Columbia University. New York, August 2007.

Thompson, Audrey. "Listening and Its Asymmetries." *Curriculum Inquiry* 33, no. 1 (2003): 79–100.

Thompson, Audrey. "Tiffany, Friend of People of Color: White Investments in Anti-racism." *International Journal of Qualitative Studies in Education* 16, no. 1 (2003): 7–29.

Thompson, Audrey. "Entertaining Doubts: Enjoyment and Ambiguity in White, Anti-racist Classrooms." In *Passion and Pedagogy: Relation, Creation, and Transformation in Teaching*, ed. Elijah Mirochick and Debora C. Sherman, New York: Peter Lang, 2002, 431–452.

Thompson, Audrey. "Not the Color Purple: Black Feminist Lessons for Educational Caring." *Harvard Educational Review* 68, no. 4 (1998): 522–554.

Thompson, Audrey. "Anti-Racist Pedagogy—Art or Propaganda?" in *Philosophy of Education 1995*, ed. Alven Neiman (Urbana, IL: Philosophy of Education Society, 1996): 130–41.

Trebilcot, Joyce. "Dyke Methods." *Hypatia* 3, no. 2 (1988): 1–13.

Trepagnier, Barbara. *Silent Racism: How Well-Meaning White People Perpetuate the Racial Divide*. Boulder: Paradigm Publishers, 2006.

TuSmith, Bonnie and Maureen T. Reddy, *Race in the College Classroom*. New Brunswick, New Jersey: Rutgers University Press, 2002.

Vasterling, Veronica. "Butler's Sophisticated Constructivism: A Critical Assessment." *Hypatia* 14, no. 3 (1999): 17–38.

Warren, John T. *Performing Purity: Whiteness, Pedagogy, and the Reconstitution of Power*. New York: Peter Lang, 2003.

Warren, John T. "Performing Whiteness Differently: Rethinking the Abolitionist Project." *Educational Theory* 51, no. 4 (2001): 451–466.

Weber Cannon, Lynn. "Fostering Positive Race, Class, Gender Dynamics in the Classroom." *Women's Studies Quarterly* 18 (Spring/Summer 1990): 126–134.

Weber Cannon, Lynn. "Classroom Discussion Guidelines: Promoting Understanding Across Race, Class, Gender and Sexuality." In *Teaching Sociological Concepts and the Sociology of Gender, Racism and Racial Inequality: Implications for Teacher Education*, 2nd Edition, eds. Marybeth Stalp and Julie Childers, Washington, DC: American Sociological Association Teaching Resource Center, 2005, 182–186.

Weir, Allison. *Sacrificial Logics: Feminist Theory and the Critique of Identity*. New York: Routledge, 1996.

Westcott, Robyn. "Witnessing Whiteness: Articulating Race and the 'Politics of Style,'" *borderlands* e-journal 3, no. 2, (2004) http://www.borderlands.net.au/vol3no2_2004/westcott_witnessing.htm (accessed July 19, 2009).

Wetherell, Margaret, Stephanie Taylor and Simeon Yates. *Discourse Theory and Practice: A Reader*. London: Sage, 2001.

Wildman, Stephanie M. with Adrienne D. Davis. "Language and Silence: Making Systems of Privilege Visible." In *Readings for Diversity and Social Justice*, eds. Maurianne Adams, Warren J. Blumenfeld, Rosie Castaneda, Heather W. Hackman, Madeline L. Peters and Ximena Zuniga, New York: Routledge, 2000.

Williams, Bernard. *Shame and Necessity*. Berkeley CA: University of California Press, 1993.

Winant, Howard. "Behind Blue Eyes: Whiteness and Contemporary U.S. Racial Politics." In *Off White: Readings on Race, Power, and Society*, eds. Michelle Fine, Lois Weis, L. C. Powell and L. M. Wong, New York: Routledge, 1991, 40–53.

Wise, Tim. "What Kind of Card is Race? The Absurdity (and Consistency) of White Denial." http://www.zmag.org/content/showarticle.cfm?ItemID=10157 (accessed July 19, 2009).

Wittgenstein, Ludwig. *Philosophical Investigations*. New York: Prentice Hall, 1952/1973.

Wolf, Susan. *Freedom within Reason*. New York: Oxford University Press, 1990.

Wolf, Susan. "Sanity and the Metaphysics of Responsibility." In *The Inner Citadel: Essays on Autonomy*, ed. John Christman, Oxford: Oxford University Press, 1989, 137–151.

Yancy, George. *Black Bodies, White Gazes: The Continuing Significance of Race.* Lanham, Maryland: Rowman & Littlefield, 2008.

Yancy, George. *What White Looks Like: African-American Philosophers on the Whiteness Question.* New York: Routledge, 2004.

Young, Iris Marion. *Global Challenges: War, Self-Determination and Responsibility for Justice.* Malden, MA: Polity Press, 2008.

Young, Iris Marion. "Gender as Seriality: Thinking about Women as a Social Collective." *Signs* 19, no. 3 (1994): 713–738.

Young, Iris Marion. *Justice and the Politics of Difference.* Princeton, New Jersey: Princeton University Press, 1990.

Zembylas, Michalinos. "Witnessing in the Classroom: The Ethics and Politics of Affect." *Educational Theory* 56, vol. 3 (2006): 305–324.

Zimmerman, Michael J. "Moral Responsibility and Ignorance." *Ethics* 107, no. 3 (1997): 410–426.

Index

About the Author

Barbara Applebaum is associate professor in Cultural Foundations of Education at Syracuse University. She received her doctorate in philosophy of education from the Ontario Institute for Studies in Education at the University of Toronto under the supervision of Dwight Boyd. She is active in the Philosophy of Education Society, the Association for Moral Education, and the American Educational Studies Association. Her research is heavily informed by feminist ethics, feminist philosophy, and critical race theory. Applebaum's work has been published in *Educational Theory, Teachers College Record*, the *Journal of Moral Education, Philosophy of Education* and *Educational Foundations*.

17163601R00133

Printed in Poland
by Amazon Fulfillment
Poland Sp. z o.o., Wrocław